A HISTORY
OF BRITAIN
IN THIRTY-SIX
POSTAGE
STAMPS

Chris West

A HISTORY OF BRITAIN IN THIRTY-SIX POSTAGE STAMPS

PICADOR

NEW YORK

www.picadorusa.com
www.twitter.com/picadorusa • www.facebook.com/picadorusa
picadorbookroom.tumblr.com

For book club information, please visit www.facebook.com/picadorbookclub or e-mail marketing@picadorusa.com.

Designer: Peter Ward
Production Manager: Lisa Viviani Goris

Library of Congress Cataloging-in-Publication Data

West, Christopher, 1940–
    [First class]
    A history of Britain in thirty-six postage stamps / Chris West.—First U.S. edition.
        pages cm
    Originally published in Great Britain in 2012 by Square Peg as:
First class : a history of Britain in 36 postage stamps.
    Includes index.
    ISBN 978-1-250-03550-9 (hardcover)
    ISBN 978-1-250-03553-0 (e-book)
    1. Great Britain—On postage stamps.   2. Great Britain—History.
3. Postage stamps—Great Britain—History.   I. Title.
    HE6183.G74W47 2013
    941—dc23

                                                            2013003852

Picador books may be purchased for educational, business, or promotional use. For information on bulk purchases, please contact Macmillan Corporate and Premium Sales Department at 1-800-221-7945 extension 5442 or write specialmarkets@macmillan.com.

Originally published in Great Britain by Square Peg, a division of Random House

First U.S. Edition: November 2013

10   9   8   7   6   5   4   3   2   1

For Imogen and Fairy
Because the future is even more important than the past.

CONTENTS

CONTENTS

Stamps tell stories.
They speak to us across generations – if only we'd stop
squeezing them into albums and worrying about their
catalogue value, and just listen to their voices instead.

Here are thirty-six that I have found most expressive:
some beautiful, some quirky, some baffling, some stained
with blood; each chosen because it inspired me in some way.
My aim is that, gathered together, their stories will meld into a
bigger story, that of Great Britain and Northern Ireland from
the early days of Queen Victoria to the present.

Welcome to Britain, in thirty-six little pieces of paper.

CHAPTER ONE

IN THE BEGINNING

PENNY BLACK, 1840

THE PENNY BLACK is the world's first postage stamp. Fittingly it bears the image of a new, young monarch: this chapter is about beginnings.

The young woman on the Penny Black inherited the crown of a brilliant but troubled nation. Brilliant in its technology and industry – thanks to engineers and entrepreneurs like Matthew Boulton and Josiah Wedgwood, this damp and not very big island off the coast of Europe had become the world's fastest-growing economy. Troubled because of the social problems this Industrial Revolution brought with it: slums, child labour, appalling working conditions and hours. Brilliant in our trading skills and naval power, and the influence these gave us in foreign lands. Troubled because of the responsibilities this brought, and our lack of understanding of how to carry these out. Brilliant in a culture of aristocratic elegance. Troubled in the corruption that can fester in closed elites.

Making sense of this dual legacy would call for creativity, courage and energy. Fortunately, the subjects of the new queen possessed these very qualities. The story of this stamp provides a perfect example.

The penny post was not a Victorian invention. Back in 1680, when London was already a big place with a population of half a million, William Dockwra had guaranteed, for that amount, delivery of a letter within four hours anywhere in the city. This proved such a success that the government quickly nationalized the system, meaning that the profits could be redirected into the pocket of the Duke of York. Fortunately for Dockwra, the Duke became king and soon after that was deposed in the 'Glorious Revolution' of 1688, having to flee the country; Dockwra found himself once again running the postal system, this time on a government salary.

Other entrepreneurs followed Dockwra's example and set up successful penny post systems in other cities. However, on a national scale the Hanoverian post was a mess. Mail between urban centres was slow; try sending something to the country and it was even worse. The arrival of mail coaches in the late eighteenth century added a dash of glamour, but the system remained clunky. A bewildering list of tariffs and surcharges made the process laborious and prices prohibitive: the average cost of mailing a single written page across Britain was about 8½d (old pence), or about 3½p in today's money, which doesn't sound much until you consider that a work-man's weekly wage was about seven shillings (35p). In modern terms, this is equivalent to paying £40 to send a one-page letter.

The only benefit to the sender was that they wouldn't have to pay this. The addressee would do that. This was hugely inefficient: recipients weren't always at home, and when they were at home sometimes refused to pay – hardly surprising at £40 per letter – or simply didn't have enough money to hand. On top of these day-to-day issues, the system was corrupt. MPs and Peers of the Realm could send post for free, and as a result businesses offered them directorships so that they could utilize this perk.

The usual cries of 'something must be done' had been echoing around for a while. But the Victorians didn't just echo, they did things.

Rowland Hill was an exceptional man. He came from one of those marvellous late eighteenth/early nineteenth-century families with a passion for education and reform. His father, Thomas Hill, ran a progressive school on the principles of 'kindness and patience', where the rules were agreed by an elected committee of boys (Thomas Hill is said to have invented the Single Transferable Vote for this purpose). Science was a core part of the curriculum, as was 'practical Mathematics', a technology class. English, history, living languages and elocution were also taught to ensure a rounded education, whereas Latin and Greek, which were endlessly flogged into pupils at Eton and Harrow, were optional.

Hill followed in his father's footsteps and was running the school by the age of 25. He didn't just run it – he designed new premises for it, which included such innovations as gas central heating, a swimming pool, an observatory and craft rooms. The new school attracted international attention and pupils from Europe as well as the UK. Alongside his educational work, Hill developed a rotary printing press, a speedometer for stagecoaches and a propeller for ships, and co-founded the Society for the Diffusion of Useful Knowledge, an inventors' club, another of whose members was Charles Wheatstone, whom we will meet again later in this story.

Hill also interested himself in public matters, writing a tract on poverty relief in the UK, suggesting ways in which poor but enterprising people could emigrate safely to

Australia. Up to that point, emigration had been a disorganized business, with unscrupulous shipowners overloading ships and underfeeding passengers. Hill recommended checks on the suitability of both migrants and carriers, and a new system whereby carriers were paid for the number of passengers who arrived safe and well in Australia. As a result of his work, he was made Secretary of the South Australian Colonization Commission. Thanks to Hill's influence, the new colony was set up with a charter ensuring religious freedom and civil liberties.

In his spare time – not that he had much – he was a distinguished amateur artist.

According to legend, Hill first became interested in Post Office reform as a boy, when the postman turned up at his family home wanting three shillings for a bundle of letters. Young Rowland had been sent into Birmingham to sell some old clothes to raise the cash. Now, as an adult with a track record in social improvement, Hill turned his attention to the topic once again, and wrote his famous pamphlet, *Post Office Reform, its Importance and Practicability*. When attempts to interest the Post Office in this failed, Hill had it published privately. It soon came to public notice, and the authorities were forced to pay attention.

Hill's vision was bold. The old system of complicated tariffs would be swept away and replaced by a simple national rate: send a letter anywhere in the UK and it would cost a penny. Rather than one sheet, which is all you could afford in the old days, you could send a letter weighing up to half an ounce (about the weight of two sheets of modern A4); any more and you only had to pay an extra penny. The system would be based on payment in advance and the old system of free postage for select groups was to be abolished.

Hill backed his vision up with clear, logical argument. First, the question of paying extra for distance. Hill looked at what economists call the marginal cost of sending a letter a long way, and found it was very low. Most of the cost lay in the overheads of the postal system, which were the same if you sent the letter from Holborn to the City or from London to Edinburgh. Then he looked at the inefficiency of payment on receipt. Finally, he argued for a low-cost service, on three grounds. One was that the Post Office would lose money initially, but soon make it up as more and more people used the post. The second was that the new system would lower the costs for British business. The third, and dearest to Hill's heart, was social. Penny post would enable families, split apart by the drift to the cities of working men and women, to stay in touch. It would also encourage literacy.

Hill was summoned to an interview with the Postmaster General, Lord Lichfield. Legend has it that the idea of a small adhesive label that could be stuck on an envelope to indicate pre-payment came to Hill during this interview. If so, then the true birthday of the modern stamp, or at least the date of its conception, is 13 February 1837, which dovetails neatly with the reign of Queen Victoria. Her diary for 20 June of that year reads:

> I was awoke at 6 o'clock by Mamma, who told me the Archbishop of Canterbury and Lord Conyngham were here and wished to see me. I got out of bed and went into my sitting-room (only in my dressing gown) and alone, and saw them. Lord Conyngham then acquainted me that my poor Uncle, the King, was no more, and had expired at 12 minutes past 2 this morning, and consequently that I am Queen.

The experts damned Hill's brilliant idea at once. Lord Lichfield said, 'Of all the wild and visionary schemes I have ever heard of, this is most extraordinary', while Colonel W.L. Maberley, Secretary to the Post Office, harrumphed, 'The plan is a preposterous one, utterly unsupported by facts, and resting entirely on assumption.' The Colonel was to become a regular thorn in Hill's side, creating difficulties for the new scheme wherever he could. Luckily Hill had another skill: the ability to handle such people.

Luckily, too, this was the 1830s, not the 1730s. A Lord and a Colonel had damned Hill's idea, but the new queen's realm had other powerful voices. Henry Cole was another of those energetic, entrepreneurial, public-spirited Victorians: amongst other things, he invented and marketed the first Christmas card, managed the Great Exhibition of 1851 and was the first director of what is now the Victoria and Albert Museum. Cole became an enthusiast for Hill's reforms and assembled the Mercantile Committee, a group of City businessmen, to lobby for them. The committee also sent petitions to parliament and drummed up support in Britain's other industrial cities via Mechanics' Institutes. These institutes had been set up by philanthropic, or at least semi-philanthropic, industrialists as libraries and places where working men could attend courses, especially in the sciences. Many thousands of people 'bettered themselves' at such places in the first half of the nineteenth century: two of the institutes became Birkbeck College in London and UMIST in Manchester.

By 1839, Hill, Cole, the Mercantile Committee and the bright, serious young men of the Mechanics' Institutes had won the day. Parliament ordered the new postal system to be set up according to Hill's guidelines and Hill himself was put in charge of the process. He was appointed to a senior job at the Treasury, which gave him a certain amount of power and temporarily kept him out of the direct line of Colonel Maberley's fire.

A competition to design materials for prepaid penny post was announced and over 2,600 entries were received. Most were for envelopes or letter sheets: only around fifty were for stamps, which were still something of an afterthought and not expected to be used very much. The winning envelope, designed by William Mulready RA, was put into production. When it came out, it was subject to a satirical onslaught – partially by political opponents of the whole penny post project, and partially because it did look rather odd: Britannia stands in front of a weary-looking lion, and one of the angels winging post to all corners of the globe is missing a leg. It was quickly taken out of use and almost all examples burnt in envelope-destroying machines designed especially for the task.

One of the stamp entries, meanwhile, came from William Wyon RA. Based on a medal he had designed earlier in the year to celebrate her first visit to the City of London, it featured a sketchy profile of the new, young queen, Victoria.

Hill was impressed. He began at once to examine the rival technologies for printing stamps. He did this with his usual thoroughness, eventually deciding on line engraving, a system where sheets of 240 stamps are printed from an engraved plate. This was the speciality of a small company called Perkins Bacon. He also set about improving Wyon's basic design. He employed an artist, Henry Corbould, to turn Wyon's original sketch into a better drawing, and worked himself on the overall layout and the intricate background of the stamp. Skilled engravers at Perkins Bacon, such as George Rushall and Charles and Frederick Heath, also had a hand in the process: the end result was a true team effort.

The finished design was approved by the Queen on 20 February 1840. Stamps went on sale on 1 May, though oddly they were not supposed to be used until the 6th. (If you have an envelope with a Penny Black on it, postmarked 1 May 1840, congratulations: you're sitting on a gold mine.)

The stamps were an immediate success. Perkins Bacon were soon working round the clock, and 68 million Penny Blacks were printed in the next ten months. Of course, there were criticisms, especially from rival printers and political opponents. Some people felt it was disrespectful and disgraceful to lick the back of the monarch's head, while others found it rather amusing. As one wag wrote:

> *You may kiss our fair Queen, or her pictures, that's clear*
> *Or the gummy medallion will never adhere*
> *You will not kiss her hand, you will readily find*
> *But actually kiss little Vickey's behind.*

Over the next few years, the newly affordable postal service boomed. In 1839, 70 million letters had been sent. By 1841 the figure had gone up to 208 million, and by 1850 it was 350 million. The amount of simple human happiness created by this change is hard to imagine: families, divided by distance, were reunited; long engagements, common at the time, were made much less painful; thoughts were shared between friends – and businesses blossomed, too.

Other nations soon took up Hill's idea. Many years later, Gladstone said of Rowland Hill's penny post (with typical late Victorian floridness): 'His great plan ran like wild-fire through the civilized world. Never, perhaps, was a local invention . . . applied in the lifetime of its author to the advantages of such vast multitudes of his fellow-creatures.'

Not bad, for a little rectangular bit of paper.

CHAPTER TWO

VICTORIA'S COMMUNICATION REVOLUTION

ONE SHILLING EMBOSSED, 1847

THE SHILLING Embossed is the stamp the Victorians used to send letters across the Atlantic on Brunel's great steamships in the late 1840s and early 1850s. As such, it forms part of a set of massive changes in communications which shrank Britain and the world in the mid-nineteenth century, in a way nobody had previously imagined possible.

Getting around Hanoverian Britain had been a struggle. Most people couldn't afford transport, so they either stayed put or walked. For those with money there were stagecoaches, but the experience wasn't pleasant: highwaymen waited on hills (it was common to take paste jewellery on stagecoach journeys in anticipation of such encounters). If they didn't meet highwaymen, passengers still often had to get out and push at the steepest gradients; on level runs where the coaches could get up speed, the vehicles swayed terribly. To move freight, you either loaded a horse or, if transporting in bulk, put it on a barge. The canals played a key part in the Hanoverian Industrial Revolution, but they weren't exactly quick, moving at the pace of the plodding horses that pulled the barges (when they weren't waiting in queues for the locks).

All this changed with the railways. Early railway pioneers were at best disbelieved, at worst ridiculed. Some experts believed that a passenger in a coach travelling at 30 mph would be asphyxiated. (Sadly, the first journey on Britain's passenger railways was a fatal one: at the opening of the Liverpool to Manchester Railway, William Huskisson MP unwisely stood on an adjoining line waiting to get into a carriage and was run over by Stephenson's *Rocket*.) Nobody was asphyxiated, however, and soon navvies were digging cuttings and tunnels and building embankments throughout Britain. The first of the great trunk lines ran from Euston to Birmingham, and opened a month into the Queen's reign. Others soon followed, the most impressive of all being the Great Western Railway of Isambard Kingdom Brunel.

If the Penny Black is an iconic image of the early Victorian era, it is matched by the photograph of Brunel in his stovepipe hat standing against the backdrop of the huge iron chains of the SS *Great Eastern*, a contemplative expression on his face, a cigar in his mouth, his clothing an odd combination of wing collar and what seem to be workman's boots. Like Rowland Hill, Brunel was both a visionary and a doer. He took an interest in every aspect of the design of his railway, from stations to signalling equipment. His vision was a passenger service – other railway entrepreneurs of his time thought essentially in terms of freight – taking travellers at speed from London to Bristol. And then onward – not just to Cornwall and into Wales, but to a more exotic destination: New York. It was Brunel's dream that you could catch a train at Paddington, travel to Avonmouth, board a steamer and sail across the Atlantic: a great iron road, from the capital of the old world to the heart of the new. So this is what he built. His Great Western Steamship Company's mighty ocean-going ships were the biggest and fastest in the world at that time. Where these ships went, mail went too. The Shilling Embossed is the stamp of Brunel's global iron road.

Alongside the postal system, railways and ocean liners, there was another element in Victoria's Communication Revolution: electrical telegraphy, the sending of messages long distance down wires.

It was a complaint in post-war Britain that 'we have the ideas, then other people put them into practice'. This was not the case in the Victorian era. The telegraph was actually invented by Germans, but its first practical use was in connection with Britain's new railways: William Fothergill Cooke and Charles Wheatstone – Rowland Hill's colleague in the Society for the Diffusion of Useful Knowledge – installed a telegraph line between Paddington and West Drayton on Brunel's Great Western Railway in 1839. Messages were sent along it using the new system of dots and dashes developed in America by Samuel Morse. In 1845, the telegraph (now extended further west) was used to tell the police that a suspected murderer had boarded a train to London at Slough. The capital's new police force, the 'peelers', were waiting for him the other end.

Once work had been carried out on how to stop cables from rusting (a kind of rubber called gutta-percha was found to be ideal), a cable was laid under the Channel in 1850. By 1857, one was laid under the Atlantic but didn't work. The Victorians set about improving the technology and, by 1866, a reliable line to America was in place. India and Britain were linked by telegraph in 1870.

Brunel plays a part in this story, too. The ship that laid the Atlantic cable was the SS *Great Eastern*, his biggest ship. A 2007 stamp shows this vessel in all its glory; a true leviathan at nearly 700 feet long with five masts and 56-foot-high paddle wheels on either side to augment its propellers. Brunel had intended the *Great Eastern* to carry 4,000 passengers from Avonmouth to Australia without refuelling, thereby extending his iron road all round the world; however, this never came about. Instead, it worked the same transatlantic route as lesser ships, then was pressed into service laying cable. Its final job was even less in line with its creator's dreams: a floating music hall docked in Liverpool. (When it was broken up, one of the masts was bought by Liverpool FC and used as a flagpole at the Kop end. It is still there.)

As we have seen, Victoria's Communication Revolution brought numerous benefits. In terms of pure economics, the greatest of these was the staggering growth in international trade. This wasn't just the result of technology, but of new ideas.

Classically, countries had protected their producers with import tariffs, as recommended by 'mercantilist' social philosophers. Adam Smith (*Wealth of Nations*, 1776) and David Ricardo (*Principles of Political Economy and Taxation*, 1817) demonstrated that this was foolish: open these barriers, and nations with differing skills and natural endowments would trade to mutual advantage. However, at the beginning of the Victorian age, nations were still unwilling to follow their advice and remove tariff barriers. This was especially the case where agriculture looked to be at risk: early Victorian England protected its countryside with the Corn Laws, which placed import taxes on wheat, maize, barley and oats. Urban radicals objected that this kept the price of bread artificially high, thus penalizing the new town dwellers, and that it encouraged other countries to introduce tariffs in response. Get rid of our Corn Laws, they said, and we can have cheaper food and foreigners will be shamed into lowering their import barriers.

To repeal or not to repeal was the great debate of the 1840s. The penny post played its part in the debate, enabling mass distribution of largely pro-repeal pamphlets – the first political mailshot in history. In the end, ironically with the help of Sir

Robert Peel, a Tory (the party of the countryside), the repealers won and a boom in international trade followed. Two decades later, economist W.S. Jevons could write:

> *The plains of North America are our cornfields, Chicago and Odessa our granaries; Canada and the Baltic are our timber forests; Australasia contains our sheep farms, and in Argentina and on the western prairies of North America are our herds of oxen; Peru sends her silver, and the gold of South Africa and Australia flows to London; the Hindus and Chinese grow tea for us, and our coffee, sugar and spice plantations are all in the Indies. Spain and France are our vineyards and the Mediterranean our fruit garden.*

The post, the railways, the great steamships, the telegraph, free trade: all these sent Victoria's kingdom hurtling forward into the second half of the new century.

Well, some of that kingdom, anyway . . .

CHAPTER THREE

THE HORROR

PENNY RED WITH IRISH POSTMARK, 1848

I N 1848, Ireland was part of the United Kingdom. One hundred and five Irish MPs sat in the House of Commons. The Irish postal system was, naturally, run from London – in 1841, the novelist Anthony Trollope, then a young Post Office employee, was sent by Colonel Maberley to Banagher in County Offaly to be a surveyor's clerk, a kind of junior manager. He worked in Ireland for ten years. The letters whose delivery he oversaw would have looked like this, bearing the same stamp one would see on a letter from Westminster to Tooting – the Penny Red, which had superseded the Penny Black that year, as the latter had proven too difficult to cancel effectively.

However, beneath this superficial unity, the islands of Ireland and Britain were very different.

Protestantism still lay at the heart of the British identity: the inquisition of Bloody Mary, Foxe's *Book of Martyrs* and the tale of the Armada formed part of the national narrative. The people of Ireland, on the other hand, were fiercely Catholic.

Economically, Ireland's factories were concentrated in the big coastal cities; the rest of the country was agrarian, with much subsistence farming and a few cottage craft industries. In 1848, the island of Britain had thousands of miles of railway linking all its main cities; Ireland had a couple of hundred miles, emanating from Dublin, Cork and Belfast, but linking none of them.

There was also the system of land ownership. As in Britain, land in Ireland belonged to a rich elite. But Ireland's elite were almost all English and either lived in England or had a grand Irish house which they visited occasionally. These absentee land-owners rented their land out to middlemen, who were often unscrupulous characters who tried to squeeze as many small farmers on to the available land as possible. As a result of this (and other factors such as the system of inheritance) most Irish peasant families lived off tiny plots. Much of the land was poor, as absentees were less likely to invest in their property in the way that landowners did on their home turf. The only crop that many families could grow in sufficient quantities was the potato. A third of the population ate nothing else.

Ireland started the Victorian era poor. To be fair to the British governing class, this problem had been noted and discussed, endlessly – since 1801, over 100 commissions had looked at Irish poverty – but, in a very un-Victorian way, nobody seemed to know what to do about it. And things were getting worse. The population was on the rise, but the potato crop was unreliable. Harvests had been bad in 1836, 1837, 1839, 1841 and 1844, yet no real attempts were being made to modernize food production, either by improving efficiency or introducing diversity. Ireland's rulers – those 105 MPs were almost all from landowning families – either didn't care, or seemed to be affected by a kind of paralysis. Maybe they thought they would muddle through, as they had with previous crop failures.

In 1845 a new potato disease, blight (*Phytophthora infestans*), arrived in Europe from North America, an unwelcome by-product of booming global trade. It devastated crops across the Continent, but nowhere was as dependent on the potato as Ireland. The harvest failed, more completely than it had for a hundred years. People faced starvation.

The Prime Minister Robert Peel made attempts to alleviate the suffering. Money was invested in public works but the funds were insufficient. Pay was low, and when shortage began to drive food prices up, wages became insufficient for the men and women building roads to nowhere. Maize was imported from America in an effort to provide an alternative source of food, but arrived in a raw state which meant that it had to go through a complex refining process in order to make it edible. However, it was often sold in its raw form. Incorrectly prepared it made people violently sick, and became known as Peel's Brimstone.

Peel was removed from office after repealing the Corn Laws and was replaced by Lord John Russell. Things got worse. Russell's chief of famine relief was Sir Charles Trevelyan – a man with a pig-headed conviction that the market was a solution for all social ills, and the belief that God had ordained this. Trevelyan had been influenced by the work of Thomas Malthus, who argued in his *Essay on the Principle of Population*, published in 1798, that population naturally outstrips food supply. Malthus' theory was that population grows 'geometrically' generation by generation (2, 4, 8, 16 etc.) while the resources available to feed them can only increase 'arithmetically' (1, 2, 3, 4, 5, and so on). The inevitable consequence of this is shortage, which in turn can be 'solved' only by famine, epidemic or war.

Malthus' main concern was to propose alternatives to these three horsemen of the Apocalypse. These included strict celibacy outside marriage, delayed marriage, birth control and 'restraint' within marriage. (The first edition of the book also advocated prostitution if unmarried men couldn't control their desires: Malthus, an Anglican clergyman, quietly dropped this from later editions.) Alongside these domestic measures, hard work would be necessary in order to increase resources. What Malthus did not intend to do was to argue 'for' famine. But unfortunately it is easy to turn his argument on its head and say that if people can't exercise enough moral restraint to keep their numbers down or work hard enough to increase resources, then famine will come – and serve them right. This was the line used by pop Malthusians like Trevelyan.

In 1846 the potato harvest failed once again, and was followed by an appallingly harsh winter. Russell instituted a programme of emergency soup kitchens, but like Peel's maize, this was initially bungled. Not enough kitchens were set up, and the soup they produced was at best revolting and, at worst, made people ill. The recipe was later improved into a kind of porridge called stirabout, made with corn meal and rice cooked in water. It kept people alive – if they were fortunate enough to live in the vicinity of a kitchen. Others were less fortunate. In that year, Nicholas Cummins, a Cork magistrate, described a visit to Skibbereen. The village seemed deserted, but on entering a 'hovel' he found:

> Six famished and ghastly skeletons, to all appearances dead, huddled in a corner on some filthy straw, their sole covering what seemed a ragged horsecloth, their wretched legs hanging about . . . I approached with horror, and found by a low moaning they were alive – they were in fever, four children, a woman and what had once been a man . . . In a few minutes I was surrounded by at least 200 such phantoms, such frightful spectres as no words can describe.

While its people were starving, Ireland continued to export

food; not potatoes, but wheat and corn. Trevelyan argued that Ireland needed the money this generated – but what Ireland needed was food, properly distributed. In earlier famines Ireland had shut its ports, and prices had fallen, allowing more people to buy food; the same was done in Belgium during the blight, with similar results.

In 1847, the harvest was blight-free and the government decided to close the soup kitchens. Instead they would improve the existing system of workhouses, in line with existing Poor Law. But too many seed potatoes from the previous year had been eaten to stave off starvation and the resulting crop was insufficient to feed the starving population. As with the soup kitchens, the workhouse improvements were inadequate. There were far too few workhouses to deal with the immediate problem. To make things worse, it was decided that the construction of new workhouses and the running of existing ones should be financed entirely by taxes raised in Ireland – another of Trevelyan's illogical *idées fixes*. So taxes were raised on the only people who appeared to have any money, the landlords.

This plan backfired. Landlords weren't prepared simply to hand over the new taxes; instead they sought to find ways of lessening their liabilities. As the tax level was based on the number of tenants a landlord had on his land, many such people were evicted – often with violence, by local thugs or by British troops. Ireland, especially in the west, began to fill with wandering, starving families. Needless to say, some young Irish decided enough was enough, and fought back. When six English landlords who had evicted tenants were murdered, the British enforced a new military crackdown. 'They send us soldiers: why can they not send food?' asked one old lady.

The workhouse system was expanded, albeit with often ramshackle and insanitary premises, and did protect many from the crop failure of 1848 and a partial failure in 1849. What it could not protect against was an outbreak of cholera. Disease had been a vicious part of *an Gorta Mór* (the Great Hunger) from the start, but the arrival of this particularly vicious and contagious pestilence added a new dimension to the suffering.

Would the misery ever end?

Thankfully the harvests returned to normal from 1850 onwards. The cholera epidemic wore itself out and the belatedly expanded workhouse system finally proved able to deal with the vast numbers of poor. To put it brutally, there were fewer mouths to feed – many Irish had emigrated to the USA or Canada (a false dawn for many, who died on the overcrowded 'coffin ships'), but the main drop in population was the result of famine and disease. It is estimated that between 1845 and 1850 these two causes killed over a million people – in what was then part of the United Kingdom, the realm of Queen Victoria whose young, idealistic face looks out from the Penny Red.

CHAPTER FOUR

VICTORIA AND THE MACHINE

5 SHILLING RED, 1867

THE CHUNKY, geometrical 5 Shilling Red looks like the work of an engineer or an ironmaster, as if you could place loads on it and calculate how much it would bear. It's a proud product of a stunningly successful machine age: by 1867 the horrors of the 1840s were history and Britain had become the 'workshop of the world'.

The postal authorities were initially reluctant to create a five shilling stamp, through fear of forgery: five bob was a lot of money in 1867. But their hand was forced. More and more people were sending parcels overseas and plastering them with shilling stamps – the known record is a wrapper with seventy-seven on. Larger denominations simply had to be issued (once the five shilling appeared, even higher ones followed, culminating in a £5 stamp in 1882 – no higher denomination was to be issued for over a century, until a £10 in 1993).

What sort of people were sending these parcels? The standard of living across Britain was rising. There was a new middle class of lawyers, doctors, accountants, factory managers, entrepreneurs and, of course, engineers. Skilled workers saw their wages increasing sharply, too, and in the year when this stamp appeared, they got the vote: the Second Reform Act of 1867 extended the franchise to every urban male householder. All these people prospered on the back of the new economic system of industrial production driven by consumer markets that Adam Smith had described back in 1776. This 'Wealth Machine' had been growing in vigour for the best part of a century, but truly got into its stride once the railways were up and running, during the period known to economic historians as the Great mid-Victorian Boom. In 1867 this boom was in full swing.

What was this Wealth Machine, exactly, and why was it was so important to the Victorians?

The obvious answer to the latter question is that it made many people better off. But there is another, more compelling reason than mere wealth: survival. Even in 1867 there were people alive who would have heard their grandparents talk about the pre-industrial age and the perpetual, overhanging threat of scarcity that had existed at that time. A generation before, Ireland had tragically proven the point. In 1867 a famine was raging in Finland, the immediate causes of which were freak weather destroying a harvest and slow and insufficiently motivated reaction from central government, but which was in essence a symptom of underdevelopment. At that time, the Finns had no Wealth Machine.

The Victorian Wealth Machine had three essential aspects. The first was industrial production: the use of mechanical power in previously manually or water-driven processes, and the division of labour, breaking manufacture into small, easily repeatable tasks in which workers then specialized. Back in 1776, Adam Smith had cited the example of a factory where

ten men split the eighteen distinct operations in making pins
and just did one or two of them. As a result, the men could
make 'upwards of forty-eight thousand pins in a day. If they
had all wrought separately and independently ... certainly
could not each of them have made twenty, perhaps not one
pin in a day?'

As well as multiplying output, industrial production stand-
ardized it. All the pins from Smith's factory would have been
of pretty similar quality, and could have been bought by
consumers safe in the knowledge of this: the pins represented
what we now call a brand. The Wealth Machine's ultimate
purpose was to serve consumers. 'Consumption is the sole end
and purpose of all production; and the interest of the producer
ought to be attended to, only so far as it may be necessary for
promoting that of the consumer,' as Smith put it. These may
sound like modern sentiments, but they were already nearly a
century old in 1867.

Another aspect of the Wealth Machine was that the interests of all consumers and honest producers should be served
by a competitive market, in which consumers could say no to
substandard or overpriced products. Smith spotted an almost
mystical social process at work here, controlled by nobody but
acting as a 'hidden hand' guiding good products towards those
who needed them. (He was well aware that producers will try
and rig markets, and that everyone needs money in their pocket
to participate in the market.)

Not everyone agreed with Adam Smith's vision. The year
1867 saw the appearance of the first volume of Karl Marx's *Das
Kapital*. Marx didn't see the Wealth Machine as a lifesaver or
a creator of general prosperity. To him it was Capitalism, a
monstrous system of class exploitation, whereby a tiny group
of capital-owners sucked value out of the increasingly mindless
labour of the rest of society, and used all means possible to
keep the power to do this, not just with the help of magistrates
and redcoats but by the manipulation of values and the

narratives of the era. Such a system was beyond reform (reform was just another tool used by capitalists to con the workers). The only possible remedy would be violent revolution – which he believed would come automatically, as for Marx history was itself a machine.

Marx can be criticized in lots of ways, but in pointing out that the Wealth Machine didn't automatically benefit everybody, he was surely right. This was a truth that some Victorians, like Sir Charles Trevelyan, didn't understand; others understood but didn't care; still others understood, cared but didn't know what to do about it. Many well-meaning Victorians were afraid that if they tinkered with the system it would grind to a halt and leave them once again at the mercy of Malthus' horsemen. Even today we still don't know how to run it perfectly: the Wealth Machine doesn't come with an instruction manual.

Marx's Capitalism needed certain values to sustain it – ruthless greed and lack of compassion on the part of the capitalists, and a kind of dim-witted subservience in the workers. Adam Smith had also said that the Machine needed values, but had come up with a very different list. For him, the values were to be shared by everybody: self-interest and shrewdness but also 'moral sentiment', by which he meant a capacity to be motivated by sympathy.

Which one of them was right? Maybe the best place to look for the values of the machine-building mid-Victorians is in the books they were reading at the time. Neither *The Wealth of Nations* nor *Das Kapital* were massive best-sellers in 1867. Samuel Smiles' *Self-Help* and Dinah Craik's *John Halifax, Gentleman* were.

The first of these originated a genre that now fills bookshop shelves. *Self-Help* is a set of true stories of people who achieved great things by their own hard work, courage, integrity and cheerfulness. To modern readers, it's a bit worthy. Mrs Craik's novel is much more fun. Its patches of full-on Victorian melodrama can be embarrassing (or funny, depending on your mood), but the classic Victorian qualities of the book's hero – industriousness, energy and determination, coupled with personal modesty, integrity and concern for other people – rise above this.

John Halifax, Gentleman is actually set in pre-Victorian times, as are many mid-Victorian classics, including *David Copperfield*, *Middlemarch* and most of *Great Expectations*. But readers in 1867 felt the book was about their time, and it was. The central character, John, an orphan scraping a living on the streets, is taken in by Abel Fletcher, a Quaker, who gives him a series of jobs, starting at the bottom with particularly unpleasant work in a tannery. John performs his tasks with diligence and rises to a position of responsibility, while 'improving' himself in his spare time (a very Victorian activity), learning to read and making models of machinery. At the same time, John proves a true friend to Fletcher's son, a disabled boy named Phineas: it is a core message of the book that success and humanity are not mutually exclusive but can go hand in hand. When John falls in love with and marries the daughter of a Hanoverian squire, she is cut off by her family without a penny. But John is given the opportunity to take over and modernize an old mill; when a scheming aristocrat dams the stream that drives the mill, John turns this potential disaster into an advantage and installs steam power:

> *'Now, my men – ready?'*
> *He opened the valve.*
> *With a strange noise . . . the steam came rushing into the*
> *cylinder. There was a slight motion of the piston rod.*
> *'Will it work?'*
> *No, it stopped.*
> *John drew a deep breath.*
> *It went on again, beginning to move slowly up and down*
> *. . . Greater and lesser cogwheels caught up the motive*
> *power, revolving slowly and majestically with steady*

regular rotations, or whirling round so fast you could
hardly see they stirred at all. Of a sudden, a soul had been
put into that wonderful creature of man's making.

To finance this, he is forced to cut his workers' wages, but takes a pay cut himself. The mill prospers and John becomes a pillar of the community.

At the same time, John Halifax is, in Victorian terms, a radical. He takes no notice of sectarian distinctions, an attitude that was a genuine challenge to the Tory Protestant orthodoxy of English life. Politically, John's entrepreneurship subverts the established economic order. Many great Hanoverian and Victorian entrepreneurs came from Nonconformist traditions.

John Halifax, Gentleman embodies the values which the Victorians – especially the growing middle class who could afford five shillings to send a parcel – believed were necessary to build a modern society and a Machine that would keep that society clear of Malthus' terrible horsemen and instead generate ever-increasing wealth. And Dinah Craik goes further, investigating which qualities were needed to keep that Machine human. In this task, perhaps, she falters. The struggle to keep the Wealth Machine human was not impossible, as Karl Marx thought, but it was far bigger and tougher than the struggle faced by John Halifax, who operated a small factory in a rural market town and was not faced by the masses of urban poor in the big manufacturing centres or, of course, in the vast megalopolis of London.

Another writer, however, was well aware of this difficulty.

CHAPTER FIVE

'NEVER BE MEAN, NEVER BE FALSE, NEVER BE CRUEL'

THREE HALFPENCE RED, 1870

THE MACHINE-LIKE 5 Shilling Red of the last chapter had been made using a new technology: surface printing. For the low-value Three Halfpence issue of 1870, the Post Office went back to the line-engraved method that had produced the Penny Black thirty years before. It was cheaper that way: they could reuse an old design first produced (but not issued) in 1860. This featured the youthful Victoria of the Wyon–Corbould profile – a woman who was now a middle-aged widow, drowning in grief at the loss of a truly loved husband.

The Three Halfpence Red was issued in the year that saw the death of that titan of British literature, Charles Dickens, a man instantly associated with the Victorian age and one who can tell us much about Victorian England and its struggles to adapt to the changes that were sweeping through it.

Dickens brought his era to life in the way Chaucer and Shakespeare brought theirs; his books teem with life, especially the life of London, which in 1870 was not only the biggest city in the world but the biggest city that the world had ever seen, having outgrown rival claimants to this title, eleventh-century Baghdad and eighteenth-century Beijing, around the time the Penny Black was issued. He was an obsessive observer of the capital. Throughout his working life he would take long walks through its slums, its docks, its elegant squares, its financial centre, its Inns of Court, its thoroughfares clogged with pedestrians and horse-drawn traffic; always watching, sensing, listening, noting.

Success came early to this great people-watcher; at 24 he was given the job of writing stories to accompany a set of sporting prints, a popular genre at the time. This appeared to be something of a coup – the artist, Robert Seymour, was better known than Dickens – but *The Pickwick Papers* soon eclipsed the prints, especially once the chirpy, streetwise Sam Weller joined Mr Pickwick and his crew. The first episode of the *Papers* sold 400 copies, the last 40,000. *Oliver Twist* followed two years later – and was even more successful. In this novel Dickens wrote about the subjects that truly mattered to him: the condition of the poor, the sanctity of home and family, and the sacred, vulnerable nature of childhood.

Dickens saw the harsh side of the mid-Victorian Wealth Machine; how some people were swept aside by it while others toiled at the bottom of it, and how others lifted themselves clear of material poverty but fell into an imaginative and emotional poverty that he found even more horrifying (Machine-enriched men like Paul Dombey are much more miserable than the likes of Sam Weller).

He was not alone in this. Henry Mayhew's *London Labour and the London Poor* (1851) consisted of interviews with a huge range of individuals who scraped a marginal living in the capital: prostitutes (of which there were tens of thousands, alongside all that Victorian respectability), beggars, street vendors, thieves and all sorts of bizarre traders such as the pure-finders who collected dog faeces for use in tanning. Many of these people were under-employed, finding work when and where they could.

Other observers such as Friedrich Engels looked at life in factories, where people did at least have regular employment – but in appalling conditions. Hours were long and breaks short. The 1847 Factories Act had limited the working week to 58 hours for women and children and banned child labour under the age of nine. But London's East End contained sweatshops where these rules were ignored. Even law-abiding factories were noisy, smelly and often dangerous: specific industries had their own health hazards, about which little was done. Matchmakers, for example, often suffered phossy jaw, a condition that began with toothache but moved on to abscesses, rotting of the jawbone, brain damage and death. (It was caused by the use of white phosphorus in match-heads, despite the existence of a safe, but more expensive alternative, red phosphorus. It was only when the law stepped in, in 1906, to ban the use of white phosphorus, that phossy jaw disappeared.)

Dickens raged against poverty in his novels, but he also sought to bring about change by personal actions. He ran a reform institution for prostitutes called Urania Cottage, which was funded by the banking heiress Angela Burdett Coutts. There were a number of institutions for such women, most of them grimly centred on drumming into the heads of the inmates how sinful they had been. Dickens and Coutts made Urania Cottage a friendly and decent place, where the women were encouraged to look forward to a better life.

However, Dickens was no Karl Marx. He disliked big social movements, fearing the de-individuating power of the mob: for him, the ultimate answer to society's ills was for individuals to reform themselves. He wrote about personal journeys: to maturity, to understanding of self and the world, to useful work and, above all, to connection to other individuals. His hatred of poverty was fundamentally based not on a passion for equality but on the fact that it prevented people from making these journeys. His most profound hatred was reserved for the cruel and the false, at any level of society.

The importance of home life was another key theme in Dickens' work. A loving home was his preferred outcome for the characters he cared about, and the failure to achieve such an outcome a mark of tragedy. Family life mattered hugely to the Victorians: the home was seen as a safe place for finer and more delicate feelings, in contrast to the competitive world outside. The tone was set by the Queen herself, whose relationship with Prince Albert was a genuinely happy one from their first meeting, through their first night together – 'a gratifying and bewildering experience' according to her diary – to their life thereafter. When Albert died aged 42 in 1861, the devastated Victoria retreated into a private world for many years, only truly emerging into public view for her Jubilee in 1887 (and even then, clad in black). Legend has it that for many years after his death she had servants lay out Albert's clothes every morning.

Roles, of course, in the Victorian home were clearly defined. Children were supposed to be mild and obedient. The wife was to be 'the angel of the house', according to the hugely popular 1854 poem by Coventry Patmore, selflessly caring for everyone. The legal position of the angel was, however, decidedly unheavenly: once a woman married, all her property became her husband's. In a *cause célèbre* of the time, Caroline Norton, largely because of family pressure, was married as a teenager to a bullying, egotistical man. The match culminated in violence and she left him. But under the law this meant that she lost the right to see her children, who were regarded as their father's property. Later, when she was left some money, her husband claimed this for himself. He even took her to court to claim the small amount she earned from writing fiction.

Because of stories like Caroline Norton's we are often snooty about the Victorians and their talk of family. But in other ways, we cling desperately to their values. Our modern Christmas, that great festival of family, is essentially Victorian. Christmas cards were invented by Rowland Hill's ally, Henry Cole. The decorated tree topped with an angel and surrounded by family presents became nationally popular after a picture of Victoria and Albert with one appeared in the *Illustrated London News* in 1846. The first crackers, made by Tom Smith, appeared the following year (paper hats and jokes were introduced a generation later, by his son, Walter). Santa Claus' red outfit was created by the American cartoonist Thomas Nast in 1862. And by far the most popular Christmas story, apart from the Nativity itself, is Dickens' endlessly reworked *A Christmas Carol.* On the subject of carols, many of the ones we sing today come from the Victorian era: some of the more sentimental ones ('Away in a Manger', 'Once in Royal David's City') but also 'It Came upon the Midnight Clear', 'We Three Kings' and 'O Little Town of Bethlehem'. 'Hark the Herald Angels Sing' got its marvellous Mendelssohn tune in 1840. 'O Come all ye Faithful' was translated from its original Latin by prolific hymn-writer J.M. Neale the next year (he later translated 'O Come, O Come Emmanuel'). 'Good King Wenceslas' is another Neale lyric, written to an old tune. There – that's nine carols. Perfect for the format of Nine Lessons and Carols, which was devised by Edward White Benson in 1880.

Dickens' own youthful idealism about marriage and the home faded – he separated from the angel in his house and had a long affair with an actress, Ellen Ternan – but he remained passionate about the welfare of children. His own childhood, in a chaotic but affectionate household (the Micawbers in *David Copperfield* are based on his parents) came to an abrupt end when he was sent out, aged 12, to work in a boot-polish factory. He doesn't seem to have been especially mistreated; the other boys who worked there – including one lad called

Bob Fagin – were not unfriendly; his pain was more at the apparent death of his dreams of being a man of letters. This ordeal lasted five months, after which he was put back on the middle-class track of education.

By the standards of some Victorian children, even when making boot polish young Dickens was fortunate. The classic image of Victorian child exploitation is that of children as young as six, covered in soot and grime from working up chimneys. A series of toothless laws tried to prevent this abuse, but it wasn't until the philanthropist Lord Shaftesbury launched a campaign against it, culminating in the prosecution for manslaughter of a sweep whose 'apprentice' had died trapped in a chimney, that the 1875 Chimney Sweepers Act made the law stick. Many more children were put to work in factories, of course, and others had to live in workhouses similar to the one in *Oliver Twist*, where they were at the mercy of Bumble-like supervisors.

At the other end of the social spectrum, the era saw a rash of exclusive new public schools: Marlborough, Clifton, Malvern, Wellington, Rossall, Haileybury, Lancing, Ardingly, Radley and Cranleigh. These catered for both the rising middle class and that level of British society – lesser landowners, military and naval officers – who could be regarded as gentlemen but who couldn't afford to send their children to Eton, Harrow or Winchester. Other, established schools, many of which had been operating since the time of Elizabeth I, quietly reconstituted themselves along public school lines, following the model set out by Dr Thomas Arnold's Rugby and immortalised in Thomas Hughes' *Tom Brown's Schooldays* (1857).

This vast divide was narrowed, a little, anyway, in the year the Three Halfpence Red appeared, when the Elementary Education Act of Liberal MP William Forster created School Boards across the country, tasked with providing universal education. It took some while for these to be set up and for schools to be built, but by 1880 the nation was ready for a further Act that made school attendance to age 10 compulsory. This was carried through despite objections from those who feared it would 'make the working classes think', and from poor parents who wanted their children to be out earning money. Probably not every child approved either.

Charles Dickens would have applauded heartily – but, of course, he was no longer around to do so. In 1865, he was involved in a railway accident at Staplehurst in Kent, when the Folkestone to London boat train came off the rails on a bridge that was under repair. He was lucky to be travelling in the first class carriage as it was the only one not to be derailed. At once he got involved in attempts to assist other passengers, at some danger to himself. The incident and his reaction to it made him even more of a national hero, but it took a toll on his health.

Until Staplehurst, Dickens lived a life characterised by that great Victorian trait, energy. Aside from the long walks, perpetual deadlines and running Urania Cottage, he also edited newspapers and periodicals, corresponded at length with many individuals, acted in amateur theatricals (to a professional standard), raised funds for Great Ormond Street Children's Hospital, and gave highly dramatic readings the length and breadth of the UK and on two tours of America, as well as looking after his large family (his ten children, his siblings and his parents), all of whom readily accepted his generosity. After the accident, his pace slowed markedly. He died in June 1870.

Dickens has been criticized for seeing industrialization and commerce as purely negative forces. Sometimes that does seem to be the message. But he was happy for his heroes and heroines to prosper within the system, provided they did so via honourable work, and protected themselves from creeping 'mental industrialization', a kind of worship of the Machine and its methods. For Dickens, humanity, in all its contrary unmechanical glory, must always be the master.

A hundred years after his death, Dickens was honoured

with his own set of stamps, joining at the time a distinguished list of non-royals to be so celebrated: Shakespeare, Churchill, Joseph Lister, Robert Burns and Mahatma Gandhi. On one of them, a 5d, Betsy Trotwood gives David Copperfield the quintessentially Dickensian advice which forms the title of this chapter, 'Never be mean, never be false, never be cruel'.

CHAPTER SIX

33 BILLION

PENNY LILAC, 1881

THE PENNY Lilac was produced not just in millions but billions: 33 billion, actually. If you put all the Penny Lilacs ever issued side by side, they would stretch for 660,000 kilometres – to the moon and most of the way back, or round the equator 16½ times. The Victorians, more sensibly, put them on letters.

The Post Office had been booming ever since the introduction of the penny post. Colonel Maberley managed to get Rowland Hill sacked in 1843 – like John Halifax, Hill was a radical, and the Colonel was able to persuade the new Tory government that he should go – but in 1846 the government changed again, and Hill was reinstated. He then had an eighteen-year run at the job, ten of them as Secretary once the Colonel had retired. Hill was a restless reformer, perpetually looking for ways to improve the system.

Part of this involved simply adding to or improving the existing networks: more post offices, more postmen. The London distribution system, which dealt with a quarter of the nation's mail, was reorganized into the sections we now know in the capital's postcodes – SW, EC, WC, SE, N (and so on) – and the effectiveness of this is shown in the fact that by 1857, London residents and businesses were receiving a staggering twelve deliveries a day: every hour, on the hour. Most towns and cities had three deliveries a day.

Hill also introduced new ideas. In 1852, Anthony Trollope, now back in England but still a loyal Post Office man, suggested the introduction of pillar boxes, which he had seen on a visit to France. These were trialled in the Channel Islands and brought to London in 1855. Originally painted green, they really became popular when it was decided to paint them red.

In 1854, Hill insisted on entry exams for the Post Office, which by 1859 had over 25,000 employees. Advertised vacancies were always over-subscribed: the work offered fair pay, decent job security, good working conditions and a sense of serving the community. And from 1865, a uniform, consisting of a black kepi copied from Parisian posties, red frock coat, waterproof cape and grey trousers.

In 1861, the Post Office Savings Bank was opened (100 years later, this event was celebrated with a set of commemorative stamps). This was another example of Hill's public service mentality: the existing banks were not interested in the business of poor people, but anyone could open an account at the POSB and millions did.

Hill retired in 1864. His successor, John Tilley, had begun his Post Office career as a clerk in 1829. He was a man in Hill's mould, who adapted the service's existing structures to enable continued growth. Like Hill, he ran the service to maximize the benefit to the public. He was a keen cutter of costs to the user, reducing the rate for newspapers and heavier letters. In 1870, he persuaded the government to buy the various small telegraph services, thus taking another part of Victoria's Communication Revolution under the wing of the Post Office. He then cut the cost of this service, too, greatly boosting its use and making the telegram a national institution.

In 1880, Tilley was replaced by Henry Fawcett, a blind economist from Cambridge (and a keen advocate of women's suffrage) who proved to be another dynamic leader. Fawcett introduced postal orders and a cheap national parcel post system that set off a boom in mail order business. He also introduced the Penny Lilac, which was effectively a replacement for that old trouper, the Penny Red, of which 20 billion had been produced between 1841 and 1880. (A Penny Brown intervened between these two stalwarts, but didn't last long.)

Twenty billion Penny Reds, 33 billion Penny Lilacs: these figures sum up the incredible success that was the Victorian Post Office. It was a triumph of imagination and sound management, of civic values such as hard work and public spirit. The latter are nowadays expected – even if we don't always find them in public life, we hope they will be there and feel angry or at least disappointed if they are not. But they had not been Hanoverian virtues. The great entrepreneurs of the pre-Victorian era may have shown them, but they did so in opposition to the boozy, dandified hedonism of the prevailing culture. The Victorians were the people who truly took civic priorities to heart.

London in the year the Penny Lilac appeared, 1881, was full of the results of this mindset: the Thames Embankment, for example, the work of Joseph Bazalgette, the most remarkable public engineer of his day, inheriting the mantle of Brunel who died in 1859. When the 'Great Stink' of 1858 made life in the city unbearable, Bazalgette was asked to repair the capital's sewerage system. Instead, he created a totally new one, with vast arterial and outfall sewers, treatment beds and pumping stations. Eighty-two miles of tunnels were dug, which meant moving 2.7 million cubic metres of earth, after which 300 million bricks were laid. The system is still in use today: Bazalgette planned for the future; the diameter of the sewers was twice what he was told it needed to be.

Rather than disrupting the already overcrowded London streets, Bazalgette created the Embankment, incorporating gardens, a road, part of the new Underground railway and, of course, the sewer. It extended all the way to Chelsea, which he reached in 1874. (You can still see one of his pumping stations between the railway bridge out of Victoria station and Chelsea Bridge.) Having hemmed in the great river, he turned his attention to helping people cross it: Albert, Putney and (finest of all) Hammersmith Bridges are all Bazalgette's designs, from the 1880s, as was the original Woolwich ferry terminal (1889).

Other civic projects of the era included the Houses of Parliament, which were completed in 1870, and the Albert Hall (1871). 1881 itself saw the opening of Alfred Waterstone's magnificent Natural History Museum in South Kensington. A visitor would come away with the impression of a mighty city that was the capital of the world's leading economic power.

But was this still the case?

In 1873, the Great mid-Victorian Boom came to an end. In the world's first truly global crash, a stock market panic in Austria spread to New York, where the bank run by Jay Cooke, the man who had financed the Union victory in the Civil War, collapsed. It then hit the UK. The subsequent economic downturn was especially harsh in the countryside, where it formed the background to the dark Aeschylean rural novels of Thomas Hardy and hastened the decline of the old aristocracy, whose income still largely came from the land.

The urban economy began to pick up as the 1870s wore on. However, it did not do so as quickly as that of Britain's rivals.

America now had its own version of the British railway revolution: the last quarter of the nineteenth century saw the Gilded Age – or Rise of the Robber Barons, to take a different perspective – when men like Andrew Carnegie, J.P. Morgan and John D. Rockefeller made previously unimaginable sums of money. American inventiveness seemed to surpass that of the British at that time. Thomas Edison had already set up his famous research lab at Menlo Park: in 1881 it turned out 50,000 of the new electric light bulbs. Alexander Graham Bell, a Scottish immigrant to the States, invented the telephone in 1876. Eadweard Muybridge, another expat Briton in the USA, invented moving pictures in 1877. Later, in the 1880s, Herman Hollerith was to invent a 'tabulating machine' that was a forerunner of the computer. Not only did the Americans invent, they commercialized. Edison was the founder of General Electric, Bell (or at least his father-in-law) of AT & T, and Hollerith of IBM.

Closer to home, Germany was beginning to catch up. United only since 1871, the new nation worked hard both to modernize its agriculture and to build manufacturing power in the areas of steel, chemicals and the use of electrical power, in what is known as the Second Industrial Revolution. (Britain was still chuffing along on steam.) Germany also innovated socially, with Chancellor Bismarck introducing old age pensions, medical care and unemployment insurance. And she began to build up her armed forces.

Still, in 1881 there was much in British life to enjoy.

Gilbert and Sullivan were turning out their comic operas, which poked camp, affectionate fun at the British establishment. There were seventy music halls in the capital. The nation's passion for sport was rising, too. The 1881 FA Cup Final at Kennington Oval marked the end of an era: Old Carthusians beat the favourites, Old Etonians, 3–0 (Sir Elliot Colvin, Bart., clearly did a better job in the Carthusian defence than the OE midfielder, the Honourable Arthur Kinnaird). Next year, Blackburn Rovers would be in the final, and from 1884 onwards all the finalists were professional teams from the north or the midlands, bearing names still recognized today (Tottenham

Hotspur was the first southern professional team to compete, winning in 1900).

In high summer there was cricket. The year 1881 was a rather routine one for the sport: W.G. Grace, titan of the Victorian game, had a quiet season and the year's top batsman was Alfred Hornby. Hornby is now best known thanks to Francis Thompson's poem, 'At Lord's', a meditation on the passage of time which ends 'Oh my Hornby and my Barlow long ago!' (Barlow, with whom Hornby opened the Lancashire batting, was actually rather dull to watch.)

Hornby and Barlow neatly sum up a dichotomy that had opened up in British society. Hornby was an amateur, a 'gentleman'; Barlow a professional, a 'player'. Hornby was expected to play a dashing game; Barlow's job was to stick around and acquire runs, boring but reliable.

The cricketing fixture of Gentlemen versus Players dates back to 1806. But by 1881, the concepts behind those terms had changed. In 1806, the concept of what made a 'gent' was pleasantly vague: it was something to do with your background, something to do with the profession you chose to take up, a lot to do with your conduct. Someone of humble origins could earn the title of 'a real gentleman' by acting in a considerate fashion (as both Samuel Smiles and Dinah Craik had been eager to point out). This became ever less possible during the late Victorian era thanks to the public schools, which tried to corner the market: a gentleman was fast becoming coterminous with someone who had attended one of these.

This change was a great loss to national life. The new schools inculcated a snobbery about 'trade' and commerce, the very things that had made Britain successful. They introduced a fixed, obvious social barrier where there had previously been a subtle, permeable one. The most obvious sign of that barrier was the divisive public school accent that led Bernard Shaw to write in 1912, 'It is impossible for an Englishman to open his mouth without making some other Englishman hate or despise him.' Back in the 1840s, Sir Robert Peel had spoken with a gentle Lancashire roll, and nobody gave the matter a second thought; even earlier, apparently, Jane Austen spoke broad Hampshire.

The accent was all part of the public school offering, which was to turn out products with a reliable brand identity that could be slotted into the machinery of government, in Whitehall or in Trincomalee. The Empire needed public school men. This 'branding' also helped new arrivals among the well-off to cement their status: send your sons to Rugby or Marlborough and your social ambitions were achieved (even if it meant the same sons now looked down on the way you had earned the money to send them there).

Politics had polarized, too. In early Victorian days, though parliament was split into Whigs and Tories, alliances often shifted between the two: for example, Lord Palmerston, a Tory, served in both Whig and Tory cabinets, and ended up heading a Liberal government. As the Queen's reign went on, however, a more modern-looking politics emerged, with two distinct parties, each led by a non-titled, charismatic, nationally known figure with a clear political style. Benjamin Disraeli was the witty, urbane, flag-waving Tory: 'Dizzy', an apparent pragmatist but secretly head over heels in love with England, its culture, its stories and its way of life (especially that of the upper classes). William Ewart Gladstone was the earnest, internationalist Liberal: 'The People's William', always looking to uplift and improve, to seek out inequity and iniquity and right them.

The two men genuinely hated each other, and didn't always keep to Queensberry rules (another Victorian sporting innovation) in debate. Disraeli, who usually won these battles, described Gladstone as 'a sophistical rhetorician, inebriated with the exuberance of his own verbosity'. Gladstone once had a go at Disraeli with 'I predict, sir, that you will die either by hanging or of some vile disease', to which Dizzy instantly replied, 'That all depends, sir, upon whether I embrace your principles or your mistress.'

1881 saw the end of this great double act; it was the year Disraeli died. Gladstone didn't attend the funeral and even managed a final insult, safe at last knowing that his opponent couldn't answer back: 'As Disraeli lived, so he died – all display, without reality or genuineness.' The ill-natured tone of 'Tory' versus 'progressive' politics had been set.

The visitor to London in 1881 would have left the city from one of the capital's magnificent stations – all Victorian (Euston, the earliest, opened a month into the Queen's reign). If they had time to spare before they caught their train, they might have bought a copy of one of the new mass-circulation magazines, such as George Newnes' *Tit-Bits*, which contained dramatic human interest stories, some true, others fictional – the children of the 1870 Education Act were now adult, and needed entertaining. Or, of course, he or she might have written home about their adventures in the capital – the Victorians wrote letters the way we send email or texts – before sticking one of the new Penny Lilac stamps on the envelope.

CHAPTER SEVEN

JUBILEE
1½d,
JUBILEE ISSUE, 1887

IN 1887 a great new set of stamps, covering ten denominations, appeared. Because they coincided with the Queen's Golden Jubilee, they became known as the 'Jubilees'. However, they weren't issued in commemoration of this grand national event, but because their predecessors had been amazingly dull.

Ten new definitives had appeared in 1884, to proud boasts that Britain would finally have a truly 'unified' set of stamps. They featured tasteful geometric designs and came in one of two sober colours, a muted lilac and an even more muted green. The public hated them, as did postal workers, who found it hard to distinguish between denominations. Stung by the almost universal criticism, the Post Office's Stamp Committee went back to the drawing board, resolving to create an issue that was colourful and easy to distinguish.

The result was the Jubilees, among the finest British definitives ever.

The most striking thing about the Jubilees was their use of two colours on a single stamp, either one colour on a coloured base or two colours on a white base. This was the first time the British Post Office had splashed out this way (and nearly the first time anyone had: America got there one year earlier). The new issue also contained a variety of design approaches – something that purists complain about, seeing unity as a supreme virtue in a stamp issue. But variety is all part of the attraction of the Jubilees, and reflects perfectly the busy world of 1887 Britain.

The issue also reflects the taste of 1887 Britain. Another purist complaint is that the Jubilees are cluttered – but the late Victorians loved clutter. Starting at the top; over the years, Queen Victoria filled her favourite residences – Osborne House on the Isle of Wight and Balmoral Castle in Aberdeenshire – with it. Heavy brown furniture, nick-nacks, chandeliers, pot-plants, curtains, patterned wallpaper (where it was visible, between the rows of gilt-framed pictures), velvet chairs dripping tassels, thick dark carpets, oriental rugs, bits of dead animal – an elephant's foot umbrella stand, a tiger-skin in front of the elaborate fireplace, a stag staring glassy-eyed from the wall. So naturally, her loyal subjects did the same.

I've chosen this particular Jubilee stamp because of the curtains, which seem to say a lot, not just as an example of period design but as a metaphor for the era.

Curtains can be theatrical. The Victorians enjoyed melodrama, complete with ingénue, scheming villain, good-hearted but naïve father and woman 'fallen from grace'. The king of this was actor-playwright Dion Boucicault, who wrote and produced such plays from the time of the Penny Black to the time of the Jubilee. (Boucicault's real name was Dionysius Lardner Boursiquot: the Victorians did names brilliantly; Dickens had a painter friend called Augustus Leopold Egg, whose professional colleagues included Charles de Sousy Ricketts, Mortimer Luddington Menpes and Rupert Charles Wulsten Bunny.) Melodrama also drove many now-unread but then hugely popular novels, such as Mrs Henry Wood's *East Lynne* (1861), versions of which featured almost permanently on the late Victorian stage. 'Gone! And never called me mother!' declaimed endless actresses playing fallen woman Lady Isabel Vane, confronting the death of her illegitimate child, the result of a fling with moustache-twirling villain Francis Levison.

Curtains can be mysterious. The 1887 edition of a popular magazine called *Beeton's Christmas Annual* ran a story by a doctor from Southsea. The doctor's story had been rejected by a number of publications, but this editor liked it and went with his instinct. It was called *A Study in Scarlet*, and featured a detective called Sherlock Holmes.

Holmes is almost as synonymous with the Victorian era as the Queen and Dickens. This is partly due to his success – people all round the world love the stories – but partly because he carries some of the unease of his era with him.

He is the supreme rationalist. His method is based on minute observations followed by rigorous logic: as he tells Dr Watson, 'By a man's finger-nails, by his coat-sleeve, by his boots, by his trouser-knees, by the callosities of his forefinger and thumb, by his expression, by his shirtcuffs – by each of these things a man's calling is plainly revealed.' He backs this up with technology, using chemical analysis to identify poisons and microscopes to examine trace evidence. Here is late nineteenth-century science – logical, empirical, leaping forward from discovery to discovery – coming to the rescue of the good guys against the bad.

However, Holmes is an emotional mess. He has no friends, apart from Dr Watson (who is almost as archetypal as Holmes: the classic public school gent; affable, loyal, unimaginative). Love never enters Holmes' life. He seems to be what we would now call bipolar. 'Nothing could exceed his energy when the working fit was upon him,' Watson says. 'But now and again a reaction would seize him, and for days on end he would lie upon the sofa in the sitting room, hardly uttering a word or moving a muscle from morning to night.' He takes morphine and cocaine.

Throughout history, men have been taught to be tough and not to give all their feelings away – apart from odd interludes when 'men of sensibility' are all the rage. The Victorians, especially the late Victorians, took the stiff upper lip to an extreme. There is a range of reasons for this, but one driving force was the Empire, which required cool, unemotional men to build and run it.

The clever thing about Sherlock Holmes' characterization is that he is not some untroubled imperialist, cheerily exhorting his doomed comrades to 'Play up and Play the Game' seconds before the spears fly, but is clearly damaged by his hiding of emotion.

Curtains conceal. If the late Victorians had trouble with emotions, they appeared to flounder when it came to sex. They drew heavy brocades around the bed, then cried 'Shame!' on anyone who talked about what went on behind them or who broke the rules of sexual engagement. This applied especially to women: that double standard, whereby a man with a healthy sexual appetite is a bit of a card but his female counterpart is a shameful hussy, was commonly adhered to. The rules were strict, too. No sex before marriage; monogamy within it; shame if you divorced.

They also had a bizarre obsession with masturbation. *Eric, or Little by Little* (1858) was a popular Victorian novel by Frederic Farrar, a clergyman who became Dean of Canterbury Cathedral. It tells of how a nice but weak public schoolboy sinks into depravity and death (the depravity is decidedly tame by modern standards). Masturbation is a key part of that sinking. 'May every schoolboy who reads this page be warned by the waving of their wasted hands from that burning marle of passion where they found nothing but shame and ruin, polluted affections and an early grave!' the book thunders.

Rather than enjoying a good bit of burning marle, the Victorians seemed to specialize in setting up situations charged with slightly off-beat sexual energy, then pretending they weren't sexual at all. Gladstone spent a great deal of time and energy rescuing 'fallen women' – but this involved odd, secret late-night encounters rather than a public, structured response like that of Dickens and Angela Burdett Coutts. Then there were all those homo-erotic spankings at public schools . . .

Explicit homosexuality was, of course, totally taboo. The Labouchère amendment to the Criminal Law Amendment Act of 1885 created the offence of gross indecency, which covered a multitude of non-sins and was used to prosecute homosexuals when actual sodomy (a separate and long-standing offence) could not be proven. It was the 'crime' proven against Oscar Wilde, and enough to get him two years' hard labour. In the next century it was the offence of Alan Turing, Enigma codebreaker, a man who should have been lauded as a war hero but was instead hounded to an early death. Such bigotry wasn't a product of Victorian society: even in the rip-roaring eighteenth century people had been hanged for sodomy, under laws which dated back to Henry VIII.

However, a number of myths have sprung up exaggerating the Victorians' sexual coyness. Did they use overhanging cloths to hide table-legs because there was something dangerously suggestive about bare legs? No, they used overhanging cloths because these were more pieces of clutter they could fill their houses with. Neither is there much evidence that Victorian women were advised to 'lie back and think of England', or that Queen Victoria refused to sign another part of the 1885 Act outlawing lesbianism, commenting, 'Women do not do such things.' Nonetheless, the Victorian approach to sex did not exactly encourage self-knowledge or tolerance of others' sexuality. In Britain, it took a while to realize the dangers of this attitude: two continentals got there well ahead of us.

Sigmund Freud is often considered a modern thinker – but he belongs firmly to the same century as Dickens and Queen Victoria. He graduated in 1873, the year the mid-Victorian boom ended. By the time the Jubilee stamps appeared, he was already working with Joseph Breuer on the case of Bertha Pappenheim (Anna O), the first person to be psychoanalysed. His patients were hysterics, people who, Freud argued, had repressed their sexual feelings totally, so that desire was forced to find strange ways of expressing itself. The route to health lay via honesty, via pulling back inner curtains and confronting truth.

Friedrich Nietzsche is another 'modern' who turns out to be pure nineteenth century: he didn't even outlive the Queen. Like Freud, he was a passionate advocate of self-understanding. Works like 1887's *On the Genealogy of Morals* show a particular hatred of religious moralizing, seeing it as a devious attempt by a scared majority to nobble original and energetic individuals. Instead, nothing should be allowed to stand in the way of *Redlichkeit*, which literally means the quality of telling the truth, but which is usually translated as authenticity.

If Adam Smith spoke to the nineteenth century from an earlier epoch, Nietzsche did the same for the twentieth. In both cases, travesties of their views led to immense suffering – Smith in Ireland via the market fundamentalism of Trevelyan; Nietzsche in mid-century Europe via the Nazis, who latched on to his martial tone plus an anti-Semitism posthumously inserted into his ideas by his sister. But more measured interpretations of these thinkers set free, and continue to set free, tremendous energies previously bottled up by ignorance and convention.

In 1887, energy was also set free by the Jubilee, which was celebrated around Britain with church services, feasts, dances, sports, processions, declamations of 'loyal' poems, peals of bells,

bonfires, picnics and fireworks. Brass bands played and choirs
sang. The weather even joined in: Jubilee day, Tuesday 21 June,
was sunny all over the country. In Badsey, near Evesham, a tug
of war between married ladies and unmarried was won by the
former, who got pudding basins as prizes. In Nantwich, a procession marched through the streets, the town band leading the
way followed by 2,000 children from church schools – Baptists,
Congregationalists, Primitive Methodists, Hallelujah Mission,
Roman Catholics, Free Church, Wesleyan, then C of E (the
order was democratically decided by ballot) – and later on, there
were races, band playing, dancing, acrobats, and a two-man
'donkey' which fell off the stage . . .

The Queen herself attended a vast banquet the night before,
which most of Europe's royalty – nearly all related to her –
attended, and on the day went in public procession to a service
of thanksgiving in Westminster Abbey, escorted by Indian
cavalry. The route was lined with cheering crowds, who
seemed to bring Victoria out of herself again. After the Jubilee,
the Widow of Windsor re-entered public life, ending her
generation-long exile of mourning for Albert.

She lived for another fourteen years, seeing sixty-year celebrations in 1897 and surviving into the twentieth century. There
is, apparently, jerky film footage of her riding in a motor car.
The most intimate companions of her later years were two
servants, John Brown and Abdul Karim. She enjoyed the
company of these loyal and forthright men; much better than
being fawned on by courtiers, irritated by her son and heir,
flattered by Disraeli or, worst of all, being lectured by Gladstone,
a man she disliked intensely. Maybe she was a little in love
with them, too – when Brown died, she had a statue of him
erected in Balmoral.

On 13 January 1901, the curtains closed on the Queen
Empress, the young figure on the Penny Black who had gone
on to reign over a nation that had grown in wealth and influence as no other had ever done. Its population doubled in that

time, but instead of facing Malthus' horsemen, most of the inhabitants of the island of Britain – not just the rich, but the middle class, skilled workers and even unskilled workers in regular employment – experienced an unparalleled increase in prosperity and opportunity. The poorest did not share in this increase. Nor did most of Victoria's subjects across the Irish Sea. But on balance, one has to applaud Victoria and her cheerful, energetic people. On being told she was to be queen, she is reputed to have promised, 'I will be good.' She kept her word.

CHAPTER EIGHT

HONG KONG HEROES

HONG KONG FIVE CENTS, 1892

T HE HONG KONG Five Cents comes from an album given to me by a great-uncle, who had filled it as a boy in the Edwardian era. The album is one where countries are listed and squares are provided to stick stamps in. Some of the pages are empty: I have no stamps from Cundinamarca, Mayotte or Stellaland. But most are not, and many of the stamps that fill them bear the heads of Queen Victoria or King Edward. Such places include Barbados, British Bechuanaland, Cape of Good Hope, Ceylon, Cyprus, Gold Coast, Honduras, Mauritius, Natal, Newfoundland, St Lucia, Selangor, South Australia, Straits Settlements, Tasmania, Uganda and Victoria. There is an 1898 Christmas stamp from Canada which features a map of the world that is largely covered in red, with the words 'We hold a vaster empire than has ever been'. (That is not quite true: in 1898, the record for the largest empire ever still rested with Genghis Khan. But Queen Victoria wasn't far behind him.)

My great-uncle, of course, was a passionate believer in the British Empire. He'd served in it, and believed that it brought justice, peace and prosperity to otherwise wild and cruel places. When I grew up, on the other hand, and was sticking stamps into my own album from an independent India, it was fashionable to rubbish the Empire: any talk of its bringing justice was hypocrisy; it had been founded on greed and cruelty, and maintained on cynicism and racism.

Who was right?

The tale behind the Hong Kong Five Cents does not set out looking good for the pro-Empire camp. The history of Hong Kong begins with trade: during the eighteenth century, Britain wanted ever more of China's tea, silk and porcelain. China, however, wasn't hugely interested in anything Britain had to offer it – as the Qianlong Emperor told its emissary Lord McCartney in 1793: 'Our Celestial Empire possesses all things in prolific abundance and lacks no product within its own borders. There is therefore no need to import the manufactures of outside barbarians in exchange for our own produce.' However the Emperor 'as a mark of favour' permitted the establishment of foreign firms at Canton (Guangzhou), 'so that your wants might be supplied and your country thus participate in our beneficence'.

The trade imbalance continued to build; Britain needed something to sell back to the Chinese in return for such luxuries. It found it growing on the hillsides of India: opium. Imports of the drug were soon booming, and ever more Chinese became hooked.

Initially, the Chinese government turned a blind eye for fear of damaging the tea trade, from which they earned substantial revenue. But by the late 1830s they had had enough, and issued edicts banning the importation. Britain's reply was to send four gunboats, which bombarded Chinese forts, debouched troops to march on Canton, and blockaded South China's two main rivers, the Pearl and the Yangtze. China had to sue for peace; in the Treaty of Nanking (really a surrender document) it allowed Britain unrestricted trade from five Chinese ports and ceded Hong Kong Island to the crown for ever.

Twenty years later saw a local tiff escalate into the Second Opium War, which ended with Britain taking more land to augment Hong Kong (Stonecutters Island and a small piece of the mainland called the Kowloon Peninsula). Finally, near the end of the Victorian era, Britain acquired some of the hinterland to Kowloon, calling it the 'New Territories'. This time, a deal was made with the Chinese and Britain agreed to lease the land for ninety-nine years – hence the need to return it in 1997.

Having acquired this colony in a largely shameful manner, Britain proceeded to govern it superbly. All those things that my great-uncle believed the Empire to have created – justice, peace, prosperity – *are* what the British Empire brought to Hong Kong. At the time of the First Opium War, Hong Kong Island was home to about 1,500 fishermen. By 1860, 120,000 people lived there (which explains why more land was wanted for the colony). By 1900 the figure was triple that. Britons made up a tiny proportion of that number: the rest were Chinese who had fled their country in search of a better life – and had found it.

James and Mabel Cantlie were two of those Britons, and their story is typical of the many who went out to the Empire and brought huge benefit to the communities they served.

James was a successful surgeon and teacher in London, who went to practise in Hong Kong in July 1887. He went out of a sense of adventure rather than any high-minded notion of imperial duty, but when he got there, his natural – and very Victorian – combination of drive and humanity drew him into public work. His wife Mabel came with him, partly because she had to, partly because she had a dream of seeing the Great

Wall of China, but once there she too found her own qualities drawn into the public arena.

The Cantlies arrived at a time when a Medical College for Chinese students was being talked about. James Cantlie summoned a meeting of interested parties, British and Chinese, to turn the talk into formal plans. When the College opened, he became its principal teacher, lecturing in general science and scientific method as well as medicine, and later became its second dean. In the twentieth century, the College grew into Hong Kong University, which is now the highest ranked university in Asia.

In 1890, dissatisfied with the quality of local hospitals, Cantlie founded one of his own next to his surgery on The Peak. At first it was tiny – he and Mabel ran it; she was both nurse and administrator. By 1892, the year the Hong Kong Five Cents came out, the hospital was a fully-fledged organization, run by two doctors. An institute for producing smallpox vaccine followed. This was government-funded, but came about thanks to a campaign by James, who was an astute lobbyist for causes in which he believed: first aid, public health, wider vaccination and improved sanitation. James Cantlie's parting gift to Hong Kong was its first public library.

While he was doing all this, Cantlie was a practising doctor, working for nothing with the poor as well as for paying clients. He carried out research into tropical diseases, including leprosy and bubonic plague. The cause of the latter was not known at that time: the risks in such research, which included visiting areas affected by the disease, are obvious.

The Cantlies had none of the traits that anti-imperialists ascribe to the men and women who made the Empire. They refused to ride on rickshaws, finding the business of being pulled along by another human being demeaning to both parties. They took an interest in Chinese medicine, adopting selected traditional remedies such as aconite (to lower patient temperatures) for use in their hospital. The best friend they made during their time in Hong Kong was one of James' first students, Sun Yat-sen – who later became President of the Chinese Republic (and who owed his life to them, after they rescued him from a kidnap attempt by Manchu agents in London). James' belief was that he was fortunate to have been educated in Britain, and he wanted to spread the benefits of his knowledge to other people who hadn't had his luck.

In the end, James became ill, exhausted by his work: serving the Empire nearly cost him his life. In 1896, he and Mabel set sail for Britain. As he did so, a band played and 'hundreds of well-wishers', British and Chinese, came to wave them off.

Hong Kong continued to boom, until the Second World War when a much less benevolent imperial power occupied it: Japan, whose legacy included mass rape, hyperinflation and starvation. Once the war was over, however, the colony soon recovered its energy, thanks mostly to its hard-working and entrepreneurial citizens, but also thanks to British officials like John James Cowperthwaite, its Financial Secretary in the 1960s. Cowperthwaite insisted on low taxation and cutting red tape, and combined this with social housing programmes for the very poor. He also protected Hong Kong from successive governments in London, who continually asked him to pay more into their exchequers and received firm, beautifully argued refusals in reply. The former rocky island and its adjoining, once-empty mainland now has a population of around seven million, more skyscrapers than any other city (including New York) and the sixth highest GDP per capita in the world.

Of course, the story of Empire is not all so positive. While James Cantlie was founding universities and hospitals and risking his life to find a cure for bubonic plague, British soldiers were using Maxim guns to scythe down African tribesmen. At the Battle of Omdurman in 1898, about 10,000 dervishes and forty-eight British were killed.

Omdurman was part of the bizarre 'scramble for Africa', whereby the European powers carved an entire continent up into totally arbitrary territories on which colonial rule was then ruthlessly imposed. Britain was arguably the least barbaric of the participants in this process (the Belgians, for example, turned the Congo into a hellish slave-state where an estimated ten million people died). But to say this is no great accolade.

Why did Britain make a mess of Africa? Maybe it was a result of this rush to take power – Hong Kong took time to grow, allowing more room for subtlety and nuance. Maybe British technological superiority was so vast by 1880 that an arrogance crept in which had not affected earlier generations of imperialists. Maybe the daft, sinister racial thinking that was an unintended consequence of the work of Charles Darwin poisoned too many minds.

But even this story has a positive side. Victorian missionary activity means that many modern Africans embrace Christianity joyfully – and authentically, not because a white man is pointing a Maxim gun at them. British education has been, and still is, valuable in the continent. Nelson Mandela studied first at a Wesleyan mission school, then at Healdtown School (established by Methodists in 1845), then at Fort Hare University, a world-class campus set up by a mixture of eminent blacks and liberal whites in 1916. Later still, imprisoned by the descendants of the Boers, he studied for a Bachelor of Laws degree under the University of London External Programme.

But neither Hong Kong nor Africa were the true heart of Empire. Apart from the UK, the biggest selection in my great-uncle's stamp album comes from India.

The story of the 'Jewel in the Crown' – the phrase is, of course, Disraeli's – began, like that of Hong Kong, with traders finding toeholds in ports. The ports belonged to another, already well-established empire, that of the Mughals (who were hardly more native to India than the British: Babur, founder of the dynasty, came from Uzbekistan and spoke Persian). However as the eighteenth century went on, the Mughals fell into decline and their rule was replaced by the anarchy of warring states.

Partly out of greed, partly out of naïvety, partly out of rivalry with the French, Britain found itself drawn into these wars. Following the Battle of Plassey in 1757 Britain was effectively ruler of Bengal. After a period when it attempted to run Bengal with a light touch, it was drawn into more wars: by the mid-nineteenth century a small island off the coast of Europe controlled most of this mighty Asian subcontinent. Or rather the East India Company did: it was only after the Indian Mutiny (First War of Independence if you're Indian) in 1857 that the British government stepped in and formally instituted the Raj. In 1877, Disraeli persuaded Victoria to accept the title Empress of India. In the late Victorian era, a series of Liberal Governors General worked hard to create a truly meritocratic governing elite combining Indians and Britons, while Tory Governors General preferred to exercise power through traditional local rulers. Either way, the Raj was not just foreigners telling the locals what to do; that would never have worked.

Was India Omdurman or Hong Kong? Maybe both. If Britain did harm, it also did good. Empire left infrastructure and institutions, such as the postal system reflected in my great-uncle's stamps (modern India has the largest such system in the world, with over 150,000 post offices). It left a global language – and a link between Britain and its old colonies which would be translated into movements of people whose story will be taken up later in this book.

And, of course, this debate is modern. Back in 1892, Empire was simply a fact of life. Schoolboys bought stamp albums, stuck in images of Queen Victoria from around the world and thought such a thing was right and that it would never change.

CHAPTER NINE

A LITTLE OF WHAT
YOU FANCY

EDWARD VII 7D PURPLE, 1910

THE BRIEF reign of Edward VII was characterized by vigour and freshness – but this was not reflected in its stamps. The 7d Purple is probably the best of them, despite its colour which the catalogue calls purple but which more accurately resembles the colour water goes when you wash a lot of paintbrushes in it. The '7' has an attractive period feel to it, reminiscent of Charles Rennie Mackintosh's graphics. The stamp is also original: for roughly half the Edward VII denominations, the Post Office was unable to come up with new designs. For the 'new' 1½d, 2d, 3d, 4d, 5d, 9d and shilling, they simply removed Queen Victoria's head from the old 1887 Jubilees and stuck Edward's in instead (a minor change meant that a crown was added to the frames, as Edward's preferred portrait of himself, by Austrian artist Emile Fuchs, shows him without one).

It's not known what 'Bertie' thought about this. Probably not a lot: he and his mother didn't get on. Victoria is supposed to have resented his role in Albert's death – it was on a trip to remonstrate with Edward about his choice of female company that Albert caught his fatal typhoid fever. She certainly disapproved of her son's refusal to be like his father.

Bertie wanted to have fun. He partied. He smoked. He chased women. Victoria and Albert made various attempts to calm him down. They put him in the Army: an unwise move, as military life just encouraged his raffishness. They sent him to Cambridge, where the party continued – and eventually got into the press. Finally Victoria found him a wife, Princess Alexandra of Denmark.

Alexandra was not the first choice. But she turned out to be perfect – for Edward. She was lively, sociable, generous to the point of extravagance, and above all tolerant. Bertie didn't stop seeing other women (he had a particular penchant for actresses) but Alexandra seemed to deal with this, and the couple had a surprisingly good relationship. She was very young when she married, but one must assume that in some way she understood the deal: kingship and fidelity don't always go together. And Bertie was always true to her in his fashion, clearly fond of her and a loving father to their children. He was a man of charm and liberality, with a tolerant, live and let live philosophy. He enjoyed life, and Alexandra did too. She made the best of her lot – which, if she looked around at the lives of most people, was very good.

When Edward became king in 1901, society seemed to lighten up. For those aristocrats who had survived the late Victorian rural slump, the era was a golden one. Their London 'Season', from mid-February to the end of July, involved endless parties in the London houses of the great families. Cynthia Asquith describes memories of 'striped awnings, linkmen with flaring torches; powdered, liveried footmen; soaring marble staircases; tiaras, smiling hostesses; azaleas in gilt baskets; quails in aspic, strawberries and cream'. This was punctuated by country house weekends where the nation's leaders would discuss politics. Come August, aristos went to sporting events such as Henley or Goodwood, then disappeared to the country for autumn and winter hunting and shooting. Land was bringing in money again.

The middle classes could enjoy life more, too. H.G. Wells' *The History of Mr Polly*, which shares a debut year with the Edward VII 7d stamp, tells the story of a nerdy, downtrodden shopkeeper with a vivid verbal imagination who bungles a suicide attempt then hits the road – on his bicycle, the great liberating force of the era – in search of 'Joy de Vive'. He finds this at the Potwell Inn, a rural riverside pub: 'my place in the world', he calls it. He sees off Uncle Jim, a local thug who runs a protection racket; at the end we find him enjoying the beauty of an English rural scene in the company of the pub's rotund, affectionate landlady. Nietzschean authenticity, the British way.

The craze for cycling followed John Dunlop's invention of the pneumatic tyre in 1888. Bicycles, or 'freedom machines' as they were known, were particularly taken up by women. Both sexes were suddenly able to explore the countryside in company of their own choosing, at their own pace. Once you got away from towns and industry, the land was still possessed of a deep tranquillity. Edward Thomas' 'Adlestrop' summons this now lost world:

> And for that minute a blackbird sang
> Close by, and round him, mistier,
> Farther and farther, all the birds
> Of Oxfordshire and Gloucestershire.

The ultimate destroyer of that tranquillity was, of course, emerging in the Edwardian era. Herbert Austin designed the first British four-wheel car in 1900, and in 1905 set up his factory in Longbridge. By 1910, the dazzling range of entre-preneurial companies that made up the Edwardian British automobile industry was producing around 15,000 units a year.

Those in search of more raucous entertainment than cycling could go to the Music Hall, which was in its heyday. Marie Lloyd was its greatest star. Her first big hit was 'The boy I love is up in the Gallery':

> *But I haven't got a penny, so we'll live on love and kisses,*
> *And be just as happy as the birds on the tree.*

Marie went on to make her name with songs like 'Oh, Mr Porter!' (a comical railway seduction story, where a young girl who'd 'never had her ticket punched before' finds herself in a compartment with a rich old gentleman), 'She sits among the cabbages and peas', 'My old man' (a darker song about being turned out of accommodation) and, of course, 'A little of what you fancy does you good'.

Bertie, unsurprisingly, was a fan. Other people weren't. The Purity Party regularly tried to get music halls closed by local magistrates. In 1913 Marie's American tour was cancelled on the grounds of 'moral turpitude'. She remained untroubled, commenting that her audiences didn't 'pay their sixpences and shillings at the Music Hall to hear the Salvation Army'.

In 1907, Marie was a leading light in the Music Hall War. The halls were run by a small group of managers, who used their power to make ever greater demands on their employees. Attempts by groups of artists to discuss improvements were rejected and in 1906 the artists formed a union called the Variety Artistes' Federation. The managers still refused to nego-tiate. The artists went on strike. Marie, who had an instinctive sympathy with the underdog, threw her weight behind the campaign and brought public opinion with her, forcing the more reasonable managers to the negotiating table. (The less reasonable ones crumbled soon after – but bided their time to get their revenge. When asked to assemble a list for a Royal Variety Performance in 1912, they did not include the genre's greatest star.)

This rise in industrial militancy was another trait of the Edwardian era. Victorian politics had been about Liberals versus Tories, but a new force was entering the fray: socialism.

The joining together of industrial labourers to make political demands was not new. The 1830s had seen the rise of the Chartists, a group of working men with a highly reasonable set of objectives such as universal suffrage, secret ballots, and that all parliamentary constituencies should be of similar size. Needless to say this was treated as dangerous sedition and the movement was harshly put down.

After the collapse of Chartism, discontent simmered in the factories but struggled to find a political voice, partly because such expression was discouraged by the authorities and, historian E.P. Thompson argues forcefully, by Methodism. There were also more positive reasons: the vote was gradually extended to most men, progress was made in factory legislation (albeit painfully slowly), and people who wanted to change things put their energies into practical solutions such as the Co-operative movement. The Victorian Wealth Machine did ultimately make life better for its operatives (real wages, i.e. wages adjusted for purchasing power, rose throughout the era, especially after 1885). Bright young men could improve themselves, while less bright but vigorous young men could help build the Empire. Most people shared a quiet, sustaining belief that things were slowly getting better.

Victorian working-class radicals had tended to be Liberals, which was also the party of free trade and enterprise. As the century ended, newer voices began to make themselves heard, arguing, as Karl Marx had for years, that free trade did not actually benefit the industrial worker and that the Wealth Machine should be controlled and owned by the state. In 1888, Robert Cunninghame-Graham became the first MP to style himself Labour. He was a colourful character, a former pupil of that hotbed of radicalism, Harrow, who then went to Argentina and became a gaucho, travelled in Morocco disguised as a sheikh and befriended Buffalo Bill Cody in Texas. In 1892, he was joined in parliament by Lanarkshire miner Keir Hardie, the first great figure of the Labour Party. Hardie's rather different life included starting work down the mine aged ten, being blacklisted by mine owners aged 23, preaching at temperance meetings, leading several strikes and founding a radical newspaper. The Labour Party was still a small one, however, winning less than 50,000 votes in the 1895 election.

The Trades Union Congress had been in existence since 1868 (a stamp was issued in 1968 to celebrate its centenary), but no real link was made between it and parliamentary politics until 1900, when Hardie led the move to create a political wing, the Labour Representation Committee. This was the effective birth of the modern, national Labour Party: in the cataclysmic 1906 election that bundled the Conservatives out of power, it won 29 seats. By 1924, this would rise to 191.

Women were beginning to speak up, too. Millicent Fawcett – wife of Henry Fawcett, the innovative Postmaster General of the early 1880s – was one of the first women to argue for truly universal suffrage (it earned her a place on a stamp in 2008). Emmeline Pankhurst and her two daughters, Christabel and Sylvia, followed. At first, the approach of the new 'suffragettes' – initially a term of derision, but one that the movement decided to take up – was moderate, with members simply stating their case. Then in 1905, two suffragettes were arrested after heckling Winston Churchill and Sir Edward Grey at a public meeting. The movement began to split between those who wanted to continue debate and those who wanted more violent action. Supporters of the latter view began to damage property, especially that of politicians. The high point of militant suffragism, with hunger strikes and Emily Davison's self-immolation at the Derby in 1913, was to come in the reign of the next King, George V.

Despite being the time when the big twentieth-century radical movements took off, for most people, even the millions still afflicted by poverty, the tone of Edwardian Britain was conservative (with a small 'c') and patriotic. If there is a theme tune to the era, it's not *The Red Flag* or *The March of Women*, but *Land of Hope and Glory*:

The tune is by Elgar, from a set of marches called *Pomp and Circumstance* (the title comes from *Othello*, when the hero bids farewell to 'all quality, pride, pomp and circumstance of glorious war'). When march number one was first played at a Promenade Concert on 21 October 1901, the audience rose to their feet and yelled for an encore. After the encore, they rose to their feet again and asked for another. Elgar had a chart-topper.

Adding lyrics to the tune was the King's idea (behind his fun-loving exterior, Bertie was a shrewd operator). The job went to A.C. Benson, a Cambridge essayist and academic, who came up with classic imperialist sentiments:

> *Land of Hope and Glory,*
> *Mother of the Free,*
> *How shall we extol thee,*
> *Who are born of thee?*
> *Wider still and wider*
> *Shall thy bounds be set;*
> *God, who made thee mighty,*
> *Make thee mightier yet.*

A writer who probably felt he should have been given this task was Rudyard Kipling. *Kim*, his great adventure story of espionage in Imperial India, was published in the same year as Elgar's march was premiered. His *Just So Stories* followed in 1902 (a hundred years later, they featured in a set of stamps).

In 1907 he won the Nobel Prize for Literature. His poem 'If...', still regularly voted the nation's favourite, appeared in 1910. Kipling's vision is a male, down-to-earth one: the ironic shrug of the man who gets things done amid all that chatter and emotion. He had a particular admiration for engineers, once scripting a ritual for young graduates in that discipline to celebrate their calling. This was an enthusiasm not in the public school spirit – the shrug and the capability were fine, but for the Edwardian gent all that study, especially of engineering, was far too earnest. (John Halifax, a Gentleman of an earlier era, would have shared Kipling's enthusiasm, of course.) Therein lay seeds of difficulty for Britain's future.

But that was a long way away. The embodiment of the exuberant spirit of the Edwardian era was the 1908 Olympic Games. No stamps were issued for this – there was nothing as showy as 'commemorative' stamps in Britain in those days. The Games were held in London; Britannia ruled the medals tables, winning the most golds, silvers and bronzes. However, the Games were not without controversy. The marathon runner Dorando Pietri came into the stadium way ahead of the field, stumbled, was helped over the line by officials, then disqualified from the race. Queen Alexandra, generous-spirited as ever, later presented him with a gilded silver cup. There were accusations of cheating in the 400 metres. The biggest row was caused by the republican-minded Americans' refusal to dip their flag at the opening ceremony in salute to the King.

Bertie smoked twenty cigarettes and twelve cigars a day. He liked a drop of champagne, too. All this – and his workload, which was greater than his playboy demeanour would lead one to believe – finally caught up with him: too much of what you fancy isn't so good for you. On 6 May 1910, he suffered a heart attack. He insisted on continuing to work on official documents, but had to retire to bed, where he lost consciousness and died just before midnight. His last moments were suitably Edwardian:

he was informed that his horse had won a race, and replied, 'I am very glad.'

The 7d Purple was issued two days before the King's death. People thought it had been specially issued in mourning, but it was just a sombre stamp at a sad time. Yet perhaps these people were right in spirit: the stamp did mark an end, of an era as distinctive as the long Victorian one that had preceded it.

CHAPTER TEN

RULE, BRITANNIA!

GEORGE V 'SEA HORSE' TEN SHILLINGS, 1913

EVEN THOSE disinclined towards militarism and flag-waving must admit that the 'Sea Horse' 10 Shillings, by Australian sculptor Bertram Mackennal with lettering by British graphic designer George Eve, is magnificent. Britannia breasts the waves, proud and defiant on her chariot pulled by three horses. Anyone sticking this on their parcel to relatives in far-flung corners of the Empire at Christmas 1913 must have felt a small shudder of national pride. Britannia rules the waves! So don't mess with her.

This wasn't just talk. The Royal Navy had been supreme since Nelson won the Battle of Trafalgar in 1805, allowing Britain to build a global empire. In 1913 it had the biggest fleet in the world: in terms of tonnage, the simple weight of ships, bigger than the next two nations, Germany and America, put together. It was still, people felt, Britain's ultimate bulwark against attack.

Such thinking was boosted by military theorists, such as the American Captain Alfred T. Mahan, whose hugely influential *The Influence of Sea Power on History* of 1890 argued that sea power was the key to all military conflict. (Mahan was a better theorist than captain: apparently, boats under his command had a number of collisions, including some with 'stationary objects'.) Mahan's book had been translated into German and become the favoured reading of the new Kaiser. Wilhelm II was a snob who was obsessed with his royal status but lacked actual leadership qualities, being impetuous, arbitrary and quick to override wiser advisers. He was also paranoid about the British, whom he disliked for various reasons, not least because it had been an English doctor that misdiagnosed his father who died soon after of cancer, and another English medic who had overseen his own birth, which was a difficult one and left him with a withered left arm. The Kaiser and his Admiral Alfred von Tirpitz determined to beat Britain at its naval game, and instigated a massive programme of warship construction.

Britain, of course, responded. Admiral Fisher, Britain's answer to Tirpitz, modernized the Royal Navy, improving conditions of service and officer training, scrapping old ships and building new vessels. In 1906, HMS *Dreadnought* was launched. It was the fastest and most heavily armed battleship the world had ever seen. The Germans immediately set about building three battleships to match it. However Tirpitz realized he could not match the Royal Navy on sheer size and had to complement his new battleships with a more guerrilla approach, building a fleet of submarines – an area in which Germany soon developed a lead. By the outbreak of war, the Royal Navy still had more subs than the Kaiserliche Marine but many of the British vessels worked only in shallow waters while the German U-boats could venture out into the deep.

This naval arms race, and the obvious threat behind it, stirred the popular imagination. Throughout the late Victorian and the Edwardian eras, a new genre of thriller flourished: the invasion novel. The original was the rather comically named *Battle of Dorking* (1871), written by a Royal Engineers officer, George Chesney, who noted the effectiveness of the Germans in the Franco-Prussian War of 1870 and wondered, as many successful novelists do, 'What if . . .?' In 1903, arguably the best novel in the genre was published, *The Riddle of The Sands* by Erskine Childers, who later became an Irish patriot before being executed by his own side. 1906 saw the most successful, William le Queux' *The Invasion of 1910*, which was serialized in the *Daily Mail*. In this, the Teutonic hordes get as far as London before being turned back by plucky Brits (a German edition was published with a different ending). Paranoia was not the unique preserve of the Kaiser.

However, many opinion formers did not share the growing mood of panic and seemed uninterested in combating it. The new Labour Party was split, with some members happy to wave the anti-German flag (Keir Hardie opposed this, but many Labour MPs found it went down well with their constituents). The Liberals were split too: though Adam Smith would not have had much time for war talk, it was a Liberal government that ended up taking Britain to war in 1914. Most intellectuals seemed more interested in their personal and aesthetic lives than politics, influenced by the philosophy of G.E. Moore, who wrote in *Principia Ethica* (1903) that 'by far the most valuable things which we know or can imagine are certain states of consciousness, which may roughly be described as the pleasures of human intercourse and the enjoyment of beautiful objects'. If there was an issue that engaged radical minds at the time, it was the women's suffrage movement, which entered a more bitter, more violent phase in the early 1910s.

Perhaps the biggest reason for the lack of concern about the drift to war was the widely held belief that since Britannia ruled the waves, winning would be easy. British military planners thought that the main British contribution to any European conflict would be to quickly sort out the Germans on the high seas and in the colonies. On land, Russia, which had by far the biggest army in the world, would charge in from the east; the French, aided by a small British expeditionary force, would stop any push the Kaiser made westward. The end result would be a few broken bones but a more peaceful Europe, with those uppity Germans back in their place. When troops set off for France in August and September 1914, they were confidently told it would all be over by Christmas – and this wasn't just propaganda.

To be fair to the British top brass, not everyone agreed with this. General Horace Smith-Dorien surprised a group of cadets on Salisbury Plain in 1914 by saying, 'We must do everything we can to prevent war. War will solve nothing, and the whole of Europe will be destroyed.'

The immediate cause of the Somme and Passchendaele (and thus of Stalin and Hitler) was a quarrel over the province of Bosnia–Herzegovina, which at that time was administered by the arthritic Austro-Hungarian Empire but which was claimed by a new dynamic Serbia for linguistic reasons: the Bosnians spoke Serbo-Croat, not German or Hungarian. The Serbs tried various ways of grabbing the province but in the end resorted to terrorism, sponsoring an organization called the Black Hand, a strange mixture of secretive military officers and dreamy, violent young men: the leader was a former bank clerk who lived with his mum.

In June 1914, the heir to the Austro-Hungarian throne, Franz Ferdinand, went to observe military manoeuvres in Bosnia. On the 28th he and his wife Sophie were to drive in an open car through the streets of Sarajevo. A carefully trained and well-armed Black Hand gang positioned themselves along the planned route.

As often in history, pure bad luck played a key role. The first two assassins panicked and did nothing. A third threw a bomb at the royal car but missed. A number of people were injured, however, and the rest of the day's formal processing was cancelled. Franz Ferdinand expressed a desire to quietly visit the wounded in hospital instead. However, nobody told the royal driver of the change of plan, so when they set off for the hospital, he started along the original ceremonial route, where a fourth Black Hand member, Gavrilo Princip, was waiting. Even then, things might have been different had the driver not been told of his mistake, stopped, and stalled trying to turn round – right in front of the delicatessen where Princip had just bought some lunch. Princip fired just two shots, but he had a steady hand and was shooting from close range. The Archduke's last words were 'Sophie! Live for our children!' – but she had died instantly and never heard them.

Austria–Hungary immediately promised vicious reprisals. Intense diplomatic activity began, to prevent these escalating into war. It failed. A month later, Austria–Hungary declared war on Serbia. The following day, Russia, eager to defend its fellow Slavs, declared war on Austria–Hungary. Two days later, Germany, an old ally of Austria–Hungary, sent an ultimatum to Russia, telling them to stop mobilizing. Russia refused: the next day, Germany declared war on them. On 3 August, Germany declared war on France – an ally of Russia, and of Britain.

That evening, Foreign Secretary Sir Edward Grey and Prime Minister Herbert Asquith sat in 10 Downing Street, drafting an ultimatum that was to be cabled to Germany in the event that Belgium, a neutral country, were invaded. The story goes that Grey looked out of the window, saw a man lighting the gas lamps in the street below and spoke the famous words: 'The lamps are going out all over Europe. We shall not see them lit again in our time.' He clearly did not believe that it would all be 'over by Christmas'.

Next morning, almost a year to the day after the magisterial Ten Shilling Sea Horse stamp had appeared to reassure the nation that while Britannia ruled the waves it was safe from conflict, German troops marched into Belgium and the First World War had begun.

CHAPTER ELEVEN

THE BRINGER OF
TERRIBLE NEWS

GEORGE V PENNY RED, 1916

T HROUGHOUT THE First World War, families of officers killed in action received the news of their death in a telegram. Families of other ranks received the news by post. They would open an envelope bearing this profile of the King, a symbol of the Britain their loved ones had fought for. Inside would be Army Form B 104–82. After a reference number they would read a hand-stamped date and address. A blank line, usually filled in as 'Madam', followed, then the typed form:

> *It is my painful duty to inform you that a report has been received from the War Office, notifying the death of:*
> *(No.)   (Rank)*
> *(Name)*
> *(Regiment)*

The information would be filled in by hand, though 'Regiment' was sometimes done with a rubber hand-stamp. The form went on:

> *which occurred*
> *on the*
> *The report is to the effect that he was*

There was a hand-stamp for 'killed in action'. Later, another pennyworth of post would arrive, containing Army Form B 104–121. This informed 'Sir or Madam' that 'an official report has been received that the late soldier is buried at . . .'

Maybe it couldn't be done any other way (though surely gentler words than 'the late soldier' could have been found): the level of slaughter was so high.

After the declaration of war, it didn't take long for Britain's official military plans to fall apart. The Russian forces that were to swarm into Germany from the east were routed at the Battle of Tannenberg. Britain's easy naval victory didn't happen, either: one of its super-battleships was sunk by German mines in October; next month the German commander Graf von Spee sank two British cruisers at the Battle of Coronel. The German Army moved easily through Belgium into France: though Allied forces stopped it short of Paris at the First Battle of the Marne, it now controlled the high ground of the Ardennes. The armies dug themselves into trenches. With the new technologies of the machine gun and heavy artillery, both of which were ideal for defending ground, the once mobile business of warfare became like an eighteenth-century prize fight where the two combatants stand in a ring slugging each other, round after round after round, until one of them collapses.

Christmas 1914, by which time the planners had said it would all be over, saw the combatants embedded in two lines of trenches running from the English Channel to Switzerland. The day itself was celebrated up and down those lines with the famous unofficial truce. We're all familiar with the iconography: the candles in the trenches on Christmas Eve; *Stille Nacht* echoing up from enemy lines; shouts of 'Hey, Fritz' and 'Hey, Tommy'; games of football in no-man's-land; pictures of sweethearts compared and items of uniform swapped – moments of humaneness and sanity.

Then madness took over again. Early in 1915, the Germans began using chlorine gas, first against the Russians, then on their western front: on 22 April French troops saw a cloud floating towards them and thought it was the smokescreen for an attack. They were ordered to stay in their places and died where they stood. From then on, gas was used by both sides, though gas canisters were never officially mentioned in orders: the British referred to them as 'accessories'. New ways of filling these accessories were soon developed: phosgene, which had to be inhaled to cause harm, and mustard gas, which only needed to touch its victim.

Figures show that gas wasn't, in fact, hugely effective as a means of killing people, because protective masks were quickly developed. But its psychological power never lessened. Wilfred Owen described the fate of a man who fails to get his mask on in time:

> *Dim, through the misty panes and thick green light,*
> *As under a green sea, I saw him drowning.*
>
> *In all my dreams, before my helpless sight,*
> *He plunges at me, guttering, choking, drowning.*

Owen savagely lambasted the notion 'Dulce et decorum est, pro patria mori' 'it is a sweet and decorous thing to die for one's country'.

When 1916 arrived, it was another year of slaughter and stalemate. On the high seas, the great naval battle of Jutland was fought – Britain lost more ships in total, but the Germans lost proportionally more and its surface fleet was never again a real threat. Instead, Germany stepped up its U-boat campaign.

On land . . . The first of July 1916 is a date that is engraved on the heart of British history. The plan was clear. At 7.30 in the morning – a dangerously late start, insisted on by French commanders – over 100,000 men along a 12-mile front were to climb out of their trenches and advance 'at a steady walking pace' towards the German lines, which commanders assumed would be empty because of an intense artillery bombardment that was to precede the attack. But the bombardment did not work: the deep enemy trenches were manned and the barbed-wire entanglements in front of them remained undamaged. German machine guns opened fire. Nearly 20,000 British and Empire soldiers died that day, the start of the Battle of the Somme.

One of the most resonant stories is that of the 36th (Ulster) Division. Little ground was gained on 1 July, but the Ulsters were an exception: disregarding orders to wait in trenches then walk, they sent men out early to cut wire, then ran once over the top. They captured their target, a fortified area known as the Schwaben Redoubt. However, the price in lives was huge: two thousand men, approximately one sixth of the entire division. And the gain was, in the end, fruitless; on either side of the redoubt no ground had been won, which left the Ulsters trapped, and they had to retreat. Of the nine Victoria Crosses awarded for gallantry on that day, four were awarded to Ulstermen. If The Great Hunger is an iconic event for one side of the struggle in Northern Ireland, the Schwaben Redoubt is the same for the other. The phrase 'No surrender', later often to issue loudly from the mouth of Ian Paisley, was originally called out by Ulstermen running towards Swabian machine guns on 1 July 1916.

The Somme offensive lasted several months. In that time, five miles of ground were won (later, in 1918, the gain was conceded in one day) and nearly 100,000 British and Empire soldiers died. To visit the Memorial to the Missing at Thiepval, in the heart of the old battleground, is an intensely moving experience: the place is quiet now, just a few visitors, still the odd wreath or note, and thousands upon thousands of names engraved on the walls of Lutyens' majestic monument.

The year 1917 was pivotal. It was also the year Britain nearly lost the war. Our allies began to crumble. A brave but unsuccessful spring offensive by General Nivelle led to mutiny in the French ranks, while Russia was engulfed by revolution. The stalemate in the trenches continued. Passchendaele was 1917's answer to the Somme, famous for its mud (the battlefield, at the northern end of the front, was barely higher than sea level). Once again, a few miles of ground were gained at the cost of over 100,000 British and Empire lives – including many from the Post Office Rifles, a company drawn from peacetime postal workers, which suffered particularly severely at this engagement. Several of the former posties died not as a result of enemy fire but from drowning in the mud.

What is most terrible of all is that these dreadful losses were in many ways a sideshow. The war that would end by Christmas 1914 had turned into a war of attrition. Who would starve and/ or revolt first? The key to that question lay – just as Captain Mahan had foretold – not in the trenches but at sea. On paper this should have been game, set and match to wave-ruling, 'Sea Horse' Britannia, but Germany's U-boats proved hugely successful weapons. As 1917 unfolded, these stealthy killers sank ever more of the vessels that were bringing essential food and raw materials to Britain. In April, over 900,000 tons of shipping was destroyed. Britain was down to six weeks' worth of grain, and the supply was drying up.

Rescue came from the Americans and their own magnificent Wealth Machine. German diplomatic skill did not match their military ability. Increased U-boat activity brought Germany into conflict with America, but rather than attempting to smooth things over, Germany made secret overtures to Mexico offering an alliance: join us, and we'll get Texas, Arizona and New Mexico back for you. This, and the attacks on merchant shipping, plus memories of the *Lusitania*, a passenger liner sunk by U-boats in 1915 with the loss of 128 American lives, were too much, even for President Woodrow Wilson who had tried both to stay neutral and to broker peace. On 6 April 1917, Britain had a new ally.

The U-boats still had to be stopped, however. The solution was to herd the freighters into convoys and to guard them with warships (cruisers and destroyers, not the great battleships, which it had originally been thought would be the key to the sea war). The Admiralty, however, resisted this, trialling the convoy system reluctantly in April and not actually implementing it fully until September. Full implementation paid off immediately, with tonnage losses dropping below 300,000 in November, and rarely rising above that for the rest of the war. Later still, as aeroplanes became capable of flying ever further without refuelling, air support for the convoys made life for the U-boats even harder.

Of course, the land war still had to be won. On 21 March 1918, the Germans launched a new series of offensives, aiming to encircle the British, capture the Channel ports and cut Britain off from her French allies. These were initially effective, prompting General Haig to issue his famous order of 11 April: 'Every position must be held to the last man: there must be no retirement. With our backs to the wall and believing in the justice of our cause each one of us must fight on to the end.'

With the benefit of hindsight we can say that the Ludendorff Offensive was a last fling, doomed to fail because of shortages of manpower, food and weaponry. But it didn't seem that way at the time. The Germans advanced on all fronts, reaching the River Marne again by July, and successfully crossing it on the 15th of the month. At that point, they were only 25 miles from Paris (almost at the same spot as a more successful invasion,

74 years later, by 'soft power': Eurodisney). However, on the 20th the French counter-attacked successfully.

There was much bitter and brave fighting to be done, but the Germans had played their last card. The Allied 'Hundred Days Offensive' began on 8 August and saw massive advances. On 5 October a new German Chancellor, Prince Maximilian of Baden, approached President Wilson to discuss surrender, which was finally signed in a railway carriage near Compiègne, about 40 miles north of Paris. The armistice came into effect at 11a.m. on 11 November.

The last British soldier to die in the fighting was Private George Edwin Ellison, shot around 9.30 on the morning of Armistice Day itself. He joined an estimated 885,000 other Britons who perished in the conflict. Army Form B 104–82 would have been dutifully sent through the post to his family.

CHAPTER TWELVE

THEN SOMEONE STOLE
THE WHEELBARROW

GERMAN 200 MARK STAMP,
OVERPRINTED 2 MILLION, 1923

I ADDED A set of German stamps from 1922 and 1923 to my collection for two reasons. One was simply that they tell a powerful story with painful clarity; the other was that their tale has great bearing on the history of Britain.

A terrible epidemic of influenza coincided with the end of the war. It killed 250,000 people in the UK. As in Ireland's Great Hunger, disease waits to batten on weakened populations – the flu was essentially a product of the war. Nevertheless, peace was seen as a time for a new start. People said this had been 'the war to end all wars'. Sadly, it did not take events long to reveal the naïvety of such hopes.

On 28 June 1919, five years to the day after the assassination of Franz Ferdinand, the Treaty of Versailles was signed, formally agreeing terms of the German surrender. Somehow, it was felt closure would be achieved by that symbolism, but actually the treaty opened new wounds. Although some historians have argued that the terms were relatively lenient – after all, what would Germany have insisted on had she won? – it is generally accepted that Versailles imposed punitive penalties from which the defeated nation could not possibly recover. British economist John Maynard Keynes, who was one of the team designing the treaty, hated what he saw and described it as 'one of the most serious acts of political unwisdom for which our statesmen have ever been responsible'.

Versailles wasn't really a treaty at all; there were no negotiations; the Germans simply had to accept the terms dictated to them. These included admitting total responsibility for the war, which, given the bizarre set of circumstances that led up to it, was hardly fair. The Kaiser was to be tried as a war criminal (he actually took refuge in Holland, which refused to extradite him). Thirteen per cent of German territory was ceded to other nations, including nearly half of her coal reserves and two-thirds of her iron ore. The German Empire was dissolved. Most damaging of all, the shattered nation was ordered to repay the entire cost of the war via huge reparations in the form of money, raw materials and agricultural produce. The exact amount was calculated in 1921 and came to 269 billion gold marks, (around $750 billion in modern money).

What was left of Germany was now a republic: a new constitution was drafted in Weimar, a graceful city which had once been the home of Enlightenment giants Goethe and Schiller. There was little grace elsewhere. A communist revolution in Bavaria was brutally put down by the Freikorps, a far right paramilitary organization, after which the communists moved to the Ruhr and established a workers' state – which was once again put down by the Freikorps. In 1922 the charismatic liberal Foreign Secretary, Walter Rathenau, was assassinated by right-wing extremists, and in 1923 the French invaded the Ruhr to ensure they got all their reparations exactly on schedule.

However, to fully understand the story told by this stamp we have to go back to 1914, when the German government decided to fund its war by borrowing rather than by the imposition of taxes. Like the British, the Germans thought hostilities would be brief. They also thought quick victory would bring booty, so any short-term debt would soon be paid off. As the fighting went on and it became apparent the war was going to be a long one, Germany persisted with its borrowing policy. By the armistice, government debt was ten times higher than it had been in 1914 and the cost of items in German shops had doubled.

Then the Treaty of Versailles was signed. The German mark tumbled on world markets – by the middle of 1920 its value had fallen tenfold. Things then stabilized: maybe the rot could have been stopped at this point – but the first money payment of Versailles reparations fell due in June 1921. The German government had no option but to buy foreign currency to fulfil this obligation, and in order to pay for these purchases began printing money. We now know this causes inflation, but at the time this was not understood.

Postal rates show the effect of these policies. When Germany joined the Universal Postal Union in 1875, the standard rate for a domestic letter was 10 pfennigs, while an international letter cost 20 pfennigs. This rate remained unchanged until 1919 – despite the fact that inflation had already begun eating away at the mark. In May 1920, the rate was 40 pf (domestic) and 80 pf (international). By July 1922, a letter cost 1 mark (100 pf) to send in Germany and 6 marks elsewhere.

The murder of Rathenau precipitated a crisis of confidence, both internally and on world currency markets. By mid-December 1922, letters cost 10 marks inland, 80 marks overseas. The authorities printed big rectangular stamps for parcels with denominations up to 500 marks. They also continued printing money, as did private banks: everyone was getting in on the act. On 15 January 1923, postal rates doubled. New stamps were issued, from 100 marks to 75,000 (the 200 mark red was originally one of this issue).

Domestic postage doubled again on 1 March and tripled (to 120 marks) on 1 July. On 1 August it increased to 400 marks. Then true hyperinflation began. On 24 August, the cost of sending a simple letter within Germany rose twentyfold. At this point, the German Post Office gave up issuing new stamps and began to overprint existing ones. They still had loads of worthless pfennig denominations: these now reappeared with various overprints, starting at 5,000 marks.

Less than two months later, the domestic letter rate was 100,000 marks. In October, it passed one million. January's issues were now as worthless as the old pfennig stamps had been, and were duly overprinted. The overprinted 200 mark stamp shown at the start of this chapter was probably issued between 10 October, when the rate went up to 2 million marks, and the twentieth of that month, when it doubled. It was still wise to get your letters posted quickly, however, as on 1 November the rate went up tenfold. On 5 November it was 500 million marks, and on the 12th 5,000 million.

Many older or retired people had their life savings – traditionally invested in government bonds – wiped out. Pensions and insurance policies became worthless: one story tells of a lawyer who had dutifully paid into a life assurance policy every month since 1903; it became due in autumn 1923; when the cheque arrived, he spent it on a loaf of bread.

Younger people in work fared better – but life was still tough. Government servants found their pay falling hopelessly behind inflation. Workers represented by unions, who could keep up bargaining pressure on employers, fared better – for a while. But their pay began to lag behind, too. What money people did earn had to be paid several times a day; workers' wives would wait for them at factory or office gates to collect the money and rush to the shops to buy food, often to find that there was nothing there or that prices had already risen beyond what they could buy. Shopkeepers would phone banks every hour to check the latest rate of inflation, and mark goods up accordingly.

Work being so erratically rewarded, theft became rife. Food was the haul of choice – urban dwellers would go on raids into the countryside. But in the end it didn't matter much what you took; anything that could be bartered had more value than money. A classic story tells of how someone went shopping with a load of marks in a wheelbarrow, popped into a shop to be told that the contents of the barrow would no longer buy them anything, and went back out to find that someone had stolen the barrow and left the money on the pavement. Currency speculation was another national pastime. The well-connected made fortunes at this – but to what end, ultimately, as their great gains on simply holding dollars for a few weeks ultimately ended up back in marks? Ordinary people could wheel and deal, equally pointlessly in the end, at illegal 'corner banks'.

How did anything function? The government continued to print money, so there was an unending supply. Industrialists could borrow to pay their workers that week (or day, or hour), and know that a few weeks later their debt would be worthless: the 100 million marks that paid a workforce one week ended up being worth the value of a stamp. People with privileged access to bank lending could buy whole companies on this principle: Hugo Stinnes, the 'Inflation King', ended up owning a sixth of Germany's private sector. Factories were actually busy, as there was high demand for goods: the one item you didn't want was cash, so whenever you got money, you spent it as soon as possible on anything you could find – you could always barter it later.

This couldn't last, of course. In the end, the whole system of making, supplying and selling goods ground to a halt, at which point unemployment, which had previously been relatively low, skyrocketed. A complete collapse of social order loomed.

It was deflected by the simple expedient of abandoning the old currency and introducing a new one. The Rentenmark replaced the old mark on 15 November 1923. There was a theoretical exchange rate – for every 1,000,000,000,000 old marks you could get one new one – but in essence the economy started from scratch. The price of sending an inland letter was once again 10 pfennigs.

But the moral damage had been done. Germany had had its Victorian values, too: solidity, thrift, hard work, loyalty. Hyperinflation made a mockery of such values, favouring selfishness and sharp practice. A helpless fatalism took over. Conspiracy theories multiplied: people like Stinnes had made fortunes from the country's darkest days; had it all been engineered by a tiny minority of bankers and industrialists? Some people pointed out that a number of these bankers and industrialists were Jewish ...

The man who benefited most from the whole business – the real 'Inflation King' – was Adolf Hitler. Without it, he might just have been another loser ranting at poorly attended public meetings. Instead, three days before the price of sending a letter went up to 5,000 million marks, he launched a coup against the Bavarian government. About 2,000 National Socialists – a party that had grown with the hyperinflation – marched on Munich's town hall. A gun battle ensued, in which twenty-one people died. The coup failed – but so demoralized were the authorities that its instigator was only lightly punished for this act of flagrant high treason, spending a few months under an undemanding prison regime which gave him the time to write *Mein Kampf*. The coup's anniversary became a sacred date in the Nazi calendar, the day the party became a serious force in German politics. (Every year from then on, they held celebrations to mark 9 November, or as they called it 'Die Neunte Elfte' or 9/11.)

It took Hitler ten more years to achieve power and six further years to plunge the world into war and to launch his monstrous campaign of racial extermination. How were these things allowed to happen in a once civilized nation? Answer: take a good look at this stamp.

CHAPTER THIRTEEN

WEMBLEY SUNSET

BRITISH EMPIRE EXHIBITION COMMEMORATIVE, THREE HALFPENCE, 1924

RITAIN DIDN'T have to worry about hyperinflation: she had an empire. And a vast one it was, too. Many people associate Empire with Queen Victoria – but in fact there was most red on the world map between 10 January 1920, when the Treaty of Versailles became effective, and 28 February 1922, when Egypt had the temerity to become nominally independent. Versailles ceded parts of the defeated Ottoman and German Empires to the UK: the poisoned chalice of Palestine from the former, various artificial African countries from the latter. In retrospect this expansion was ridiculous. But in many ways the British Empire felt solid at the time. The loyalty and bravery of troops from all corners of it had been noted and admired.

So – time to celebrate this extraordinary international entity. A number of global exhibitions had been organized in the late

Victorian and Edwardian eras. Paris had hosted two, in 1896 and 1900, at which countries of the world had built pavilions where they showed off their culture and industry. Why not have one for the Empire? A company was formed to create a British Empire Exhibition.

Wembley Park was chosen as the location. It had been the site of a bizarre attempt in 1890 to outdo the French by creating a tower bigger than Eiffel's: the tower had reached 155 feet before the project ran out of money and it had been demolished in the Edwardian era, after which the 216-acre park around it had reverted to waste ground. In 1922 the Exhibition company bought the land and building began.

The first and biggest piece of construction was Wembley Stadium, with its famous twin towers, redolent of Thiepval (the architect, Maxwell Ayrton, had been a student of Lutyens). This was opened for the 1923 Cup Final, so famously misman-aged: fans poured into the ground virtually unchecked, forcing some to spill out on to the pitch. It's amazing that nobody was killed – there were about 900 minor injuries and twenty-two people were taken to hospital. The classic image from that day is of a lone policeman on a white horse clearing the playing area, but the biggest calming influence on the crowd was the arrival of the King and the singing of the National Anthem. In the end, people stood by the pitch as well as filling the stands and the game went ahead, Bolton beating West Ham 2–0. (The first goal, by David Jack, knocked out a spectator pressed close against the back netting.)

While the site was being prepared, plans were going ahead for two special Exhibition postage stamps. These would be the first commemoratives (stamps issued to celebrate a specific event) to appear in the UK. The rest of the world had been producing these for decades: Peru is generally regarded as having been the first, in 1871, celebrating the 20th anniversary of the country's first railway. America's Columbus issue of 1892 was particularly admired. However, the King, who was a keen philatelist, did not approve, considering the concept flashy and 'un-English'. But the King was also aware of the power of propaganda, and was talked round. A competition was announced, and the Stamp Committee awarded the prize to a modernist design by Eric Gill. The King overrode the decision, choosing instead this lion by Harold Nelson. George V wasn't noted for his artistic taste – he once burst out laughing at an exhibition of French Impressionists – but he was, surely, right here: the traditional appearance of Nelson's stamp suits the Exhibition perfectly.

The event opened on St George's Day, 23 April, 1924 and ran throughout the summer. Entry cost one shilling and sixpence (children 9d). There were pavilions from most of the fifty-eight nations of the Empire, the Australian and Canadian ones being the biggest, mirroring the vastness of the two dominions. The latter contained a huge statue, carved out of butter, of the Prince of Wales on horseback. Smaller, more eye-catching pavilions included India's (designed like a Mughal palace), South Africa's (a Dutch settler's house), Malaya's (with dome and minarets), West Africa's (a fort) and Burma's. The last of these was especially popular, with beautiful carved teak spires, a Buddha and an exhibition of fabulous precious stones. Elephants were on display and could be fed by the visitors.

Along with the national pavilions were three huge palaces dedicated to Industry, Engineering and the Arts. In the Palace of the Arts was a doll's house made for Queen Mary to a design by Lutyens, containing one-twelfth-size models of the rooms in Buckingham Palace. There was real wine in the tiny bottles in the kitchen; the locks on the miniature doors worked; loos flushed (there was even one-twelfth-size loo paper). Tiny bound books contained stories specially written by eminent authors, including Hardy, Kipling and Conan Doyle (George Bernard Shaw refused to allow his work to appear in this format).

The Exhibition also had amusements. You could promenade

in 'Floral Street' past trees in tubs. There was a roller-coaster: Donald MacFadyen, a young Merchant Navy officer and regular visitor to the Exhibition, described how 'you could get a sixty mile an hour gale rushing down the giant racer, with the girl of your choice clinging tight and screaming her head off'. Visitors could travel round the grounds in revolutionary electric minibuses called Railodoks, and eat in a range of restaurants, smartest of which was the Lucullus, where MacFadyen admired the deep carpets and the 'slow precision' of the waiters.

If you were at Wembley on 30 June, and lucky enough to be in the main post office around 3p.m., you would have witnessed a formal ceremony as the Prince of Wales bought the five millionth British Empire Exhibition stamp. The stamps could only be bought at the exhibition site, where there were a number of outlets and vending machines. The latter, made by the British Automatic Stamp and Ticket Delivery Company, were not always reliable, and are responsible for a number of damaged specimens. Later, the stamps went on sale at one London office.

From 21 July to the end of August, a nightly Pageant of Empire took place beneath Wembley's twin towers, featuring 15,000 performers, as well as 300 horses, 500 donkeys, 730 camels, 72 monkeys, 1,000 doves, seven elephants, three bears (no Goldilocks) and a macaw. The procession was accompanied by music, centring on Elgar's setting of a suite of poems by Alfred Noyes, a writer best known for the Edwardian classic, *The Highwayman*. The suite told the story of England, starting in the time of Good Queen Bess as Shakespeare arrived in London with 'a knapsack of quiet songs' and 'merchant adventurers' set out from Plymouth. Different parts of Empire were celebrated, and finally the war dead were remembered:

> *Grieving for the grief that crowned her*
> *England bows her glorious head.*

Donald MacFadyen wasn't impressed by the pageant. He doesn't say why, but I suspect that so much Englishness did not go down well with this loyal Scot.

The Exhibition was a huge success: so much so that it was reprised the following year (a fresh pair of stamps, dated 1925, were duly issued). All in all it received 27 million visitors. But the image it portrayed, of a glorious, busy, happy family of nations, was one-sided.

The Empire was a luxury Britain could no longer afford. In 1913 national debt had been around 30% of GDP; in 1919, it was 175%. Many of the markets Britain had exported to in the Edwardian era were now shattered: where would the money come from to repay that debt? Or the money required to run the Empire, which, despite its indirect economic benefits, was also a huge cost?

The Empire's problems weren't only financial ones. British rule had been partly enforced with the Maxim gun, but had also worked because a critical mass of people in the governed countries had seen the benefit of it. This critical mass was beginning to erode. Mohandas Karamchand Gandhi is the classic example: as the son of a high official and a graduate of University College London, he should have been a bulwark of Empire, but a series of unpleasant encounters with some of its dimmer enforcers turned him into a passionate anti-imperialist.

The Amritsar massacre of 1919 was, perhaps, the tipping point. Gandhi had called for a mass strike all over India. In the Punjab, the authorities tried to prevent this by deporting activists from the province. A demonstration against this got out of hand; shots were fired and a British lady missionary was attacked by a mob (she was rescued by Indian bystanders). Martial law was declared, which included a ban on public gatherings. However, many people were unaware of this and gathered for a religious festival in Jallianwala Bagh, a public garden enclosed by high walls. General Reginald Dyer appeared at the Bagh with ninety troops. He blocked the only effective

exit and gave no order to the crowd to disperse – just shot at
them for ten minutes, round after round, until he had run out
of ammunition. Many tried to save themselves by jumping into
a well, where they died. After the massacre, the wounded were
left unattended, since a curfew was in place in the city. It is
estimated that over a thousand people were killed.

There were men like Dyer all over the Empire. Around the
time when people were flocking to Wembley and feeding the
elephants in the Burmese pavilion, Eric Blair, a young super-
intendent in the Imperial Police, was posted to a remote rural
town on the Irrawaddy. Eleven years later he published a novel
based on his experiences called *Burmese Days*. It is a hymn of
hate to Empire, vividly drawing the miserable, incompetent,
nasty-minded British expatriates who surround, and eventually
destroy, the hero, an idealistic young man on his first posting.
The attitudes of the Britons to the Burmese range from
patronage to sheer loathing, and they extend their malice into
local society: part of the plot deals with the Machiavellian
attempts of an equally unpleasant Burmese to attain his ultimate
desire – membership of the previously exclusive European Club.

The book's author – he is, of course, George Orwell – went
on to even greater heights. Actually, on returning from Burma
in 1927, his first move was not to write about the Empire but
to seek out injustice at home. He didn't have to look far. Despite
the unified pageantry of Wembley, Britain was a divided society.
Lloyd George, the wartime Prime Minister, had promised the
returning troops 'Homes fit for Heroes', and partially delivered
on this promise: the 1919 Housing Act had ordered local
authorities to build council houses and provided funding for
this; the results can be seen in most English villages (down
the road from the war memorial). But the housing shortage in
big cities continued. Jobs fit for Heroes had proven even harder
to achieve, as the government had spent little money on industrial regeneration (it had precious little money to spend).
Inflation had set in, soon outpacing wages. The coal industry

faced particular problems, with shrinking markets and depletion of the richest coal seams. In 1925, the mine owners responded by threatening to cut wages. The trades unions responded with justified fury: two years to the day after the Prince of Wales bought the five millionth Wembley stamp, Britain was brought to a halt by the General Strike.

This divided, indebted nation could not support Empire any longer. Not with Reginald Dyer and the cast of *Burmese Days*; not with the rising protests of the brightest and best of the governed; not with its own post-war economic difficulties. The British Empire Exhibition so proudly celebrated by Harold Nelson's roaring lion was both a partial view and a view that looked backwards, not, as was trumpeted at the time, forward. Young Donald MacFadyen understood this, even when he was bombing down the roller-coaster with the girl of his choice. He wrote: 'Wembley; the end of the spacious days; the grand finale'.

CHAPTER FOURTEEN

THE BIRTH OF MODERNITY

SILVER JUBILEE COMMEMORATIVE, TWOPENCE HALFPENNY, 1935

THE SILVER JUBILEE commemorative twopence half-penny is as modern a stamp as Harold Nelson's lion was traditional. It is modern in its imagery – gone is the hierarchical boastfulness of Empire. It is modern in its design: the blocks of colour, the simplicity and the almost 3D effect are all new to British philately. It is modern in its technology: the Silver Jubilee issue was printed using a new method, photogravure, which enabled much clearer lines and subtler shades.

It was designed by Barnett Freedman. Born to poor Jewish immigrants in London's East End, Freedman fought poverty and chronic asthma to win a place at the elite Royal College of Art, becoming Britain's finest lithographer, responsible for book covers, packaging, adverts, posters and this wonderful stamp.

Britain, and the world, had changed massively since 1924.

America, its economy undamaged by the First World War, had boomed, especially in the second half of the 1920s, and this in turn had helped other nations to grow. Management techniques pioneered by F.W. Taylor made industry more efficient (though arguably less pleasant to work in). New consumer goods appeared, which more and more people could afford to buy – it was a self-reinforcing cycle of prosperity and expenditure.

The changes weren't just economic. The tunes at the Pageant of Empire had been martial, orchestral, stirring, but essentially sedate. In 1925, new music hit Britain: the Charleston, with its syncopated rhythm, manic tempo and wacky – or incredibly sexy, if done by Josephine Baker – dance. An even cheekier one, the Black Bottom, danced to a similar Charleston-type rhythm, followed the next year.

In the hands of the goofy, pre-packaged and rather aptly named Paul Whiteman Orchestra, the new jazz was still light entertainment. In the hands of some of Whiteman's sidemen, especially Bix Beiderbecke, and other cornet/trumpet players like Louis Armstrong and James 'Bubber' Miley, it became art. It created beauty that amazed, troubled and lingered, and it did so in the context of the dance floor, the speakeasy, of having fun rather than sitting politely in a concert hall. Its musicians were subversive, too: Bix and Bubber both drank heavily and eventually died of this, and most of the great players were black: a challenge for many at a time when racist attitudes were common.

Like the Jubilee stamp, the popularity of jazz also owed a great deal to technology. The BBC had started radio broad-casting in 1922 (the very first official broadcasts were by the Post Office, but it was soon agreed that a new body was needed). Early 'crystal' radios were unreliable, however, and it wasn't until 1926 that the medium took off, with the arrival of a valve receiver that could run off the mains. At the same time, gram-ophone use boomed, thanks to the availability of cheap units made by companies like HMV and Decca.

Technology also boosted the film industry, which flourished in the late 1920s. Charlie Chaplin's *Gold Rush* came out in 1925; 1927 saw the first talkie, Al Jolson in *The Jazz Singer*.

Motor cars were everywhere. By 1928, there were two million in Britain. This necessitated the construction of fast new 'arterial' roads, such as the Great West Road Brentford bypass. Along this were, and still are, marvellous art deco factories – finest of all being the Firestone tyre factory (until it was vandalized by its then owners in 1980).

More and more of these cars were driven by women. The old world of Empire had been male; the Britain that was emerging in the 1920s was much less so. The Post Office provides a classic example of this change. Before 1914, it had largely been a male preserve, despite the efforts of leaders like Henry Fawcett both to recruit women and to reward them fairly. By 1918, almost half its workforce was female. Though many women stepped – or were pushed – aside when men came back from the front, others did not. Female suffrage, a contentious issue before the war (in 1914 many women said they did not want the vote) became uncontroversial as it drew to a close. In February 1918, Lloyd George gave many women over 30 the vote, and in 1928 all women over 21 joined men in a genuine universal franchise.

Married women were still expected to be the homemakers – but technology was beginning to make this an easier task, especially for the middle classes. Gas cookers were replacing the old wood or coal stoves. Vacuum cleaner salesmen were knocking on doors. Among the young, the 'flapper' had appeared, with her ever-shortening hemline, heavily made-up eyes, cropped hair, flat chest and maybe even a cigarette; determined to live life on her own terms. Of course, most women didn't flap, but they did put on a little more make-up, wore slightly shorter skirts and felt a bit freer in the face of male power.

The decade that had begun in the gloomy shadow of war looked as if it would end on a high, but people should have known that the Wall Street Crash was going to happen the moment a financial expert proclaimed, 'Stock prices have reached what looks like a permanently high plateau.' The American market peaked on 3 September 1929, then plummeted on Black Thursday, 24 October. Various other Black days of the week followed and, apart from the odd weak rally, Wall Street headed downward till July 1932, by which time it had lost a staggering 89% of its value. The London Stock Exchange was not quite as badly hit, but Britain's economy still went into a slump.

This slump was both deep and, more worrying, long. The country seemed stuck in it, unable to pick itself up. Valuable export markets shrank (on top of this, nations were suddenly reintroducing import tariffs), the home market was trapped in a vicious circle of shrinking demand and output, and unemployment climbed remorselessly, passing 2.5 million by the end of 1930 and nearly touching 3 million in 1933. The system of national unemployment relief collapsed under the strain. It had been based on contributions to a kind of insurance fund, and only paid out for six months. But now hardly anyone was finding work. A new system was introduced, which promised to pay claimants indefinitely. But to keep its cost down, payouts were smaller and a 'means test' was introduced, to ensure recipients did not have savings or secret sources of income. The snooping associated with this was bitterly resented by many honest people.

For many, the Great Depression was a shock almost as strong as the war. The mighty Wealth Machine that had made Victorian Britain rich and silenced Thomas Malthus had survived the Somme and Passchendaele, but now seemed to have conked out, like a flivver halfway up a hill ... Things were especially bad in the north. George Orwell spent part of 1936 living in the slums of Sheffield, Barnsley and Wigan. *The Road to Wigan Pier* is a sobering read for anyone keen to eulogize the good old days.

An attempt was made to brighten things up, in the south at least, via public art. Some came courtesy of corporate advertisers, especially Shell, but much came from enlightened government bodies. London Underground had been leading the way since the 1920s, when managing director Frank Pick had started commissioning stylish but functional new stations such as Arnos Grove and East Finchley (he also commissioned Harry Beck's diagrammatic tube map, an expanded version of which we use today). The Post Office followed: Pick's equivalent, Stephen Tallents, joined in 1933.

Tallents had been given a brief to improve the public image of the Post Office (and of the government that controlled it): it was an early exercise in what we now call PR. But above this, he had a simple, Rowland-Hill-style sense of public duty; he wanted to commission attractive things to make national life a bit more pleasant. The results include Rex Whistler's Valentine's Day Telegram, Giles Gilbert Scott's Jubilee phone box (the classic smaller red phone box) – and Barnett Freedman's stamps.

Tallents also employed a film unit. One of their products is *The King's Stamp*, a 20-minute film about Freedman and his design of the Jubilee issue. Part of the film flashes back to the Victorian era and mocks it: the world of the Silver Jubilee 2½d did not want to be connected with that of the Queen Empress.

Night Mail is the unit's best-known film. The star of this documentary is the Travelling Post Office, the passengerless express that left Euston for Glasgow six days a week at 8.30 p.m. precisely. On each journey, half a million letters crossed the country, some from start to finish, others snatched en route from gantries overhanging the line or loaded or unloaded at Crewe, where a series of lines interconnected – woe betide the feeder train that arrived late here and thus upset the entire system. 'The Postal', as the express was called, was an aristocrat of the rails: local services were shunted aside to make way for it. All the time, letters were being sorted on board. The film shows us how – and lets us into a vanished world of Bakelite telephones, manually cranked railway signals, strict but cheerful hierarchy, men in trilby hats smoking pipes and, above all, steam engines. However, the film's conclusion, as the train crosses Scotland's southern uplands, is thoroughly modern: played to dissonant music from a young Benjamin Britten and the words of a fine poem by W.H. Auden.

At the time he wrote his poem, Auden was a self-proclaimed communist. The flight of the intelligentsia to extreme political ideas was a feature of the new, modern era. On one level, it was due to the apparent breakdown of the economic system. But men like Orwell saw the effects of this breakdown more clearly than most, and didn't embrace totalitarianism. The drift to extremism was a symptom of a deeper malaise.

The First World War had left a hole in the Western moral universe – a fact noted by bright non-Westerners such as the Cantlies' friend Sun Yat-sen, whose admiration for the West dimmed markedly after 1914: how could 'civilized' countries have indulged in this slaughter? The promoters of the British Empire Exhibition had wanted visitors to fill this hole with puzzled, respectful grief. Others filled it with the buzz of jazz, cars and cocktails. Those such as Eric Gill and the poet T.S. Eliot, chose to return to traditional Christian faith. Another great modernist poet, Ezra Pound, flew off to the far right. But many more artists and intellectuals marched to the far left. (Auden later recanted his views, disgusted by the cruelty of the communists he fought alongside in the Spanish Civil War.)

Wiser, surely, than falling into goose-step with Stalin, Hitler or Mussolini was to have a good long look at the Wealth Machine and work out how to fix it. John Maynard Keynes, back from Versailles and teaching at Cambridge, realized that, in a situation like the Great Depression, the government could get the stalled economy moving again by spending money, even if it meant borrowing or printing it: they'd get it back later via taxation on increased economic activity, and in the meantime, society would benefit. Keynes, well aware of the lessons of Weimar, never said this was *always* the right thing to do: later, his views were misapplied, for which he can hardly be blamed. Another economist, Joseph Schumpeter, argued that the decline of outdated industries was a healthy part of a natural cycle of 'creative destruction' whereby the economy reinvented and reinvigorated itself. Entrepreneurs should be encouraged to create fresh, vital businesses based on new technology and new market understanding, which would drive recovery, as they had in the 1920s.

In the end, recovery did come, slowly and selectively. In London and the South-East, it was driven by light manufacturing: the Hoover building on the A40 is magnificent testimony to this. In the Midlands it was the automobile, of which Britain now made more than any other European country. More generally, things picked up once the threat of war forced government to put Keynes' ideas into practice, suddenly spending money on armaments.

Despite these difficulties, the Royal Jubilee celebrated in this stamp was a cause for national merrymaking. This took forms the Victorians would have recognized instantly (apart from some odd four-wheeled machines chugging along in the ceremonial precessions): not everything in Britain had changed by modern 1935. Treeton and Orgreave in Yorkshire had a church service, a carnival procession, maypole dancing and crowning of the May Queen, tea for children in the school hall, sports on the colliery canteen field, entertainment for old folk – interrupted by the King's Jubilee Broadcast, which was relayed to the hall – and a bonfire and fireworks to round off the celebrations. The Rother Vale, Treeton Prize Band provided music throughout the day. Down south, in Datchet near Slough a procession of people in Victorian outfits rode penny-farthings. Bloxham, near Banbury, renamed Tank Lane 'King's Road' in honour of the event. The procession in Hampton, Middlesex, was the 'best ever seen in the town'. And so on, all across the United (for the day anyway) Kingdom.

To the philatelist, George V is something of a hero. He was an avid and thorough collector, slowly building the royal stamp collection started by his uncle Prince Alfred into one of the finest in the world (it is so large, nobody knows exactly how many stamps are in it). However, in other ways, he is not an easy man to warm to. He was ill-tempered and lacked interest in art or science. His favourite hobby was shooting; he once killed 1,000 pheasants in a single day. His children were scared of him.

But he had his strengths. George V never pretended to be anything he wasn't, once commenting, 'I am only a very ordinary sort of fellow.' He was a moderating influence on politicians: when Stanley Baldwin wanted to crush the General Strike with force, he counselled calmness, adding, 'Try living on their wages.' He dealt well with Ramsay MacDonald's Labour government of 1924, unruffled by republican noises in the party ranks. He saw through Hitler instantly. He brought the monarchy closer to the people, appearing more often in public, and living a private life much more like that of his subjects than that of his flamboyant father. In the end, he was popular, as the Jubilee celebrations showed.

The smoking habit the King had acquired during the First World War finally caught up with him. Suffering from septicaemia, he was hospitalized then sent to recuperate in a home on the south coast, near Bognor – renamed Bognor Regis after this visit. The atmosphere here was congenial, and he recovered. When illness struck again, someone tried to cheer him up by saying he'd soon be well enough to visit Bognor again. Irascible to the end, he replied, 'Bugger Bognor!' They were his last words.

CHAPTER FIFTEEN

BETRAYAL

EDWARD VIII ½D, 1936

ISSUED ON 1 September 1936, the Edward VIII ½d was a fine, contemporary stamp showing the profile of a handsome young king with a determined look. It seemed to promise a modern monarch for modern times. But only two months later, Edward had abdicated the throne. During most of the time this stamp was in use, he was an exile from his own country, and he continued to be so for nearly thirty years. The story of the stamp itself can shed light on how and why this came to be.

If former East Ender Barnett Freedman was a daring choice of designer for the Jubilee stamp, the choice for the new king's definitives was even more radical. Hubert Brown was 17 years old. He was a schoolboy in Devon, who designed the stamp in his spare time and sent it to Harrison and Sons, the Post Office printers, in March 1936. Brown was clearly influenced by Freedman's work: his pencil design is shaded, as the Jubilees but no other British stamps had been. But Brown de-cluttered the design in a way that not even Freedman had dared to do. Sometimes it takes a totally fresh pair of eyes to really change things.

It should have been a marvellous story. A young artist capturing the spirit of a new age and getting the ultimate credit for this – his work acknowledged (and used) nationally! Unfortunately it didn't happen that way. Brown didn't even get a reply after his idea was submitted. The first thing he knew about its acceptance was when the stamps went on sale. When his father wrote to complain, the Post Office replied that *they* had designed them, pointing out small differences between Brown's drawings and the end product. This was a fraudulent defence: with all stamp designs, the monarch has the final choice and makes this choice from a small, pre-selected set. As the options presented to the King were variations on Brown's idea, Brown has as much right to be credited with this issue as any designer does for any stamp. Luckily, Mr Brown senior was a fighter and kept up a battle to have his son's work recognized. Eventually, he won: in the Stanley Gibbons catalogue, the credit now reads 'Designer: H. Brown, adapted by Harrisons'.

The new stamps proved controversial. Professional artists like Eric Gill, who previously saw themselves as radical free spirits, suddenly morphed into reactionaries, huffing about amateurism in stamp design. The public, however, felt differently. In a 1937 *Stamp Lover* magazine, a reader in Brighton presents the results of an informal poll in the office where he worked. The results are fascinating: the younger people loved them; the older ones did not.

Welcome to that modern phenomenon, the Generation Gap! Of course, there have always been gaps in perceptions between generations. Yet at some times changes in environment – music, technology, politics – stretch that gap to breaking point. The 1960s was one such time; the 1930s was another.

Edward VIII was a modern young man. He liked jazz. He had love affairs. He didn't just accept ideas, he wanted to think for himself. He also had a streak of narcissism, a little of which is evident perhaps in this stamp. It certainly shows in other pictures of him. If you are fortunate enough to visit the Isles of Scilly, go to the Scillionian Club and look at the picture of Edward, then Prince of Wales, at the Club's ceremonial opening. He sits surrounded by respectable, dark-clad, essentially Victorian old men, glowing like an emanation in his light suit, a look of horror on his face. *I don't belong here*, he seems to be saying. *Get me out!* Would this overgrown adolescent have turned into a good monarch? We never got the chance to find out.

Edward met Wallis Simpson in 1931. Wallis was a breath of modern air into King George's essentially Victorian court: she was bossy, irreverent, sexually liberated – and American. She had already been through one marriage and was now in another, though this did not stop her flirting with other men, including the Prince. He fell in love with her in early 1934, and she (though many commentators suggest she was less committed than he was) fell in love with him later that year.

Needless to say, this did not go down well with the King and the equally conservative Queen Mary. A considerable social stigma was still attached to divorce; it was worse, even, than being American and bossy. It was against the teachings of the Church of England, of whom the Prince would be head when he became king. (Remarriage of divorcees with living spouses has only been sanctioned by the Church since 2002.) And there were rumours that Wallis had had affairs with dubious characters: a car salesman and senior figures in Fascist regimes, Italy's Count Ciano and the German ambassador to Britain, von Ribbentrop. The British establishment had taken a violent dislike to Wallis, so may have cooked up these rumours. But it is certainly true that she socialized with these people.

When George V died, people in the know – the public was

unaware of the affair – hoped Edward, like Shakespeare's Prince Hal, would change his lifestyle. He didn't, but neither did he totally abandon his royal role. On one official trip to South Wales, he visited a town where the local steelworks had recently closed, leaving thousands of men unemployed. 'Something must be done to find them work,' he said. Old-fashioned monarchs didn't say things like that. Modern ones, it seemed, did. But this did not go down well with the establishment. What things did he have in mind? Probably getting the government to spend money on work-creating projects. Critics of Edward point out that this solution was that of Oswald Mosley, leader of the British Union of Fascists. But it was also the solution of the immaculately liberal John Maynard Keynes – and was what the government ended up doing, though out of panic rather than calculation.

Nonetheless, Edward's comment was one more nail in the coffin of his monarchy. Battle lines were drawn. On one side were the King and a few supporters, including Winston Churchill. On the other side stood most of the ruling elite. Many of the latter figures were old: Stanley Baldwin, the Prime Minister, was 69; the Archbishop of Canterbury, a fierce opponent of the King, was 72. The battle of Hubert Brown's stamp was being fought again: modernity versus tradition; the generation gap at one of its wider moments.

Matters came to a head when Wallis got her divorce from husband number two on 27 October (technically it was a decree nisi, which meant she would be free to marry six months later. Just in time for the coronation!) The King tried to persuade his opponents that he should have a morganatic marriage, whereby his wife would not formally be queen. This compromise was turned down. Attempts were made to persuade Wallis to abandon the King: reluctantly she gave in, but he refused to accept this. In the end, Edward was left with a simple choice.

On 11 December, he broadcast a speech to the nation which Churchill had helped him write:

At long last I am able to say a few words of my own. I have never wanted to withhold anything, but until now it has not been constitutionally possible for me to speak.

A few hours ago I discharged my last duty as King and Emperor, and now that I have been succeeded by my brother, the Duke of York, my first words must be to declare my allegiance to him. This I do with all my heart.

You all know the reasons which have impelled me to renounce the throne. But I want you to understand that in making up my mind I did not forget the country or the Empire, which, as Prince of Wales and lately as King, I have for twenty-five years tried to serve.

But you must believe me when I tell you that I have found it impossible to carry the heavy burden of responsibility and to discharge my duties as King as I would wish to do without the help and support of the woman I love.

From then on, it was downhill for the handsome young man on the halfpenny stamp. He went into exile, hoping to return soon, but instead was publicly snubbed: the new king refused to allow any of the royal family to attend his brother's wedding, and it was made clear that he would not be welcome back in the UK. A few months after this rebuff, Edward visited Hitler and gave him a Nazi salute. Later on there were rumours that he betrayed British war secrets to the Germans, but these claims have never been substantiated.

Treachery runs through this story. Edward VIII was betrayed by the British elite: a way could have been found round the Wallis problem if the will to do so had been there. Did he betray his country in return? Probably not, as he was later allowed back into British life, a tiny bit, anyway: he was invited to the current Queen's coronation in 1953 and the Investiture of the Prince of Wales in 1969. One must assume that clearance for such invitations would not have been granted had there been any serious evidence that Edward was a traitor.

This still leaves the question of what kind of monarch he might have made. The ideal monarch is undemonstrative, grounded, a careful considerer of all positions rather than a fanatical advocate of any one. Such a person is a bulwark of solidity, perspective and sense against the rampant egos of politicians. Edward would probably have made a better politician than he would a monarch.

And what of Hubert Brown? He never became a big-name designer. Like many talented young people, he had to decide between the rather perilous life of a creative artist and something more reliable; he chose the latter. When the Post Office sought to track him down many years later, in effect to say sorry for appropriating his design, they found him living 'in a good small detached house in the best part of Torquay'. He was 'a retired man, in comfortable circumstances with a nice car, but no telephone'.

No telephone? How un-modern of him!

CHAPTER SIXTEEN

TOTAL WAR

GEORGE VI 2½D BLUE WITH 'CENSORED' POSTMARK, 1940

IN NAPOLEONIC times, if you weren't in the war zone, life went on as usual (Tolstoy's hero Pierre Bezukhov even went to spectate at the Battle of Borodino). In the First World War, people back in Britain had tragically little idea of the reality of the trenches. The Second World War was different. It involved everybody.

It did so in the most obvious way with Goering's bombing raids on British towns and cities. It did so via a conscript army (something that had only been the case for part of World War One). It did so with a vast extension of government powers into previously sacrosanct areas of life: one of Churchill's first actions on becoming Prime Minister was to pass the Emergency Powers Act, which suspended traditional liberties like Habeas Corpus and effectively nationalized British industry. It did so via rationing, which was much stricter than in the previous war: clothes, meat, tea, milk – almost anything nice. This envelope shows yet another way: post was rigorously censored. There were about 20 censor offices around the UK, with the main one based at Aintree. In total, these offices employed around 10,000 people, carefully opening and checking all mail to or from service personnel, lest recipients of letters might blab out information that could be picked up by enemy spies.

Despite this new, total war, life went on. The BBC rather reluctantly broadcast the new swing jazz, the music of the young people who fought the war, with its walking bass, driving drums and not a banjo to be heard. Radio listeners could laugh with *ITMA* (*It's That Man Again* – cocking a snook at Hitler, but also at British officialdom's love of acronyms), a wacky, fast-paced comedy show based on stock characters with catch-phrases, and with each episode written just before being broad-cast to ensure bang-up-to-the-minute references.

Relationships between the sexes, especially the young, changed: men about to be sent off to fight did not want to die virgins, and the heightened level of danger in everyone's life added intensity to affairs. Once in khaki, the only way to communicate with your loved one(s) was by post. But there were 10,000 censors watching . . . In an interesting example of officialese being turned on its head and used against its orig-inators, letter writers developed a code using acronyms – there were SWALK ('Sealed with a Loving Kiss') and HOLLAND ('Hope our Love Lasts and Never Dies'). Less romantically, NORWICH meant '(K)nickers off Ready when I Come Home' and EGYPT meant 'Eager to Grab Your Pretty Tits'.

In the late 1930s, few people in Britain wanted war. Memories of Passchendaele and the Somme were strong, and modern conflict threatened something even more terrible: aerial bombing. But the case for peace grew ever weaker as Hitler marched into the Rhineland, Austria and Czechoslovakia, ripping up agreements as he went. Kristallnacht, 9 November 1938, when synagogues and Jewish property were vandalized and Jews beaten, murdered or arrested, showcased the brutality of the regime to anyone who hadn't got the message yet. In 1939, Hitler turned his attention to Poland, which he invaded on 1 September, having agreed a week earlier to carve the country up with his former arch-enemy Stalin.

British Prime Minister Neville Chamberlain, who had tried to restrain Hitler by negotiation, issued an ultimatum. Obloquy has been heaped on him, but he was not a coward or a buffoon, just a man of peace at a time of war. On 3 September, the nation crowded round its radios to hear him broadcast from 10 Downing Street:

> *This morning the British Ambassador in Berlin handed the German Government a final note stating that, unless we heard from them by eleven o'clock that they were prepared at once to withdraw their troops from Poland, a state of war would exist between us. I have to tell you now that no such undertaking has been received, and that consequently this country is at war with Germany.*
>
> *You can imagine what a bitter blow it is to me that all my long struggle to win peace has failed. Yet I cannot believe that there is anything more or anything different that I could have done and that would have been more successful . . .*

People feared immediate bombing raids, but in fact hostilities got off to a slow start. The first casualties came at sea, from U-boat attacks on British shipping. On land, Britain quietly built up an Expeditionary Force in France, while Hitler carried on picking off the targets that suited him – Denmark, Norway, Holland, Belgium. British troops were sent to protect Norway, but were overpowered. Chamberlain took the blame for this and was booted out of office on 10 May 1940, to be replaced by Winston Churchill. On the same day, Hitler invaded France and the war began in earnest.

It nearly ended soon after. German tanks poured across the French border, blasting their way past opposition still thinking in terms of trenches and barbed wire. Three weeks later, the mighty Expeditionary Force found itself surrounded and being squeezed by an ever tighter noose around the Channel port of Dunkirk. It is still a mystery why Hitler didn't finish the Force off. The most convincing explanations are that he wanted to preserve his resources for attacking France – he liked to invade countries one by one – and that he thought the Luftwaffe would do the job of destroying the British at Dunkirk. The Luftwaffe certainly made Dunkirk hell, but the Navy, Merchant Navy, and anyone with a boat set out to rescue the trapped soldiers – and succeeded.

In words one cannot imagine Chamberlain mustering, Churchill rallied morale after this defeat with his famous 'We shall fight on the beaches' speech.

France soon fell and Britain was next on Hitler's list, with Operation Sealion scheduled for autumn 1940. For the operation to succeed, Hitler needed air superiority over south-east England as well as the Channel. On 12 August – Adlertag, Day of the Eagle – Germany launched a full-on assault on Britain's radar stations and fighter bases. For weeks, the skies of Sussex and Kent were arabesqued with vapour trails as Hurricanes, Spitfires and Messerschmitts duelled like medieval knights. The fifteenth of September was a crucial day. Goering launched a massive daylight bombing raid on London, hoping to draw the RAF into a huge, one-off battle. Up to a point, he succeeded: the RAF did change tactics and reply in force – but the Luftwaffe lost the fight, with sixty of their planes shot down to Britain's twenty-three. The day is celebrated in David Gentleman's fine 1/3 stamp of 1965, showing vapour trails in a clear blue sky over St Paul's Cathedral.

Hitler switched his strategy to the night bombing attacks of the Blitz, but Operation Sealion was indefinitely postponed: the first Act of the war was over. Nevertheless, things still looked dire. Britain was short of many things: food, raw materials, finance. The stamps of the time show the effects of this: the main definitives were reissued in washed-out colours to save ink, the striking ultramarine 2½d which inspired this chapter turning to the lightest of blues.

Late 1940 and early 1941 saw Germany almost starve Britain with the help of the U-boats it operated from bases in newly captured France. However, Britain was able to crack the Enigma code used by the U-boat commanders, and thus locate these elusive hunters more effectively – though they continued to menace shipping for the next two years. The code-breaking was done at Bletchley Park, a run-down country house in the middle of what is now Milton Keynes. Much of the technology for achieving this was provided by the Post Office. At the heart of Bletchley Park was arguably the world's first computer, the Colossus, built by Post Office engineer Tommy Flowers and his team.

In 1941, the Axis Powers made huge strategic mistakes. On 22 June 1941 Hitler turned on his new friend and invaded Russia; on 7 December Japan bombed Pearl Harbor, bringing a reluctant America into the war. Despite these, 1942 was largely a year of Allied defeats. February saw the fall of Singapore. Rommel's Afrika Korps swept across North Africa. In August, a commando raid on Dieppe by largely Canadian forces led to massive casualties and showed how far the Allies still were from being able to land an invasion force in northern Europe. Only at the end of that year did good news finally come in: Rommel fell ill and his replacement was trounced by Montgomery near El Alamein, a small seaport in northern Egypt. On the announcement of this victory, church bells rang out all over Britain – including those of Coventry Cathedral, where the tower was all that remained of the noble Gothic building that had been blitzed in November 1940. Oddly, a stamp has never been issued in Britain to celebrate this first victory of the war; there is a fine Australian one from 1992, commemorating the contribution to El Alamein of the 9th Australian division, but nothing British.

The year 1943 saw hard-won gains. The U-boats in the Atlantic were finally overcome, thanks to a combination of new weaponry, continued code-breaking and the appointment of a submariner, Max Horton, to combat them. In July, American troops landed in Sicily. Hitler's Russian campaign suffered its crucial defeat in the biggest tank battle ever fought, near Kursk, south of Moscow. Intercepted messages from German High Command, decoded at Bletchley Park, played a crucial role in this victory.

At the end of 1943, Churchill, Roosevelt and Stalin met at the Soviet Embassy in Tehran to discuss both the war and plans for the post-war world. The conference should have been a triumph for Churchill, but was a disaster. Stalin, on home ground, was particularly arrogant. Roosevelt went along with him, partly because he was unwell, partly because he was awed by Stalin, and partly because both men knew the post-war world would contain two superpowers, neither of them Britain. At a dinner to round off the conference, Churchill presented Stalin with a sword from King George VI, which Stalin's aide promptly dropped. Stalin made a deadly serious comment about liquidating 50,000 German staff officers after the war, to which Roosevelt jokily replied that maybe 49,000 would be enough. Churchill did not join in the laughter.

Still, the Allies had to work together. In early 1944 German resistance in Italy was finally overcome at Monte Cassino. A Japanese attempt to invade India was stopped at Imphal and Kohima. And on 6 June, British, American and Canadian troops landed on five beaches in Normandy, having successfully fooled Hitler into thinking their attack was a feint. Four thousand Allied soldiers died on that day, but by evening the beachheads had been secured. By the end of June, the Germans had retreated from the whole of Normandy, and on 25 August allied forces marched into Paris. Hitler ordered his commander, General von Choltitz, to leave the city 'in rubble': the General disobeyed.

Hitler still had aces up his sleeve. As Allied troops advanced across France, he launched the V1 flying bomb, nicknamed the Doodlebug, on London. An even more sinister weapon, the supersonic V2 rocket, followed in September. Luckily, the V2 proved inaccurate (British intelligence also managed to fool the Germans into thinking the rocket was over-shooting, so most fell short of London: by the time they had worked this out, its launching grounds were overrun by Allied forces). Finally, like Ludendorff in 1918, Hitler launched a last counter-offensive in the Ardennes, the Battle of the Bulge. It failed. The Allies marched on.

While this was happening, Bomber Command launched huge 'area bombing' attacks on German cities. This was total war taken to a new level. The destruction of Dresden on 13–15 February 1945 is notorious: estimates of civilian deaths vary wildly from 25,000 to 250,000. The man responsible for this policy, Arthur Harris, made his way on to a fine stamp in 1986. Many people were uneasy about this commemoration, though for others the gesture was more a tribute to the brave young aircrew who manned the bombers, which was one of the riskiest jobs in the entire war.

But of course, far greater atrocities were committed by the other side. On 15 April 1945 British troops liberated a concentration camp near the village of Belsen. The liberators were battle-hardened men, accustomed to the horrors of war – but nothing they had experienced in combat prepared them for what they saw that day. Eyewitness reports tell of trenches full of bodies in various stages of decomposition, huts crammed with a mixture of the dead, the dying and people too weak to move, crowds of emaciated survivors in lice-ridden rags, and the entire ground littered with excrement and corpses. Many soldiers who arrived in Belsen that day were so traumatized by the experience that they never uttered a word about what they saw, even to their families.

Belsen, with its 60,000 inmates, was a small part of the hellish slaughter machine that Hitler had constructed: it fell to Soviet forces to discover Auschwitz, Treblinka, Belzec, Sobibor, Chelmno and Majdanek, where an estimated six million human beings died. But the camp at Belsen entered British consciousness in an especially powerful way.

Meanwhile, the Nazis were fighting their last defensive battle, on the Seelow Heights about 60 miles east of Berlin. By 19 April, these defences were breached. For many months Hitler had been living a fantasy life in a bunker surrounded by sycophants, barking out orders based on falsified estimates of troop strengths and resource levels. On 30 April, the truth finally caught up with the Führer: he committed suicide, surrounded by the blood-soaked wreckage of the nation of which he had imagined himself the saviour. A week later, Germany formally surrendered: the total war was over.

CHAPTER SEVENTEEN

VICTORY!

2½D VICTORY
COMMEMORATIVE, 1946

A T THREE o'clock on the afternoon of 8 May 1945
(VE Day), Churchill broadcast to the nation,
announcing the surrender. Celebrations broke out at
once. In London, crowds gathered in Trafalgar Square and
thronged up the Mall towards Buckingham Palace chanting
'We want the King!' George VI, his family and 'Mr Churchill'
appeared on the balcony. Later that evening, the monarch made
his own broadcast.

*In the darkest hours we knew that the enslaved and
isolated peoples of Europe looked to us. Their hopes were
our hopes, their confidence confirmed our faith. We knew
that, if we failed, the last remaining barrier against a
worldwide tyranny would have fallen in ruins.*

But we did not fail. We kept faith with ourselves and

with one another, we kept faith and unity with our great
allies. That faith, that unity have carried us to victory
through dangers which at times seemed overwhelming.

The fun went on all night. People caught trains up to the capital, partied, jumped on early trains back and appeared bleary-eyed at work. British reserve came down for a moment; everyone was everyone else's friend. A wonderful new era had begun.

For some, of course, the celebrations were more muted – those with loved ones fighting or imprisoned in Burma, for example. The war with Japan carried on another three months before coming to a dramatic and terrifying end when atom bombs obliterated Hiroshima and Nagasaki. The new era wasn't, perhaps, going to be as wonderful after all.

Economically, Britain was in a terrible mess. Its infrastructure was a bomb site. Its merchant fleet had been decimated. Its reserves of gold and of foreign currency were gone: from March 1941 the country had been effectively bankrupt, after which it had been propped up by America via a system called lend-lease, whereby the US lent money and materials but never actually asked for the loans to be repaid. However, soon after the war ended this prop was pulled away and was replaced by a traditional, and actually rather harsh, loan.

The results of this in everyday life could be seen in the continuation of rationing. Even in 1948, clothes, soap, canned fruit, meat, cheese, butter, tea, sugar, milk, jam, bread and potatoes were still controlled. Britain had fallen into a deep hole, and could only climb out of it very slowly.

The victory stamps issued in 1946 – the 2½d for postcards and a 3d for letters – reflect this sober reality. They came out to commemorate the first anniversary of VE day rather than hot on the heels of victory itself, and their emphasis was on reconstruction rather than celebration, portraying themes of agriculture, housing, industry and trade.

Between VE Day and the appearance of these stamps, Britain had acquired a new government. An election, called immediately after victory was announced, took place on 5 July. Churchill, leader of the Conservatives, had expected to win on the strength of his personal popularity, but Labour triumphed by 145 seats. The new men in power – particularly the new Prime Minister, Clement Attlee, and William Beveridge, a civil servant with Rowland Hill's talent for devising effective social institutions – had radical plans for a new Britain. These are reflected in the motifs on the 2½d stamp.

First, the tractor. The market for agricultural produce was effectively nationalized. Rules were put in place, whereby the government guaranteed both to buy fixed amounts of the main agricultural products and to pay fixed prices for them (fixed well in advance).

Housing, especially public housing, was to be expanded in a massive programme. This meant new building in bomb-damaged cities, but also the creation of 'New Towns', where people from former slum areas could start new lives in space and fresh air. More generally, the lives of families would be improved: education for everyone up to the age of 14 was to be compulsory and free.

Then there's the factory. The government had a range of ideas for industry. These included taking over what Nye Bevan called 'the commanding heights of the economy' – the mines, railways, power, iron and steel industries. In effect, this meant carrying on what had become wartime practice but making it official: the old owners would be bought out by the govern-ment. National employment levels would be kept high: a target of 3% unemployment was set, and if the figure dipped below this, money would be pumped into the economy. For those still out of work, there would be a national insurance system: everyone would pay into a 'pot' and people would get assistance if they were either laid off or sick.

The cargo ship was perhaps the least relevant symbol: Britain had so few left after the war. Would the country ever be a great trading nation again?

Maybe the stamp's designer, H.L. Palmer (a staff artist at Harrison and Sons, now part of De La Rue), would have been better replacing the ship with a stethoscope. The healthcare system of the Victorian and Edwardian eras had been based on charitable hospitals. GPs had charged for their work, though the kinder ones had often waived fees for the poor. The system came close to breakdown in the 1930s, when the Great Crash had taken away huge chunks of the endowments which had previously financed the hospitals, and unemployment had resulted in a worsening of public health.

William Beveridge's biggest idea was to replace the old system with a state-owned National Health Service, that would take over the old hospitals and employ all GPs. It would provide free treatment for everybody. Beveridge hoped that the cost of the new service would fall over time as people became healthier as a result of it and of other improvements in welfare. This belief did not last long: by 1951, the government had to introduce charges for prescriptions and eye tests to meet the NHS's rapidly escalating cost.

But the idea was, in essence, a brilliant one. It has been copied (in outline at least) by all the world's advanced economies apart from America – whose healthcare system now gobbles up half as much again of GDP as anyone else's and still does little for the poor. Like the penny post, this is an area where Britain led the world.

The nationalization of industry proved less effective. The new public bodies turned out to be leaden-footed and bureaucratic. The new bosses turned out to be indistinguishable from the old ones and worker morale remained low. Rather than revitalizing them, the nationalized boards presided over the decline of the coal and railway industries.

All of these interventions cost money. Some funding came from taxation, which had risen sharply during the war and was not lowered after it. Some came from borrowing; the government issued low-interest bonds, which proved to be lousy investments for bondholders and sowed the seeds of future inflation for everyone else.

Still, by and large, the reforms of the 1945 government, represented by the symbols on the 2½d Victory stamp, brought about huge change for the good. When Seebohm Rowntree carried out a survey of poverty in York in 1951 – carrying on a tradition of such surveys started by his father Joseph in the Victorian era, all of which had shown poverty doggedly persisting – he found it had largely disappeared. Even the Conservative Party came round to the new institutions, especially 'rising young men' like Harold Macmillan and Ian Macleod. Since then, Beveridge's welfare state – scarcely imagined before World War Two – has become an accepted part of British life, with political debate almost always centring around who can manage it better rather than whether it should exist.

CHAPTER EIGHTEEN

THE AUSTERITY GAMES

1/- OLYMPIC GAMES
COMMEMORATIVE, 1948

L ONG BEFORE war broke out, it had been decided that London should host the 1944 Olympics, which were, of course, cancelled. Britain was offered the 1948 games, and, after some debate as to their affordability, accepted.

A set of four stamps celebrated the event, each by a different designer. Percy Metcalfe's 2½d shows the globe surrounded with a laurel wreath above an Olympic symbol that looks as if someone – a weightlifter or a wrestler, perhaps – has sat on it. The 3d, designed by Abram Games, who was later to design the logo for the Festival of Britain, symbolized speed: a face breasting an imaginary finishing tape against a background of a globe and the Olympic rings. S.D. Scott's 6d design is a simple Olympic symbol plus laurel leaves. The shilling stamp, my favourite, is by Edmund Dulac, a designer with a long pedigree including the stamps for George VI's coronation and (with Eric Gill) the era's definitives. Here Winged Victory waits with a laurel wreath in her hand to crown the champions – and she's hovering right over Britain!

Despite these confident stamps, the games were not going to be showy. It is estimated that Hitler spent the equivalent of over £6 million on his propagandist 1936 Olympiad. Britain set a budget of £750,000. This was expected to be recouped from ticket sales and sponsorship – and was. No special stadia were to be built: Wembley would be the main arena, even though it only had a dog track (this was upgraded). The ice rink next door would become the Olympic swimming pool. The Victorian velodrome at Herne Hill got a quick makeover – which did not include floodlighting (when races ran on into dusk one evening, officials drove cars into the venue and used the headlights instead). Olympic villages were set up at an old army camp near Richmond and at RAF bases at West Drayton and Uxbridge; other athletes were billeted with families or stayed in school dormitories or in the halls of residence of University of London colleges. This accommodation was free, but athletes were expected to bring their own towels. Travel to venues was via a mixture of hired buses and free passes on London Transport, though competitors in the cycling events were expected to ride their own bikes to Herne Hill. The event soon came to be known as 'The Austerity Games'.

The austerity was not helped by a resurgent and unattractive aspect of British life. The central planning mentality of both the war and the post-war governments had created a fearsome bureaucracy that was slow, uncommunicative and self-righteous, serving the public good in theory but actually making life far more difficult than was necessary. This almost resulted in the games starting with incomplete facilities. The Ministry of Works held up work on the boxing ring by dithering over a Control of Iron and Steel Order. Gifts of wood from Sweden and Finland, required for the renovation of the seating at Wembley, got stuck in Customs. More wood from abroad,

Canadian fir for the diving boards, was delayed by the Board of Trade.

If this nearly messed up the practicalities (in the end, dynamic individuals like Lord Burghley, Harold Abrahams and Sir John Elvin, the owner of Wembley, got things moving), a more theoretical piece of nit-picking threatened to damage British participation in the games: an obsession with amateurism.

Remember those 1881 cricketers, Hornby and Barlow? Hornby had had a private income; Barlow hadn't. Cricket had dealt with this, operating a subtle system where professionals and amateurs – players and gentlemen – could share a field, even if they had separate dressing rooms. British athletics in 1948 had no such system: professionals were banned and that was that. Some Eastern European countries put their best athletes in the army and then allowed them to train like pros. America had a system of university sports scholarships. Britain did neither, and instead went to absurd lengths to root out professionalism as if it were a contagious disease.

It wasn't just being paid to compete that was unacceptable; even sports teachers were deemed to be professionals. Denis Watts, the UK's champion long-jumper, was not allowed to participate because he had applied for a PE instructor's job from which he was yet to earn a penny. British athletes couldn't accept the tiniest gifts from commercial organizations (although the rules were stretched to allow Dunlop to lend cyclists tyres for the event, as long as they were returned afterwards). Some argue that amateurism was what made the 1948 Olympics fun, but in fact, the so-called 'ideal' simply generated hypocrisy, class bias and a smug mediocrity that filtered into many areas of British life and did great damage. The 1948 Games were fun because young, lively and talented people got together to compete in a friendly spirit, not because aspiring sports teachers were banned.

The opening ceremony took place on 29 July, a baking hot day. The athletes paraded round Wembley Stadium: 3,714 men and 385 women, from fifty-nine nations (with memories of Belsen and the Burma railway still too strong, Germany and Japan were not invited; the USSR refused to send a team, thinking the games would be a 1936-style showcase for America). At 4p.m. precisely, George VI declared the Olympics open and 2,500 pigeons were released into the stadium. A twenty-one-gun salute was fired, terrifying the pigeons. The Olympic torch entered the stadium and the flame was lit.

The Games ran for two weeks, the first in blazing sunshine and the second in almost constant rain with athletes splashing through puddles and crowds sheltering under raincoats. In the end, winged victory did not spend much time crowning British heads. That obsession with amateurism didn't help, and the nation was still physically exhausted from war and the continuing shortages. The USA won most medals; Sweden, a neutral nation in the war, came second in the table. Britain, despite fielding more athletes than any other country, came 12th, winning just three gold medals, none of them on the athletics track.

However, nobody seemed to mind. The crowds were happy to take excellence to their hearts, wherever it came from. Fanny Blankers-Koen, a 30-year-old mother of two from Utrecht, won four golds – and could have won more, if there had not been a rule preventing women athletes from competing in more than three individual events. Micheline Ostermeyer of France won gold in the discus and shot-put: she was also a concert pianist and celebrated the latter win with a performance of Beethoven the same evening. Between them, these two unassuming superstars raised the profile of women's athletics (despite perpetual attempts by the head of the IOC, Avery Brundage, to denigrate it).

Among the men, the ungainly but unstoppable 'Czech Locomotive' Emil Zatopek lapped all his opponents in the 10,000 metres and won silver in the 5,000. But perhaps the greatest hero was 'Jumping Jim' Halliday, a British weightlifter who had been a POW in Burma and came home weighing 4½ stone. He ended up winning a bronze medal.

Of these heroes, Zatopek went on to win three gold medals at the 1952 Games in Helsinki. Later still, he supported the 1968 Prague Spring – and for this, he was sent to work in a uranium mine for six years. The truth is that the London Olympics, with their international optimism, were a bright match-flare of goodness in a world that was already darkening again. One great evil had been removed from it; another had not.

The wartime allies had fallen out almost immediately after VE Day: at a conference in Potsdam in July 1945, Stalin had walked all over Attlee and Harry Truman, laying down boundaries for Germany and refusing to hold elections in countries occupied by the Soviet Union. The fate of countries he had annexed during the war – Estonia, Latvia, Lithuania and Moldavia – was not even discussed. Soon after, Churchill made his famous comment about an Iron Curtain being drawn across Europe. The 'Cold War' had begun.

Where elections in Stalin's bloc were allowed, they were rigged. In February 1948, a coup was staged in Czechoslovakia; the next month, Jan Masaryk, a key figure in Czech resistance to Soviet occupation, mysteriously fell out of a window. On 1 April, the Russians began delaying traffic into West Berlin, which was under joint British, French and American occupation. By July all routes into the former capital were closed. The Allies responded by airlifting essential supplies into the city: while the Olympics were taking place, 200 planes a day were flying into RAF Gatow.

Stalin was also building an atom bomb. *Pervaya Molniya* (First Lightning), as powerful as the weapons used on Hiroshima and Nagasaki, was tested on 29 August 1949. It worked.

British scientists had been involved in the Manhattan Project, but after the war America barred its research to outsiders. Britain had to develop its own atomic weapon, or accept it was no longer a global power. Even for a Labour government, this was too bitter a pill to swallow. Ernest Bevin exploded at a cabinet meeting: 'We've got to have this thing over here, whatever it costs. We've got to have the bloody Union Jack on top of it.' Britain might have come 12th in the Olympics medal table, but in a new event, the global arms race, it still coveted the bronze.

The amazing human capacity for innovation turned to the creation of ever more sinister weapons. American scientists were already working on the hydrogen bomb, which essentially used a first-generation atom bomb to trigger an even more destructive reaction. Russia would follow, and so, dragged on by a mixture of fear and outdated pride, would Britain.

So were the Austerity Games, with their make-and-mend internationalist cheeriness, a sham, a half-told tale, just like Wembley's British Empire Exhibition twenty-four years earlier? Shouldn't a stamp that truly represents the era show the Angel of Death, not Winged Victory?

A pessimist might think so. But in the end, surely, the greatest weapon against both tyranny and hydrogen bombs is a shared sense of humanity – which is what the Olympics are essentially about. As Emil Zatopek put it: 'After all those dark days of the war, the bombing, the killing, the starvation, the revival of the Olympics was as if the sun had come out. Suddenly there were no frontiers, no more barriers, just people meeting together.' In their delightfully bumbling way, and without having the slightest intention of doing anything so portentous, Britain's cheery, uncomplicated Austerity Games made a statement as powerful as Hitler's had done in 1936.

CHAPTER NINETEEN

GLORIANA

1'3 CORONATION
COMMEMORATIVE, 1953

EORGE VI had been a popular monarch. He had earned this popularity by walking through the bombed East End (despite initially being booed), by staying in Buckingham Palace during the Blitz, and by keeping a sense of quiet dignity throughout the war: the perfect foil for the bombastic, energizing Churchill. Partly because he had insisted on living in the draughty palace, but also because he smoked like a chimney, his health was not good, and he died in 1952 at the age of 56. He was succeeded by his 25-year-old daughter Elizabeth.

There was a buzz of excitement about the accession of the new queen. Comparisons were made with Elizabeth I, whose reign had been one of national growth and glory. A new Elizabethan age had dawned: if this magnificent stamp was anything to go by, it would be one to be proud of.

But what form would this age take? It could not be an age of Empire: though the Commonwealth was still a significant entity, its days were essentially over. It could not be an age of global leadership: as Stalin and Roosevelt had known at Tehran but Ernest Bevin hadn't yet taken on board, there were just two superpowers in the post-war world. Could it be a golden age of British science? In the year this stamp appeared, arguably the most important scientific discovery of the century was made at Cambridge: the structure of DNA, finally worked out by Francis Crick and James Watson (who just beat Rosalind Franklin and Maurice Wilkins to the discovery – another British-based team, from Kings College London). However, science was becoming a global pursuit; the big American universities were beginning to attract greater funding than even Kings and Cambridge. What about British culture? Benjamin Britten's opera *Gloriana*, written for the coronation, celebrated the first Queen Elizabeth, but its strange harmonies did not appeal to the average listener. Shakespeare's Elizabethan audiences had come from all backgrounds; culture in 1953 seemed the domain of an elite, with the equivalent of the man or woman in the Globe stalls preferring Hollywood movies, West End musicals and Frank Sinatra.

Still, the optimism was there. Britain needed it. The climb out of the economic hole left by the war had been a slow and painful one, salved by the welfare state but also slowed by other policies of Attlee's government, such as nationalization.

Elizabeth's coronation took place on 2 June 1953. The weather was foul but tens of thousands of people lined the route between Buckingham Palace and Westminster Abbey anyway, including a couple who had sailed all the way from Australia to be there. They saw magnificent processions to and from the Abbey, featuring members of the royal family, various branches of the forces and Commonwealth heads of state – Queen Salote of Tonga proved particularly popular, sitting in her open coach beaming with pleasure despite the pouring rain. At the heart of it all was the young monarch in the gold State Coach, wearing George IV's Diadem, the crown in which she appears in the Dorothy Wilding photograph that adorned the other coronation commemoratives and all the other stamps of the first fourteen years of her reign.

The coronation ceremony is a piece of pageantry with deep historical roots; William the Conqueror would have been familiar with the outline of the ritual. The monarch is first presented to the congregation, who are asked if they are 'willing to do homage' to her. She then swears an oath to govern British territories 'according to their respective laws and customs'. She is then presented with a bible and receives Holy Communion. Following that, she takes her place on King Edward's Chair (Edward I, crowned in 1272), where she is anointed by the Archbishop of Canterbury on hands, head and heart – a part of the ceremony which is carried out away from public view (or at least under a canopy). She is presented with the *colobium sindonis*, a relatively simple garment which reminds her that her power comes from the people, then with the sword of state, a symbol of justice, with the orb, a Christian symbol, and with a ring that symbolizes the marriage between monarch and nation. Two sceptres follow, one topped with a cross, the other – the one shown in this stamp – the Sceptre of the Dove, symbolizing fairness and mercy. Then, literally, comes the crowning moment: the Archbishop places on her head St Edward's Crown (or at least, a replica of it: Edward the Confessor's original was lost by King John in the Wash in 1216). The congregation call out 'God save the Queen'. Homage is then paid. The first person to do so was the Duke of Edinburgh, a moment that brought a smile to the Queen's face. Finally the Archbishop blesses her:

The Lord give you faithful parliaments and quiet realms;
sure defence against all enemies; fruitful lands and a
prosperous industry; wise counsellors and upright

> *magistrates; leaders of integrity in learning and labour; a*
> *devout, learned and useful clergy; honest, peaceable and*
> *dutiful citizens . . .*

In 1953 many people found the ceremony, with its potent symbolism and connection to a millennium of history, a source of huge pride. It left them with a refreshing reminder that they were a part of something vast, complex and purposeful, and lucky so to be. And it wasn't experienced only by the fortunate few in the Abbey. One thing William the Conqueror would not have recognized was the presence of television cameras. It could be argued that the Coronation was the first truly national event, experienced moment by moment by a huge proportion of the population. There were only about 2.5 million TV sets in the UK at the time – not surprising, as they cost around £80 (about £1,700 in modern money) – but anyone with one of these machines invited friends and relatives to share the experience. It is estimated that well over 20 million Britons ended up watching what we would now consider ghostly images on the small, bulbous screens, and hearing the elegant commentary of Richard Dimbleby. The Coronation was a family occasion as much as a national one.

If this was not enough to cheer everyone up, it was announced on the same day that a British-led expedition had been the first to reach the summit of Mount Everest. Neither Edmund Hillary, a New Zealander, nor Nepali Sherpa Tenzing Norgay were actually Britons, but they had planted a Union Jack on top of the mountain (along with the flags of Nepal, India and the United Nations. Hillary also planted a cross, and Tenzing left some food, a traditional Buddhist offering, and a blue pencil given him by his youngest daughter Nema).

The economy began to pick up around this time, too. Several staples were still rationed, but the control system was slowly being dismantled. On the day of the Coronation itself, everyone was allowed chocolate bars. Meat was becoming plentiful in the shops, even though its rationing was not formally ended until July 1954 – the last item to come off the list, an occasion celebrated with bonfires of grey-covered ration books.

These events – the Coronation, the conquering of Everest and the withering away of rationing – should have had a uniting effect on the nation. But in fact a battle was brewing between two visions of Britain. On one side was the old guard: traditional in taste and behaviour, focused on nation and Empire, hierarchical, conservative with a small 'c' and often with a big C too. On the other were the forces of change: restless, youthful, intellectual, liberal in outlook but not Liberal in the traditional sense – more likely to be socialists than to share Gladstone's view of the Wealth Machine as a socially liberating force.

An early skirmish had been the Festival of Britain in 1951, an event celebrated in two fine stamps (especially Abram Games' 4d). For the old guard this was a triumphalist show of socialist modernism. Looking back, it's hard to see how it could have been read this way: the Festival was a gently nationalistic event, if one with an emphasis on the ability of technology to transform the future. It might have lacked military bands and poems by Alfred Noyes, but that hardly made it sinister leftist propaganda. However, Churchill hated it, and when a Conservative government was elected towards the end of the Festival's run, he couldn't wait to be rid of it. When the icon of the Festival, the aluminium, needle-shaped, seemingly hovering Skylon, was taken down, it was unceremoniously dumped into the River Thames, where it sat on a mudbank until it was taken away for scrap. It apparently ended up as ashtrays.

The Coronation on the other hand, though a genuinely unifying national event, worked its magic in a firmly traditionalist tone. The Queen had six maids of honour carrying the train of her robe up the Abbey aisle; four had double-barrelled names. The other two had triple-barrelled names. The committee organizing the event, headed by the nation's senior peer, the Duke of Norfolk, was full of aristocrats. (Another member was the Honourable George Bellew, who had designed a beautiful high-value definitive stamp for George VI.) Peers were also involved in the ceremony itself, swearing loyalty to the Queen before donning their coronets.

Along with this, there was a powerful reaction against the bureaucracy which had come so close to messing up the Olympics, and which many people associated with socialism. If this is change, many people thought, then we'll stay as we are, thank you ... And across the Iron Curtain, regimes purporting to be 'progressive' were showing their true colours: a fortnight after the Coronation, a two-day strike in East Germany was brutally put down by Russian tanks, to oratory redolent of another of George Orwell's books, *Nineteen Eighty-Four*, about 'foreign provocateurs and Fascist agents'. Tradition, it seemed, was a safer bet.

The Coronation 1'3, the swan song and masterpiece of Edmund Dulac – the great designer died before it appeared in post offices – is probably my favourite British stamp. It is elegant, eloquent and perfectly proportioned. The symbols of the four nations that make up the United Kingdom are subtly worked into the background, and the wording is kept out of the way of the visuals – running up and down the sides of the stamp, it frames the image of the monarch, and reminds me of the columns of a Georgian country house.

Yet there is a radical twist to it. The stamps of Queen Victoria and Edward VII always show them in profile. At the beginning of George V's reign, experimental stamps were issued with the King in three-quarter profile, but these did not prove popular. A number of criticisms were made – the imperial lion on the design was decidedly mangy, for example – but many people disliked the informality of the pose. They felt the image of the monarch turning towards them rendered him too ordinary. At the beginning of George VI's reign, Dulac threw away the rule book and had George and his queen nearly but not quite face us in their 1937 coronation stamp. However, the rest of George's stamps went back to profile. Now the new, young monarch looks us straight in the eye: a message, perhaps, that the new Elizabethan era will be more populist and less sedate than many people hoped.

CHAPTER TWENTY

WHITEHALL FARCE

46TH INTERNATIONAL PARLIAMENTARY CONFERENCE 4D COMMEMORATIVE, 1957

H OT ON the heels of Dulac's brilliant New Elizabethan stamp came . . . er . . . nothing. No commemoratives appeared for four years until finally, in 1957, two issues crept out, one celebrating the 50th anniversary of the Boy Scout movement, and this one, the 46th International Parliamentary Conference 4d, which has to be one of the most boring and inept stamps ever produced. The standard 4d definitive – a pleasant enough design, by Michael Farrar-Bell – has had lettering squeezed inelegantly into the sides. It looks as if someone has then thought 'Oh, drat, we left out the 46th' and has desperately looked around for a place to put it.

It looks that way because that is precisely what happened. The Parliamentary Conference is a roving event that takes place in a different world capital each year. In 1957 it was London's turn. Colonel Malcolm Stoddart-Scott, a Tory MP connected with organizing the event, thought there ought to be a stamp for it. The Postmaster General disagreed, but Stoddart-Scott persisted and the PMG finally gave way just a few weeks before the conference was about to begin. With no time to commission a professional artist to do the design, Frank Langfield, the man in charge of the production of postage stamps, had to rustle one up himself. Langfield was a practical man, but no designer. 'I got a sheet of 4d [stamps] and ... with a mapping pen drew the lettering around the frame,' he admits. When he sent it off to the printers, they realized he'd left out the '46th' and stuck it into the only available space.

The Wodehousian feel to this story says a lot about the state of late-fifties Britain. The nation had decided to stick with the old guard, but they were making a mess of things.

It was beginning to be pointed out that the country's economic performance, while adequate, wasn't exactly brilliant. Britain seemed to be lagging behind France, Holland, Belgium and – harshest of all – the two countries it had defeated in war ten years ago, Germany and Japan.

The nation of Dickens and H.G. Wells' easy-going Mr Polly was also showing an unattractive lack of liberality. Immigrants from the colonies encountered discrimination. There were attempts to 'root out' homosexuality: Alan Turing, one of the heroes of Bletchley Park, was driven to suicide after being charged with gross indecency. There was an enforcement of conformity, a mood of deference to old-fashioned rules and roles (one of the best-selling books of 1956 was a guide to upper-class usage by the impeccably posh Nancy Mitford). This all had a whiff of fear about it. Maybe the Cold War, with the hydrogen bomb lurking in the background, was the cause of this fearfulness. Or maybe just concern about how far Britain would fall now it had been firmly and finally pushed off its slot as top dog. People muttered darkly about what had happened to the once-mighty Romans.

The Suez debacle of autumn 1956 summed it all up.

Completed in 1869, the Suez Canal was another of those amazing Victorian world-shrinking achievements: linking the Mediterranean with the Red Sea, it slashed the journey time from Europe to India and the Far East. A chunk of it had been bought by Disraeli in 1875. In 1882 Britain had invaded Egypt and taken over the running of the Canal. After Indian independence in 1949, its imperial significance decreased – instead it became a superhighway for oil from the Arabian Gulf to booming Europe.

In 1953, Colonel Gamal Abdul Nasser seized power in Egypt, and at once claimed ownership of the Canal. On 26 July 1956, he took it, sending in troops to occupy the Canal Zone. This was a provocation Britain found impossible to resist: comparisons with Hitler and Mussolini were made, and the shame of Chamberlain's failed attempts to placate the former revisited. The French felt similar rage, as did Israel. These three countries hatched a plan: Israel would invade Egypt, and Britain and France would send in troops, ostensibly to keep the warring sides apart, but actually to retake the Canal.

On 29 October, Israel invaded. Britain threw her hands up in mock horror and piled in, bombing parts of Cairo (hardly a logical way of keeping two fighting nations apart, especially as the victims of the bombing had also been victims of the invasion). British commandos and French paras were sent into the Zone. The Canal was almost captured . . .

But the rest of the world was not having it. The Soviet Union used the crisis as a cover for brutal suppression of dissent in Hungary. Saudi Arabia cut off supplies of oil. America threatened to start selling the British government bonds they had bought as part of the Marshall Plan to boost European economies – an act which would, after a short time, have bankrupted the UK.

The operation was halted. It was a humiliation, in terms both of geopolitical power and of moral status. Suddenly Britain looked like a playground bully who'd been caught picking on a vulnerable pupil and dragged off, looking very small and stupid, to face the head. It was a terrible fall for the nation that had stood alone against Hitler only sixteen years before.

Of course, some people in Britain were delighted by the fiasco. Not everyone had welcomed the invasion – the 'Law not War' rally in Trafalgar Square the day before it was one of the best attended political events in modern British history. Afterwards, there were plenty of Britons eager to rub the faces of the old elite in the mud.

Protest was in the air. 1956 was the year of the Angry Young Men. Writers like John Osborne and Kingsley Amis railed, not so much against the incompetence of Suez, as at a general feeling of stuffiness in British life. They liked neither the worthy, technocratic Festival of Britain version of the future, nor the Coronation version with its triple-barrelled maids of honour. Instead, they wanted honesty in public life and in personal relations; they wanted vitality, to live with energy and passion.

One place they looked for these was booze. Another was jazz, particularly trad jazz, played in the twenties style of Beiderbecke or Armstrong. The world of jazz at that time was split between lovers of trad and lovers of modern, the cerebral, highly technical music of American virtuosos like Charlie Parker or Dizzy Gillespie. The Angry Young Men spurned the intellectualism of the latter, looking to the former for emotional sustenance. But they were intellectuals, and there's something rather inauthentic about their blanket rejection of modern. The same intellectualism led them to look down on a third strand of popular music that was in the ascendant at the time: rock'n'roll.

Rock'n'roll was the music of choice of most young Britons in the mid-to late fifties – and was, though the Angry Young Men didn't spot this, the true heir to the jazz of the twenties: fresh, approachable, tuneful and accompanied by new dances that you had to be young and fit to do well. The first great rock'n'roll track to hit the UK was Bill Haley's 'Rock around the Clock', which exploded into the charts in November 1955. Next year saw the triumph of the genre, with the arrival of Elvis Presley: 'Heartbreak Hotel', 'Blue Suede Shoes', 'Hound Dog' and 'Love me Tender' (none of these classics got to Number One in the British charts, being kept out by such now-forgotten acts as the Dream Weavers and Ronnie Hilton, but the new generation had taken Elvis to its heart).

The problem with rock'n'roll in the UK was that we didn't seem to be very good at it. We tried, but somehow British home-grown acts didn't cut the mustard. Likely-looking lads from working-class backgrounds were chosen and packaged by London recording companies. They were usually given formulaic names: first name boy-next-door, second one rebellious/romantic – Tommy Steele, Billy Fury, Marty Wilde, Tommy Quickly, Johnny Gentle (the antithesis, I assume, of Tommy Quickly). More promising for young Brits wanting to make their own music was skiffle, a fast-moving blues for which you only needed a cheap guitar, a washboard and a bass made out of a tea chest. The king of skiffle was Lonnie Donegan, who emerged from the world of trad jazz. Skiffle was fun to play, but little new material was being written for it, the repertoire being almost all traditional American songs like 'Cumberland Gap' and 'Rock Island Line'. (Donegan later recorded a British novelty song, 'My Old Man's a Dustman' – the first record I ever bought, from Woolworth's in Stevenage.)

On 6 July 1957, a couple of months before the Parliamentary Conference Commemorative 4d appeared, the annual church fête took place at Woolton, a suburb of Liverpool. It was a big event, with a parade led by the band of the Cheshire Yeomanry with other floats following – Scouts, Guides, Brownies, a troupe of morris dancers, schoolchildren in fancy dress and the 13-year-old Rose Queen on her motorized throne. Bringing up the rear was a coal lorry, decorated for the day, carrying a local skiffle group. The gala that followed the parade featured the usual stalls and sideshows, plus a demonstration by the City of Liverpool Dog Unit and, on an outdoor stage, more performances from the skiffle group. After their first set, the group's young leader was introduced to a friend of a friend, who also played the guitar. The two teenagers said 'hello' to each other, and that was nearly the end of the encounter, except for the fact that one of the lads in the band couldn't tune his guitar and the new arrival showed him how, impressing the leader. A week later the newcomer was asked to join.

The band's leader was called John Lennon, and the new arrival Paul McCartney.

CHAPTER TWENTY-ONE

PRODUCTIVITY

NATIONAL PRODUCTIVITY YEAR 3D COMMEMORATIVE, 1962

THIS MODERN-LOOKING stamp sweeps us into the 1960s. The first of many by one of the country's finest designers, David Gentleman, it celebrates an attempt to propel Britain into a new age of prosperity, driven by excellence in all the arts of industrial wealth creation. How successful that attempt would be was another matter ...

The new decade began quietly. The old guard seemed to have shaken off the disaster of Suez. Harold Macmillan, an Old Etonian with a restrained, lugubrious manner, was Prime Minister; Sir Anthony Eden, the man responsible for Suez, had been ditched shortly afterwards. Rock'n'roll, in its pure, finest form, hadn't lasted much longer than Sir Anthony – after one last classic, 'Jailhouse Rock', Elvis had been drafted into the US Army and was never quite the same again: more anodyne entertainment seeped back into the charts (in one late-fifties classic Doris Day told listeners to accept whatever would be, would be). In 1959, an election had been held, where the now usual pre-poll pumping of money into the economy had created a mood of optimism – Macmillan gave his famous 'You've never had it so good' speech – and the Conservatives kept power with a huge majority. (Inflation was cranked up another notch, but who cared about that?)

The next year, 'Supermac' made another famous speech, about winds of change blowing through Africa – but the winds he had in mind were gentle zephyrs not hurricanes. Having finally woken up to the true cost of Empire, Britain divested itself of its African possessions as decorously as possible. By and large, it was done without bloodshed, Kenya being an exception. Most people knew it was inevitable.

Still, the discontent hadn't gone away. Even without the burden of Empire, and despite the consumer goods available on hire purchase now filling the shops, if you peeked across the Channel, you'd get a shock: mainland Europe's economy was now clearly performing better than Britain's. Britain's soul-searching became ever more intense. Why was the country doing so badly?

One explanation was 'poor productivity': an hour of British work produced less than an hour of work elsewhere. Looking back, that sounds more like a symptom than a cause, but it was decided that something needed to be done. So 1963 was to be National Productivity Year. Plans were announced in the House of Lords on 12 July 1962:

> *First, to strengthen the determination of all organisations*
> *concerned with industry to take an active part in*
> *improving the country's efficiency and in maintaining its*
> *place among the leading industrial nations of the world;*
> *secondly, to foster a more favourable climate of opinion to*
> *better methods and their proper use; thirdly, to bring clearly*
> *before everyone the nature and value of services that exist*

to help him; fourthly, to promote discussion and research
into the needs of industry; fifthly, to encourage mutually
agreed co-ordination among bodies, to secure an even more
concentrated and purposeful contribution to the problems of
industry; and, finally, to bring into being a means of
regular consultation and discussion, which will continue
after the Productivity Year is over.

This announcement unintentionally says a lot about the deeper reasons why the country was underperforming. The entrepreneurs who had made Britain a great economic power had vision, imagination, passion, energy, spark, fizz, as well as great technical skill. The compiler of the above 142-word sentence appears to lack all of these. Such qualities had been sucked out of British business. Organization was the order of the day. Big was beautiful. The government encouraged firms to merge in order to be more efficient. Sadly, business history reveals that many mergers result in culture clashes that increase inefficiency.

The ghost of Rugby School's Dr Thomas Arnold was rattling its chains, too – or rather its classics textbooks. Gentlemen, remember, did not study vulgar things like engineering, and certainly didn't work in industry. This prejudice extended throughout the educational system; one major reason that our workforce was less effective than Germany's was that German workers had a better technological education.

'The unions' were blamed, at least in part, for this malaise. It has to be admitted that they didn't help matters, seeming to spend as much time fighting each other as they did managing working conditions. Endless demarcation disputes slowed life in British factories to a snail's pace. But at heart this was a crisis in vision, in leadership. If your leaders can't come up with anything more enthralling than the NPY manifesto above, then why not spend half the afternoon arguing about who makes the tea?

Business had its own demarcation issues, with neat cartels dividing up markets and keeping prices pleasantly (for the producers) high – just as Adam Smith had predicted back in 1776: 'People of the same trade seldom meet together, even for merriment and diversion, but the conversation ends in a conspiracy to raise prices.' The Restrictive Practices Act of 1956 had done little to change this.

Overhanging all this was a vague sense that, because Britain had won the war, it was entitled to take it easy. If 'wops and dagoes' (the description of Europeans by the 1950s chairman of the Football Association, Alan Hardaker) were a bit more productive than we were, so what? However hard they worked, they'd still be foreign. National Productivity Year was going to have its work cut out.

The organizers of the Year did get one thing right – they commissioned David Gentleman to design the stamps. Gentleman had strong views on aesthetics: away with the elaborate and fussy, and in with clean lines and simple images. He was less keen on what he called the 'Stalinist' theme of this issue, but a gig is a gig, and he got on with it and produced an attractive, punchy set, of which the 3d is his (and my) favourite.

Sadly, the production of the stamp was less impressive: the issue is noted for the number of errors available to collectors. Versions of both the 3d and 1/3 exist without the Queen's head. The 3d also has a bizarre set of errors where white blobs on the UK map makes it look as if National Productivity Year has caused huge inland lakes to form: they appear on some stamps in Yorkshire, where Beverley and York have been submerged (viewed close-up, it also turns Spurn Head into the beak of a rather ferocious eagle), on others in Scotland, where it is Galloway's turn to be inundated (and Britain suddenly looks like a T Rex with a Scotland-shaped hat). In other errors Kent has crumbled into the sea, and the Queen has a nasty white spot on the end of her nose. Couldn't Britain do *anything* right?

Rather than ushering in a sudden boost in productivity, 1963 saw more blows crashing down on the old guard. First, John Profumo, Secretary of State for War, was found to have been having an affair with Christine Keeler, a free-spirited girl who had other lovers, one of whom was a Russian naval attaché (another was a drug dealer, bringing new dimensions of seediness into the proceedings). Profumo then lied to parliament about the affair. Even the Tory press was becoming much less deferential, so the media had a field day – Keeler was stunningly good looking, as Lewis Morley's famous photograph of her sitting astride an Arne Jacobsen chair shows. Speculation about other sex scandals became rife ('We've never had it so often!' chortled *Private Eye* magazine). Profumo subsequently devoted his life to charitable work in London's East End – but the damage was done.

A second scandal erupted when Kim Philby, a senior figure in the Foreign Office, turned out to be a Russian spy. The establishment had already been rocked by the defection of two agents, both public school and Cambridge educated, in 1951. Now a third man was added to the list of gentleman traitors. Philby lived out his days as a lonely alcoholic in a miserable Soviet block of flats, though after his death he was made a Hero of the Soviet Union and even featured on a 5 kopek commemorative stamp.

Though it was already doing a fine job in self-destruction, the old establishment found itself on the receiving end of a new 'satire boom'. There was *Private Eye*. The show *Beyond the Fringe* sent up aspects of Macmillan's Britain (Macmillan bravely went along to see it). TV got in on the act, with *That Was the Week That Was* regularly attracting 12 million viewers despite its late-evening slot on BBC2.

And then along came the Beatles.

At the beginning of 1963 few people outside Liverpool had heard of the group. By the end of the year, they were everywhere. But it wasn't so much the success as its nature that was unsettling to traditionalists. Audiences went wild for the Fab Four in a way people just hadn't done before (Beatlemania went far beyond the admiration of earlier generations for Sinatra or Elvis). Audiences couldn't control their screaming – or their bladders: daughters of women who'd stoically survived the Blitz were wetting theatre seats at the sight of four lads they didn't even know. It all seemed terribly un-British.

The band had had to work hard for its success: no post-victory sense of entitlement for them. After the Woolton fête, John Lennon and Paul McCartney spent hours at each other's houses, practising their guitars and swapping chords. Buddy Holly had set a trend for self-penned material and they were soon writing songs of their own. The band acquired another member and guitar fanatic, George Harrison (John's Aunt Mimi thought he was a bad influence, as he was from a rougher part of town). Then the adventure nearly came to a sudden, dreadful end when John's mother was run down and killed by an off-duty policeman. John retreated into stoical silence, plus the occasional drunken fight, but his love of music pulled him out of this hole, and the band began to perform once again. A gig in a local strip club got them a residency in Hamburg, despite complaints by British musicians already established there that they didn't want 'a bum band like the Beatles' lowering the standards. Hamburg, of course, made them, with long hours on stage, the need to 'mach Schau', and the wild antics that created a group culture.

Back in Liverpool, and now a tight, unusual, energetic live act, they found a manager, Brian Epstein, owner of a local record shop. After much traipsing up and down Tin Pan Alley with demo tapes, Epstein landed them a record deal with a novelty label, Parlophone, a tiny and very unimportant part of the EMI empire. With a new drummer called Ringo Starr, the band cut their first single on 4 September 1962, the Lennon–McCartney composition *Love Me Do*. Largely thanks to Epstein's buying boxloads of records, it inched on to the chart.

They were then given a corny but catchy 'instant hit' to record by their label, but refused, insisting on recording their own material. *Please Please Me* got them a slot on a popular TV show and on 2 March 1963, the single reached Number One.

From then on, success compounded success: a best-selling album also called *Please Please Me* (recorded in one day), a string of chart-topping singles and an appearance on the annual Royal Variety Performance on 4 November. Then in 1964, Beatlemania hit America. Traumatized by the assassination of John F. Kennedy, the country needed something new and fresh to re-engage its spirit. In April 1964, Beatles records were at Numbers one, two, three, four and five in the US.

The music, of course, drove this success, but the band also had what we now call attitude. They were funny and irreverent, particularly John Lennon, who had a real hatred of much of what the old guard stood for and wasn't afraid to express it. Alongside this, Lennon had a deep sensitivity: the inconsistencies of his nature continued to pull him in all sorts of directions for most of his troubled life. As with Bix Beiderbecke, Louis Armstrong and 'Bubber' Miley, the Beatles crossed that line between popular entertainment and the initially unsettling but ultimately more fulfilling world of art, especially in their classic albums (the covers of which featured on a 2007 set of stamps).

Artistic excellence was not achieved at the expense of commercial success. By August 1964, the Beatles had sold 80 million records around the world. This figure passed the 100 million mark in 1965, 150 million in August 1966, 300 million in 1969 and 545 million in October 1972. Sales are now estimated at 1.3 billion – and rising: new generations of fans have discovered the music and love it.

Now *that's* productivity!

CHAPTER TWENTY-TWO

The Cairngorms SCOTLAND 1s6d
L ROSOMAN HARRISON AND SONS LTD

OFF WITH HER HEAD!

BRITISH LANDSCAPES 1s6D COMMEMORATIVE, 1966

THIS PLEASANT, quiet-looking design is in fact the result of probably the biggest changes ever made in UK stamp-issuing policy. Behind that, it tells of huge shifts in British society.

Harold Macmillan's health began to suffer in late 1963, and he resigned from office. The Conservative Party responded to the new Beatle-inspired national enthusiasm for youth and classlessness by appointing as its new leader the 60-year-old 14th Earl of Home. Sir Alec Douglas-Home (he had to downgrade his rank in order to become PM) was a decent, thoughtful man, but he was out of touch with the times, his grouse-moor image already history. He was defeated in the 1964 election by Labour's Harold Wilson, the intellectual son of a Yorkshire chemist and a schoolteacher, who became the youngest Prime Minister since Lord Rosebery back in 1894.

Actually, Wilson was in many ways a conservative person, with his pipe, perpetual Gannex raincoat, love of HP Sauce, holidays on the Isles of Scilly (halfway, perhaps, between Sir Alec Douglas-Home's grouse moor and Tony Blair's Tuscany) and middlebrow taste in art: though he awarded the Beatles MBEs, his favourite music was Gilbert and Sullivan. Politically he was more of a centrist than a man of the left. Nevertheless he brought in a new era.

The new Postmaster General, Anthony Wedgwood Benn – now better known as Tony Benn – was a more dynamic figure. His first move was to widen the criteria for issuing stamps. Up to that time, policy had been to confine issues 'to marking outstanding national or international events and Royal and postal anniversaries'. However the Post Office knew that what people wanted was nice-looking stamps. Of late, a rather odd selection of 'outstanding events' had been chosen for cele-bration: National Nature Week, the 20th International Geographical Congress and the International Botanical Congress were completely non-outstanding events that allowed the Post Office in 1963 and 1964 to depict animals, landscapes and flowers. Benn saw the silliness of this, and announced new criteria in Parliament:

> *To celebrate events of national or international importance, to commemorate appropriate anniversaries and occasions, to reflect Britain's unique contribution to the arts and world affairs, to extend public patronage of the arts by promoting philately, and* [last but not least] *to raise revenue.*

He contacted leading stamp designers, asking them to suggest ideas for new issues. David Gentleman replied with a list that included famous men and women, transport, plants and regional landscapes. The last of these brought this stamp into being (though it is not Gentleman's design, but by Leonard Rosoman).

Gentleman had other ideas for change, too. Designers were

getting fed up with the requirement to fit the large Dorothy Wilding portrait of the Queen into their stamps. He suggested a smaller, cameo picture of the Queen – or something even more radical, leaving her head off altogether and replacing it either with the words 'Great Britain' or with some other icon such as an outline of a crown or the royal arms.

This last suggestion was music to the ears of the republican Benn. He asked Gentleman to prepare some ideas. It was now 1965. Sir Winston Churchill had just died and the Battle of Britain anniversary was coming up, so Gentleman duly produced queenless mock-ups of stamps to commemorate these events.

The designs created a furore. It was not long ago that trad- itionalists had objected to Shakespeare appearing on a stamp: the monarch should be the only named individual to be so honoured, they argued. Removing the Queen altogether was several steps too far – as Benn found out. In a rather comical scene, he enthused to the monarch about the new designs, laying them out on the floor of Buckingham Palace, starting with a set featuring racehorses to whet her appetite. The Queen watched politely and later communicated her disapproval to the PM.

Nevertheless, a cameo proved acceptable, and made its first appearance in the British Landscape issue. (For a while, two sizes of cameo were used; later, the smaller one – exemplified in the stamp featured in the next chapter – won the day, and has been used ever since.)

Shortly after this, Benn was promoted to Minister of Technology, and the PMG's job went to Edward Short, who was less of a firebrand. Benn wrote in his diary that it was obvious that he would have to abandon his hopes of getting the Queen's head off the stamps.

It wasn't the only hope the Wilson government had to abandon. One key differentiator of the new government had been technology. Wilson had wowed the 1963 Labour confer- ence with talk of the 'white heat' of a scientific revolution in which a new Britain would be forged. This enthusiasm can be seen in a number of technology-celebrating stamp issues that followed. The first, from 1966, shows items that have largely now fallen out of favour – a gas-guzzling car, a hovercraft (whatever happened to them?) and the nuclear power station at Dounreay (which closed in 1994 and will take forty years to decommission). The year after, another issue followed, featuring less controversial advances – radar, penicillin, jet engines and TV. Stamps for Concorde and Post Office technology appeared in 1969.

This was a genuine leap forward from the technophobic world of the grouse moor: Isambard Kingdom Brunel would have approved highly. Yet the government never really worked out how this revolution was to be achieved. Research establishments were set up, science places were created at universities – but not enough thought went into how this work could be put to practical use. Meanwhile, active harm was done by the Technology Ministry with its continuing policy of encouraging corporate mergers.

As the decade went on Britain's new love affair with science began to pale. *Tomorrow's World* continued on the BBC, with its modern jazz theme, but elsewhere the Formica was starting to peel. In March 1967, the supertanker *Torrey Canyon* hit the Seven Stones rocks near Wilson's beloved Scillies, spewing oil on to over 200 miles of British and French beach. On 16 May 1968, four people died in a building collapse at Ronan Point, one of the modernist high-rise tower blocks that architects had assured everyone would be so wonderful to live in. By the end of the 1960s, the benevolent technocrat who would solve society's problems had morphed into the mad scientist in Bond movies or TV shows like *The Avengers*.

Another great enthusiasm of the Wilson government was planning. A Department of Economic Affairs was set up, much to the disapproval of the Treasury, who thought that economic affairs were its job. A National Plan was duly delivered.

Absurdly optimistic – and, like most such plans, inflexible – as its golden targets slowly sank beneath the ever-changing waves of reality, it was quietly shelved.

Away from all the technology and planning, a different set of policies, which had hardly been mentioned in Labour's 1964 manifesto, proved itself to be fully in tune with the times.

Roy Jenkins was one of the ablest politicians of his era. He cuts a strange figure: the son of a coal miner, he talked – and lived – like an aristocrat, enjoying his vintage claret and the odd love affair, including one with Jackie Kennedy's sister (like Edward VII, he managed to keep his own marriage intact despite his philandering). He had a formidable intellect, and wrote a string of political biographies, one of which, *Gladstone*, won the Whitbread Prize. Jenkins had set out his stall in 1959, in a book called *The Labour Case*: 'Let us be on the side of those who want people to be free to live their own lives, to make their own mistakes, and to decide, in an adult way and provided they do not infringe the rights of others, the code by which they wish to live.' As Wilson's Home Secretary, Jenkins was able to put these ideals into action.

Divorce became easier to obtain, with the process now less about one person's 'fault' and more about two adults accepting that they were not compatible. The traditional grounds for divorce remained – adultery, desertion, insanity or cruelty (the last of these widened to mental as well as physical bullying) – but a new one was added, that of separation: either the couple had lived apart for five years, or they had lived apart for two years and both agreed that the marriage was irreparable.

Homosexuality was finally decriminalized – in England and Wales, anyway: Scotland and Northern Ireland had to wait till the 1980s for this legislation.

Abortion was legalized, too. Whatever one's view on this practice, illegal 'back-street' abortionists or, even worse, botched home attempts at abortion had been responsible for the terrible suffering, and in some cases death, of many unfortunate young women, often the most vulnerable and sexually ignorant. Action was needed, but previous governments had just looked the other way.

Ancient laws censoring the theatre were abolished. Since Victorian times, all performances had had to be cleared by the Lord Chamberlain's Office. This body had in its time banned plays by Ibsen, Miller, Pirandello and Strindberg. It was responsible for the ruling that women could appear naked on stage but were not allowed to move, and had once removed the phrase 'up periscopes' from a play on the grounds that it might encourage homosexuality.

All these changes distanced the state from private decision-making. With the abolition of capital punishment the state also lost its right to take life except in war. 'The rope' had been controversial ever since the 1950 hanging of Timothy Evans, a man who turned out to be innocent. Doubts were also expressed about the convictions of Derek Bentley (1953) and James Hanratty (1962). The last hangings in the UK took place in August 1964, of Peter Anthony Allen and Gwynne Owen Evans, two petty crooks who bungled a robbery and killed the victim: the proceeds of their crime had been a watch and possibly a small amount of money.

Jenkins' changes still attract controversy. Opponents say they sent signals to society, encouraging the subsequent break-up of social order and family life. There may be some truth in this, but overall Jenkins' reforms were brave, healthy and humane.

The Labour Case also said that the party should be 'on the side of . . . brightness'. At the start of the decade, many British movies were still made in black and white – including the Beatles' first and probably best, *A Hard Day's Night*. Soon this became the art-house exception and colour the norm. British colour TV began in 1967: the first broadcast was of a fourth-round Wimbledon match between Roger Taylor and Cliff Drysdale (Taylor won in five sets). This change also affects British stamps. The Landscapes issue was a relatively sober affair, but compare vividly colourful sets like the 1963 National Nature Week, 1965 Salvation Army, 1966 Christmas or 1967 British Birds to the monochrome efforts of the 1950s, and the difference is obvious. Part of this simply stems from improved printing technology, but there is more to it than that. The new Britain that was emerging wanted brightness, and in the mid-sixties got it.

The British Landscapes issue captures another trend that was accelerating in the 1960s: regionalism. The Queen Elizabeth high value definitives, first issued in 1955, had featured castles from the four nations of the UK. The first stamps specifically for regional use had appeared in 1958 (in Scotland, Wales and Northern Ireland, anyway: England had to wait till 2001). But the Landscapes issue was the first commemorative explicitly to cover the four nations: alongside the Cairngorms, it featured the Sussex downs, a valley in Antrim and Harlech Castle.

In response to fears that the language was dying out, 1962 had seen the founding of the Welsh Language Society. Four years later, the Welsh Nationalist Party, Plaid Cymru, won its first parliamentary seat in a by-election. A year after that it was Scotland's turn, with Winifred Ewing winning the previously unassailable Labour bastion of Hamilton. As a result, Harold Wilson set up a Royal Commission to look into ways of devolving government. This thorough, though snail-like body finally reported in 1973, recommending regional assemblies. The assemblies were even slower to come into being: referenda were held in Scotland and Wales in 1979, and both rejected them (Scotland on a technicality: 52% voted for a regional assembly, but too many people abstained to make the vote legally binding). It was not until the Blair government of 1997 that they came back on the agenda.

Being British has always been about having more than one identity. The English, the majority nation by a big margin, are inclined to forget this. This is unwise. However, the next stamp in this history of Britain is unashamedly English . . .

CHAPTER TWENTY-THREE

'THEY THINK IT'S
ALL OVER . . .'

WORLD CUP WINNERS
4D COMMEMORATIVE, 1966

ALL NATIONS have special moments of pride. These are not the vulgar, manufactured swanking of Hitler's Olympics; they simply fill people with a sense of how good it is to belong. Outsiders aren't excluded from such moments; they are invited to join the celebrations, in the knowledge that another time they will have their such moments, too, and good luck to them when they do. Britain had such moments on VE Day and on the day of the Coronation. England had one on 30 June 1966.

The hosting of the 1966 football World Cup got off to a bad start when the cup was stolen when on display at a stamp exhibition in Westminster Central Hall. A ransom note was sent; the police set a trap and a man was caught – but he did not have the trophy, know where it was or reveal who his accomplices were. A national search was launched and the cup was eventually found, wrapped up in newspaper and dumped in a hedge, by a man walking his dog on Beulah Hill in south London. The dog, Pickles, became a national hero while his owner was largely ignored. (The cup was stolen again in Brazil in 1983 and has not been seen since.)

England's first game was as lacklustre as the security at the stamp exhibition, a drab 0–0 draw with Uruguay in front of a three-quarters-full Wembley. This did not surprise many: Football Monthly had selected Portugal, Argentina and Hungary as most likely cup winners, adding that England's chances were 'not that good'. However, the team picked itself up for the remaining two games of the group stage and won them both 2–0, thus qualifying for the quarter-finals. From there on, it was a knockout competition. In a nasty game against Argentina – a team with whom England's sporting (or in this case unsporting) rivalry goes back long before the Falklands War – the home team scraped through by one goal to nil, helped by the fact that the Argentinian team ended the game with ten men. The semi-final was against Portugal, one of the most attractive and dynamic teams in the tournament. Facing opponents of this quality, England raised its game, going 2–0 up with goals from Bobby Charlton. Portugal's star player, Eusebio, then scored, and England fans had a nervous eight minutes till the end of the game (12 years old and a fearless viewer of *Doctor Who* and anything else the TV could throw at me, I hid behind the sofa at this point). But there were no further goals. England was in the final!

The other finalists were West Germany. The press build-up in the UK was largely free of the 'don't forget the war' silliness that England v. Germany encounters now evoke, probably because many people still remembered the war and were keen to move on from those memories. The game itself was a thriller. Germany scored first, then England went 2–1 up, after which they seemed to have things under control until Germany scored in the last minute. Setbacks like that can break teams' morale, but England manager Alf Ramsey exhorted them: 'You've won the World Cup once, now go out and win it again.' And they did, scoring twice in the half-hour of extra time. Both goals were controversial. Did the first one really cross the line? Forward Roger Hunt, who was closest to the goal, insists that it did; he had also been in a position to nod the ball back into the net if he had thought otherwise, but turned away in celebration. The second goal, giving Geoff Hurst a hat-trick, came in the dying moments of the game when three fans had already burst on to the pitch, eliciting the famous lines from commentator Kenneth Wolstenholme: 'They think it's all over . . . it is now.'

The great image of the game is of Bobby Moore, the England captain, hoisted on the shoulders of his team-mates, holding the cup. Moore was probably the finest defender of his time, and an astute captain with an uncanny ability to read a situation – but when he died at the early age of 51, tributes to him cited above all his gentlemanliness. The upper-middle-class takeover bid for the concept of gentleman had not totally succeeded: Moore was just a decent man who understood that decency is strength, and people in all walks of life appreciated that.

The World Cup win was in many ways the icing on an already scrumptious cake. People use the phrase 'Summer of Love' to describe summer 1967, but in my view they are a year out. 1966 was the true Summer of Love. The weather was gorgeous; The Kinks produced the perfect record to go with it, 'Sunny Afternoon', which topped the chart. Like the Beatles, the Kinks were a very British band, adding to American electric blues UK traditions of observational comedy and Music Hall. The Beatles spent summer '66 recording their album *Revolver*, with songs like 'Eleanor Rigby', the irresistible 'Yellow Submarine' and John Lennon's 'Tomorrow Never Knows'. The last of these, the final track on the album, opens the door into the rest of the decade, through which we tumble, Alice-like, into heaven knows where (but it's going to be interesting . . .)

Summer 1966 was the high point of Swinging London. The famous *Time* magazine article on this subject appeared on 15 April, characterizing the decade as one ruled by youth and arguing that London ('the scene') was the centre of this rule. A totally new style seemed to have emerged out of nowhere – yellows, pinks and purples, interweaving in swirls; velvet jackets, long hair, floaty dresses, boots . . . A sexual revolution was taking place, too. Gone were the old hang-ups; lovemaking was a joyous and natural business, no longer to be hushed up or sniggered at. Gone, too, of course, was the old risk of unintended pregnancy: the contraceptive pill had been available on the NHS since 1961, but it had taken a while for it to be trusted and widely used.

Oddly enough, bright old Victorian military outfits, granny glasses and Union Jacks came out of cupboards to go with this new style. Britain had found a way of holding on to its traditions yet seeing them in a witty, ironic light as it moved forward into a new era. The nation that had once ruled militarily was now putting on old army uniforms to light one of those funny, rather sweet-smelling cigarettes and wander down the King's Road, and reconquering the world with what is now called soft power, via sport, music and fashion.

Critics have said that Swinging London was the preserve of a tiny elite of successful media-savvy individuals – but this is to miss the point. The feeling spread and lifted the spirits of those sufficiently young at heart to enjoy it, whether they lived just off the King's Road or in Newcastle under Lyme. Like twenties jazz, it did this through mass media: TV shows, movies, records and radio. Many would have heard 'Sunny Afternoon' on one of the new pirate radio stations, whose 'disc jockeys' operated from boats moored outside UK territorial waters (anywhere over three miles off the coast). Wonder-ful Radi-o London–'Big L'–broadcast its weekly Fab 40 from just off ultra-respectable Frinton.

Summer '66 might have felt like it would never end, but of course it did. On the morning of 21 October, a slag-heap collapsed on to the school of Aberfan, a Welsh mining village, killing 116 children. This cast a shadow over the national mood, and made Swinging London suddenly seem rather frivolous. As 1966 turned to 1967, the old order began to fight back. The police raided the home of Rolling Stones guitarist Keith Richards and discovered drugs. Found guilty of possession, Richards was sentenced to a year in prison, vocalist Mick Jagger to three months – both unusually punitive for the offences. Pirate radio disappeared from the airwaves, thanks to the Marine Broadcasting Offences Act, the brainchild of Anthony Wedgwood Benn in one of his less liberal moods.

Society began to polarize in a manner that was deeper and nastier than jailing the Stones or silencing Big L. A new political party was formed in 1967, the supposed year of love and peace: the National Front, a far-right organization that preyed on the fears of the white working class. On the other side of the spectrum, two movements were building, equally uncompromising in their opposition to 'centrist' or liberal ideas, the New Left and the counterculture.

The New Left was powered by a revival of interest in the work of Karl Marx. Marx' economics was largely ignored this time; he was rediscovered as a sociologist, especially his views on alienation – does the Wealth Machine turn us all into machines, too? – and ideology, his belief that the capitalist system pervaded and perverted all areas of thought and discourse.

New Left thinkers pointed to the shameful continuation of poverty in what was becoming an ever richer world. In 1963 Britain had issued two attractive stamps by Michael and Sylvia Goaman, celebrating the Freedom From Hunger campaign. Five years later, this campaign had not succeeded: terrible famines were occurring in Bihar and in the stillborn secessionist state of Biafra in south-eastern Nigeria. The New Left also had a specific issue to rally around: America's war in Vietnam. Harold Wilson had skilfully kept Britain out of this conflict, in the face of strong US pressure to send troops, but the issue still brought protestors out on to London's streets. A demonstration outside the US Embassy in March 1968 saw violent clashes with police.

The counterculture shared the New Left's ideological feeling that everything about the existing system was polluted and should be rejected. But it was distrustful of formal politics: its call to revolution was internal. If people changed, society would follow. It attacked on various fronts. One was through sexual liberation. The counterculture carried on where Swinging London had begun, criticizing old prudery, taboos and hypocrisies. It did so with a messianic intensity that now feels way over the top – books like Richard Neville's *Play Power* seem more embarrassing than liberating. But things did need to change: in the previous era, the general level of ignorance on sexual matters and the scared moralizing that went with it made many lives miserable. The messages of Freud and Nietzsche still hadn't got through to most Britons.

Less admirably, the counterculture also taught liberation through drugs, which were supposed to lead people to a new, higher consciousness. For some individuals this happened, but for many others, the misery of breakdown or addiction awaited. Among musicians destroyed by drug use were Pink Floyd co-founder Syd Barrett and Fleetwood Mac's brilliant Peter Green. John Lennon spent much of 1966 high on LSD but found more mental torment than liberation. Later he gravitated to heroin.

The counterculture sought higher consciousness in more refined ways, too. Organized religion, especially Protestantism, had been a constant factor in British life throughout the first half of the twentieth century: statistics of all kinds – numbers of baptisms, communicants, confirmations, church attendance – show this. There was even an increase in churchgoing after

the war: in 1954, Billy Graham's 'Crusades' attracted millions
of people around the country. But around 1956, the figures
began to tumble. They have never recovered. For example, in
1960, nearly 200,000 adolescents were confirmed in the Church
of England; by 1980 that figure was below 100,000 and by 1997
it was just over 40,000.

Atheists – most 'progressive' thinkers in, say, 1964 probably
fell into that category – would argue that at last the blinkers
had been removed from people's eyes. But for many, the decline
of organized religion left a God-shaped hole in their lives. The
Beatles, especially George, became painfully aware of this,
rejecting swinging London for Rishikesh (via Bangor) and the
teachings of a Hindu guru, Maharishi Mahesh Yogi. The counterculture created a new and unexpected alternative religious
revival, as many other young people set off on similar quests.
Some ended up in cults (in other words having their spirituality
organized again); others found or made for themselves a faith
that was both fulfilling and personal.

Most ambitious of all, perhaps, the counterculture sought
to bring about a new, alternative society. The free music festival
was the perfect expression of this ambition, and Woodstock
(1969) the perfect example of this. Though it was an American
event, many of the acts performing were British: The Who
closed the second day, Joe Cocker and Ten Years After played
on the third day, and the whole festival was wound up by Jimi
Hendrix, born in America but now firmly part of the London
scene. It was a massive success. Half a million people shared
a cramped space, had fun, and sent a message out to the
Vietnam warmongers: there really is another way.

Later the same year the Altamont Speedway Free Festival
hoped to repeat the experience. Like Woodstock, it took place
in the States, but was in many ways a British event, partially
organized by, and starring, the Rolling Stones: it was supposed
to be a celebration of what had become an Anglo-American
culture.

Security at Woodstock had been run by a man called Wavy Gravy and his 'Please Force', who were instructed to be polite to festival-goers. The organizers of Altamont gave the job of security to another group with countercultural associations, the Hell's Angels. They apparently paid the Angels in beer. As the gig went on, the audience took more drugs and the Angels drank more beer. Fights broke out, both between Angels and audience and within the audience. People began chucking bottles. When the Stones came on stage, some members of the audience tried to rush the stage, one of whom appeared to be carrying a gun. He was intercepted by an Angel who stabbed him five times; the man died on the spot.

The counterculture lives on and has infiltrated British life in many ways. The nation is now infinitely more at ease with sex than in the uptight 1950s. Alternative spirituality is now thoroughly mainstream. But Altamont marked the end of the grand social vision, the ideological belief that the right kind of revolution in personal consciousness would naturally bring everyone's innate goodness to the fore. Few things are less likely than Kenneth Wolstenholme attending the Altamont festival, but if we imagine for a moment that he did, he could have watched the battle between stoned concert-goers and Hell's Angels and repeated his famous line of the last seconds of the World Cup final, now reframed as a comment on the noblest ambitions of the counterculture: 'They think it's all over . . . it is now.'

CHAPTER TWENTY-FOUR

LIFE ON MARS

'MACHIN' DECIMAL
DEFINITIVE, FIRST DAY
COVER, 1971

STAMPS TELL stories. Usually, they are excellent witnesses of their era. However, sometimes they miss the point totally. The 1970s saw the introduction of a new set of definitives, the 'Machins'. These stamps are elegant, simple, solid and certain. The 1970s, on the other hand ... It is often said that the sixties were the pivotal decade in post-war British history, when the old order was swept away and the country we know today emerged. However, for many people the seventies were the time of the most radical and disorienting changes.

It is, of course, artificial to cram history into neat decades. Arguably both sixties and seventies belong to a much slower, longer revolution in British life, which started back in the 1950s with the rumblings over the Festival of Britain and turned into clear revolt in 1956, with Suez, the Angry Young Men and rock'n'roll. It went on long after the 1970s, only ending (if such things ever do end) in 1997, with the election of Tony Blair and the catharsis of the Diana tragedy. Over that time, the country became more tolerant, diverse and liberal, lost deference to (almost) all the old ruling class, loosened the stiff upper lip and acquired a measure of emotional intelligence – but at the same time became more pragmatic about economic matters. It was revolution the British way: no statues pulled down, no little red books, raging demagogues not taken seriously, minimal violence, but at the end of it all, huge change. The extent of this change hurt people like my parents who belonged to the old world and by the 1970s felt very out of it. Life on Mars, they might have called it, if they had been fans of David Bowie (which, unsurprisingly, they weren't).

A significant milestone in this revolution was the demise of the old currency. Britain had counted its cash in pounds, shillings and pence since time immemorial – along with other wonderfully arcane weights and measures: the furlong, the bushel, the stone, the ounce, the rod, the pole and the perch. As part of its modernizing 'white heat' spirit, the Labour government decided to get rid of the old money and replace it with decimal coinage.

The idea had been around for ages: Anthony Trollope, Victorian father of the pillar box, has a character enthusing about it in one of his novels. Various committees had recommended the change throughout the first half of the twentieth century. Finally the decision was made and Chancellor Jim Callaghan put it in his 1966 Budget. The Conservative Party, at that time eager to seem 'with it', made no objection. The old system was rather complicated, and, as inflation crept up, the penny and even the shilling were becoming ever less useful units. (Still, for the history lover there was something nice about reaching into your pocket and pulling out a coin with Queen Victoria on it.) So, goodbye half-crown, florin, sixpence, penny and halfpenny, and hello new pence or 'p'.

The switch-over took place on 15 February 1971. Some of the old coins mapped easily on to the new system: a sixpence was worth 2½p, a shilling 5p, two shillings 10p. New coins were issued for ½p, 1p and 2p. Old pennies and the bronze, twelve-sided threepenny bit remained legal tender for a few months, though they could only be used in amounts that worked in the new currency. For most people, the change was pretty painless: the older generation suffered most, both in confusion and in the loss of a cultural anchor. People who found the new pennies worked in old 6d slot machines were delighted.

No new stamp designs were commissioned for decimal currency, as a new definitive range had only recently been introduced. For the first fifteen years of the Queen's reign, Britain had used a set by various designers, which depicted riffs on the theme of the emblems of the four nations that make up the UK, all framing the standard portrait of Her Majesty by Dorothy Wilding. Critics say the 'Wilding' stamps are too fussy – but, homely and pretty, they speak of their era, the early fifties, which still hurt from the war and which craved a few frills round the edge of all the prevailing austerity. As the nation grew ever more prosperous, something new was needed.

In 1963, sculptor Arnold Machin had created a bust of the Queen to be used on coinage. This was adapted for the new stamps – just as William Wyon's 1838 coin design had been adapted for the Penny Black (the Queen, aware of this historical link, had insisted that the new standard letter rate stamp be black). It was an excellent choice. Machin's design is still in use today, forty-five years after its introduction. It has appeared in every value from 1p to 50p (except for 21p), on many values between 50p and £2, on a £5 stamp, on first and second class (large and small), on regional issues and on a stamp for letters to Europe. Almost all of these have been in attractive, strong colours (X292 in the Stanley Gibbons catalogue, '26p drab', possibly wasn't much to write home about – or with – but most of the range has been tremendous).

New Machins were, of course, issued for Decimal Day – the first ones appearing on 15 February. Needless to say, collectors were keen to get First Day Covers of this new issue. But they couldn't, as the Post Office was on strike. The Union of Post Office Workers had asked for a 15% pay rise in October 1970; the government had offered half; the strike had begun in January and was to last into March, the longest strike since 1926 (and a taste of things to come).

At this time, Britain was essentially run by various boards and councils, where leaders from government, industry and the trades unions worked together for the national good. The best known of these was the NEDC, the National Economic Development Council – but its nickname, Neddy, hardly inspired confidence, conjuring up a weary donkey trudging round in a wheel.

This faithful old creature was about to meet its nemesis. From the mid-fifties to the mid-sixties, inflation had risen, but so gently that hardly anyone noticed, and in the late sixties/ early seventies, it actually fell. But between mid-1972 and early 1975, inflation skyrocketed in a way it had never done before in British history, rising from about 4% to 25% in three years. The parallel was inevitable to anyone with any knowledge of history: Weimar Germany.

Various preconditions had set this up. These included the inflationary legacy of UK politicians' attempts to buy votes at election time (a standard tactic since the 1950s), the global inflation caused by America's borrowing to finance the Vietnam War, and unrelenting pressure on wages by the British unions. Trades union power had been growing throughout the 1960s but the unions also fought among themselves, creating a pressure to outbid one another when asking for pay rises. Following the postal workers' 1970 claim for 15%, the mighty National Union of Mineworkers asked for 43%. When this was refused, strike action was called. The miners had more power than the postmen. Not only did they stop producing coal, they sent 'flying' pickets round the country to stop coal being unloaded at docks and moving from depots to power stations, steelworks and other major users. A state of emergency was announced;

industry was put on a three-day week to save electricity; in the end, the government did a deal, as they pretty much had to.

While this was going on, unemployment was rising. In early 1972 it hit the million mark for the first time since the 1930s. There was a new government in power: Wilson had been replaced by Conservative Ted Heath, now perhaps best remembered as a yachtsman with heaving shoulders and a Santa Claus laugh. Heath, a fundamentally liberal man, was genuinely dismayed by the unemployment figures. He was also a politician and was thinking ahead to the next election. In mid-1972, he and his Chancellor Anthony Barber started to reflate the economy. But, of course, it was inflated enough already: the new spending just made prices rise even faster. John Maynard Keynes, whose name became associated with such foolishness but who never said 'You can throw money at the economy whenever you feel like it', would have been turning in his grave.

Then OPEC, the world's oil producers, joined in. They had long been unhappy about the prices they were getting for their product – prices that were not rising in line with the Vietnam-induced global inflation – and had been planning to form a cartel. In 1973, war broke out in the Middle East. Furious with the West's siding with Israel, the Arab–Iranian members of OPEC put an embargo on sales of oil. The price of the liquid gold on which so much of the British economy relied quadrupled almost instantly.

Back home, more unions were winning more pay rises. The miners found themselves dropping down the relative pay scale again; by 1974, they were ready for another strike. The government came up with similar responses – state of emergency, three-day week – but added a new one: a snap election, called on the theme, 'Who runs the country?' The electorate decided 'Not you, Ted' and voted Harold Wilson back in; a settlement with the miners was soon reached. The Conservative Party would not forget this humiliation. Meanwhile, another dollop of kerosene had been chucked on to the fire of inflation, which was now threatening to turn into a conflagration.

While the currency was threatening to go into free fall, traditional industries seemed to be losing the plot, too. The Post Office, once a solid earner, had been making small annual deficits for a while: in 1974–5 it recorded a huge loss of £308 million. The British automotive industry fared even worse. This had once been the finest in Europe. By the mid-1970s, it was centred round a lumbering corporation called British Leyland, which had been cobbled together in the merger mania of the sixties, when an ailing company (British Motor Holdings) was dumped on a profitable one (Leyland) in the hope that the latter would sort it out. In the end, the opposite happened: the rot spread through the whole company. British Leyland factories were riven by strikes; its cars were poorly engineered, inelegant rust-buckets. In 1975, the company went bankrupt.

The song *Life on Mars* was actually released as a single in June 1973. A look at the singer would have created more puzzlement in older people: Bowie was at the height of his gender-bending phase, resplendent in lipstick, mascara, rouge and a bizarre haircut, yet robustly heterosexual if some of his lyrics were anything to go by.

Of course, to younger, more flexible people, the Martian atmosphere was fine. There were good times to be had; there always are. Roy Jenkins had wanted Britain to be on the side of experiment, of letting people be 'free to make mistakes' – so we were making mistakes. Hell, if the Chancellor of the Exchequer couldn't manage the economy or the board of British Leyland manage their business, why shouldn't the rest of us stick silly bits of glitter in our hair, listen to glam rock, or take the odd substance we shouldn't?

But in the end, mistakes are there to be learnt from. There was a feeling that in mid-seventies Britain, especially among the nation's rulers, mistake was compounding mistake and nobody was learning anything.

Not the message one gets from Arnold Machin's magisterial stamps.

CHAPTER TWENTY-FIVE

OUR WAY

SILVER JUBILEE
COMMEMORATIVE, 8½P, 1977

I N THE end, inflation didn't ratchet up as it had in Germany. Britain didn't print endless banknotes, and Harold Wilson did an uneasy deal with the unions to moderate pay demands. But it had been a close-run thing. The economy was still struggling. Across the Channel, people looked on in puzzlement and talked about Britain as the sick man of Europe, a term once applied to the now-defunct Ottoman Empire. The country seemed to have lost its sense of direction, of pride, of identity. This handsome stamp, from 1977, appears to fly in the face of the reality of its era, like the Machin definitive. Or does it?

Two apparently opposed reactions to Britain's growing woes appeared around the same time. One was loud and rude, and purported to come from the inner-city high-rises though actually grew out of the suburbs; the other was intellectual and patrician, though not quite as patrician as it sounded. The people behind these reactions loathed each other, but secretly shared a passion.

The Sex Pistols were the Angry Young Men of the mid-seventies. The band was essentially the creation of entrepreneur and artist Malcolm McLaren, who believed in the value, both commercial and artistic, of shock. The Sex Pistols certainly managed that, spitting at their audiences, fighting on and off stage, and generally head-butting every taboo they could find. They weren't much good at playing their instruments (the most musical of them, Glen Matlock, was sacked), but created a compelling stage show that was more theatre than music, decked in the bizarre punk fashions of McLaren and Vivienne Westwood: chains, cigarette burns, piercings – McLaren was fascinated by the interaction of sex and cruelty.

The band hit the national spotlight on 1 December 1976, when they were interviewed on ITV. The interviewer, Bill Grundy, didn't exactly help the situation by asking them to 'say something outrageous'. Steve Jones, the Pistols' guitarist, duly obliged with 'You dirty f***er ... What a f***ing rotter.' The band then landed two record deals, both of which they blew by outrageous behaviour, though they got to keep the money.

Just as it had been for the Angry Young Men, the big personal issue for the Sex Pistols was how to live a life that was vital and honest. Along with the Bill Grundy interview, the most famous piece of Pistols footage is of Sid Vicious, Matlock's replacement, singing 'My Way'. This is often interpreted as a send-up, but actually he is simply doing what the song says, doing it His Way: sneering, furious, at full volume. Vicious (John Simon Ritchie, to give his original name) had a strong belief in personal freedom. But he was also a very troubled individual. Like the New Left and the counterculture, punk saw conventional society as the enemy of vitality, honesty and freedom. But Sid Vicious' biggest enemy was himself. He was prone to outbursts of uncontrollable rage, at himself and others. And then there were the drugs ... Sid thought they made him more authentic. In fact, they destroyed him. In a terrible climax to his life, his girlfriend and fellow user Nancy was murdered, possibly by him, and he died of an overdose, aged 21. Punk's Altamont.

One can think of few characters less like Sid Vicious than Margaret Thatcher. However, they both shared a belief in the value of individual freedom. For Thatcher, freedom lay safely within the law and in the removal of the state from economic activity. In 1974 she co-founded the Centre for Policy Studies (CPS) with Sir Keith Joseph. The CPS challenged the prevailing belief that the economy could be steered by government, and instead argued that government intervention just messed things up – individuals and businesses knew better how to spend their money than politicians did. Instead of macroeconomic tinkering, the government's economic tasks were to ensure sound money – to make sure the currency was not debased by inflation – and to create a culture where enterprise was encouraged and rewarded.

Of course, most people in 1976 neither stuck safety pins in their nose nor buried their head in CPS leaflets on controlling the money supply. They just struggled on. In September of that year Britain nearly ran out of cash and had to negotiate a loan from the International Monetary Fund, a body set up to rescue basket-case economies.

The year after that was the Queen's Silver Jubilee. With the country in such a mess, many people doubted whether it was wise to make much of a deal about this. The government decided not to fund any celebrations – though the Post Office did commission a set of stamps from Dick Guyatt, a professor at the Royal College of Art (among his students had been David Gentleman). The issue beautifully echoes Barnett Freedman's 1935 classic, while having a style and voice all of its own. But did anyone care? The nation didn't seem very interested in the Jubilee; it was too busy struggling to pay the weekly bills. In the end, a committee of well-connected individuals raised money and planned some celebrations. In May 1977, the Queen and the Duke of Edinburgh made an extensive tour of the country, as often as possible having walkabouts, when they dispensed with protocol and met the crowds. This proved surprisingly popular.

The main Jubilee celebrations were on 6 and 7 June. On the evening of the 6th, the Queen lit a special bonfire at Windsor Castle. The plan was for a ripple of light to spread across the kingdom via a chain of beacons on high places: once the Windsor one was alight, people who could see it would light theirs, then people who could see those would light theirs, and so on. It didn't quite work that way, but the atmosphere was cheerful: beacon-lighters felt linked to others around the country – and to history, as the idea had been based on the system put in place to warn Queen Elizabeth I about the Spanish Armada.

Next day, the royal family attended a service at St Paul's and a lunch at the Guildhall, then processed back to Buckingham Palace, the Queen and Prince Philip travelling in the Coronation Coach. Crowds gathered to watch – including people who'd camped out overnight in the inevitable rain to get good places: estimates of the numbers were around one million. On the same day, street parties were held up and down the country. At these, people thoroughly enjoyed themselves and discovered a new sense of belonging, to their communities and to the nation. Britain didn't have to have an Empire or be global top dog: its people could simply be who they were and enjoy themselves. 'Doing it Our Way.'

Not everyone joined in the fun. The Sex Pistols released an anti-Jubilee single, 'No Future'. In Derek Jarman's film, *Jubilee*, Queen Elizabeth I is teleported to 1977 Britain and encounters a dystopic world of damaged, marginalized individuals. Both these works are impressive in their own way – but they miss the point of summer 1977. The Jubilee lifted a sense of national gloom, and gave Britain the belief that it deserved something better than the mess in which it seemed to be mired.

But it was still in that mess. Inflation began to rise again, as sharply as it had back in 1973. The government tried to insist on a 5% limit for pay settlements, but this was ignored by many private sector employers. A strike by the drivers of oil tankers threatened to cause as much disruption as the miners' strikes of '72 and '74, and was bought off with a 15% rise. Public sector unions pressed for similar rises. A day of action in January 1979 brought more workers out than any call since the General Strike of 1926. Unofficial wildcat strikes followed around the country: not only were unions competing with one another, but union branches were trying to outdo one another in militancy. Soon nearly half the hospitals were treating emergency cases only. In Liverpool, a strike by gravediggers meant bodies weren't being buried. In London, refuse collectors were on strike; bags of rubbish piled up on the capital's streets and squares . . .

Enough! A vote of no confidence in the government of James Callaghan was tabled in parliament, and passed by one vote. The resulting election took place on 3 May 1979, and resulted in a 43-seat majority for the Conservatives – now under Margaret Thatcher, who had been voted leader in 1975.

Some present this election as a conscious, determined swing to the right. But figures show that far-right parties didn't prosper – the National Front fielded over 300 candidates and got under 200,000 votes. What people voted for was change. A woman prime minister, for one thing. And a new set of ideas for another. Would they work? Nobody knew, but surely they couldn't fare any worse than the previous ones. Or could they?

CHAPTER TWENTY-SIX

LIVERPOOL AND MANCHESTER RAILWAY 1830

VICTORIAN VALUES

LIVERPOOL AND MANCHESTER RAILWAY 150TH ANNIVERSARY COMMEMORATIVE, 12P, 1980

THIS STAMP appeared soon after Margaret Thatcher's victory. At first glance, it has little to do with this, but actually it is particularly appropriate. The railway it celebrates was a classic piece of commercial entrepreneurship of the kind the new Prime Minister admired. And it speaks of an era she clearly respected. She did not invent the slogan 'Victorian Values': it was suggested to her in 1983 by a TV interviewer, Brian Walden, when summarizing her attitudes. However, she replied 'Exactly. Very much so' to his suggestion. Positives like enterprise, hard work, family, a sound currency, patriotism – but also a stony-faced intolerance of commercial failure: these values lay at the heart of the Thatcher revolution, and were ones that most Victorians would have recognized and applauded.

The question was, would these work in a 1980s economy?

The revolution got off to a bad start. Inflation-busting measures were put in place: interest rates were raised and no fresh
money was pumped into the system. But inflation kept rising.
Instead, the measures hit manufacturing. Unemployment
reached two million and Thatcher's popularity in the polls
tumbled to 23%, a record low for any prime minister. She faced
a revolt in her own cabinet.

However, she remained resolute, making her famous
comment 'You turn if you want to. The lady's not for turning'
at the 1980 party conference. And, slowly, the medicine began
to work. Inflation peaked at 22% then fell as sharply as it had
risen. Soon it was back to 5%. Apart from a brief spike in the
late eighties, it has never risen above that level since.

But the cost was high. In 1982, unemployment passed three
million, a figure not seen since the Great Depression. The
Thatcherites' Schumpeterian belief was that after this shock,
fresh jobs would be created by newly incentivized enterprise,
and unemployment would fall again. They proved to be half
right. The second half of the 1980s saw a boom in certain parts
of the country, but not in others, for example where towns
relied on the old heavy industries like steel and shipbuilding.
Or coal.

By 1980, many British mines were either running out or
working small, inaccessible seams: the industry, which had been
contracting steadily since the late 1950s, was heading for a
crisis, and would have been whatever government had been in
power. Sadly, a legacy of ill feeling exacerbated the situation.
The Conservatives wanted revenge for the defeats of the seventies. The miners' union elected a firebrand leader, Arthur
Scargill, who was also fixated on 1974: he wanted a rerun and
another win, complete with the collapse of the government.
The Conservatives appointed Ian MacGregor, a man with a
reputation for ruthless trimming of workforces, as head of the
National Coal Board. A strike became inevitable. It started in
March 1984. Violence on the picket lines soon became

commonplace. One of the worst examples took place at Orgreave. Back in 1935, the colliery had hosted patriotic celebrations for the King's Silver Jubilee. In June 1984, it witnessed a battle between 10,000 miners and as many police.

Winter would be the big test. Could the miners cause the electricity industry to falter, as they had in the seventies? The answer was no: new legislation had curbed the power of flying pickets, and electricity generators had stocked up on coal. Lack of wages began to tell, too: men started to return to work. A year after the strike had begun, it was called off. Defeat was painful. At the start of the strike there had been 170 pits open. Forty of these were closed in 1985–6, after which a slower but still steady decline set in: Treeton, for example, was closed in 1990. Employment in the industry fell from 190,000 in 1984 to 20,000 ten years later. Its current level is around 5,000.

Part of the way in which Mrs Thatcher wanted to encourage new jobs to replace the lost ones was privatization, selling government departments in the hope that they would become more entrepreneurial. First to go were legacy stakes in private companies such as BP and British Aerospace. Then the privatizers moved on to state monopolies, including the telecommunications part of the Post Office, now renamed British Telecom. In 1984 just over half of this was sold to the public – or at least went on sale: in fact only a third ended up in the hands of small investors. British Gas followed in 1986 – a string of TV adverts reminded viewers to tell Sid the sale was on – and water utilities in 1989. Another part of this campaign was the Right to Buy: council houses were sold to their tenants. It was an aim of both these exercises to spread ownership, of shares and of property. They succeeded, but this did not, of course, do much about poverty. However, Right to Buy did move the dividing line in society down, creating more home-owning 'haves'. Had it been matched by construction of new homes for the remaining 'have nots', it would have been a truly impressive measure.

The Falklands war was another defining aspect of the Thatcher years – and one the Victorians would surely have approved of. On 2 April 1982, Argentina invaded the islands. The invasion was swift and successful: unsurprising, as the British garrison consisted of eighty-five serving troops and about forty volunteers. Diplomatic efforts to get the invaders to leave failed, so Britain resorted to force. The war was nasty but relatively brief (it lasted 74 days) and limited: no attempts were made to bomb the Argentine mainland. Nearly a thousand combatants died, around a third of them British. Another third were on board an Argentine cruiser, the *General Belgrano*, which was sunk by a British submarine. The sinking remains controversial – but war is war: by the time of the sinking, Britain had suffered several serious losses, and both sides knew this was going to be an unpleasant conflict.

Other aspects of 1980s Britain would have shocked the Victorians no end. They might have recognized the young, upwardly-mobile professionals, or yuppies, that burst on to the scene in the Thatcher era. They would have been surprised, however, at how many of them were female.

With the Queen quietly occupying the throne and Margaret Thatcher in Number 10, there was a new confidence among women, especially in the workplace. The old 'rules of work' were changing, partly because the traditional 'male' jobs were vanishing and being replaced by service industries, where tact and emotional intelligence were key values – though an appearance of forcefulness still helped: power dressing became a requirement for the eighties businesswoman, involving simple, well-made outfits with bright accessories and shoulder pads that looked as if they'd been borrowed from American footballers. In all walks of life, language began to change, with the universal 'he' and 'him' disappearing. Terms from feminist activism crept into everyday parlance – life was getting tougher for the 'male chauvinist pig'.

The rise of such activism mirrored a bigger shift in the

nature of British politics. After the 1979 defeat, the Labour Party imploded: its old approach had been buried under the rubbish bags of the Winter of Discontent and a new one had to be found. At first it sought revitalization by moving to the left, but in doing so it became more marginal and ideological. Other groups sprang up around it that would once have fed into the Labour Party but now stood up and proclaimed their message for themselves. Gay Power was one such group. After facing centuries of bigotry and oppression, in the 1980s the gay community and lifestyle began to become more open and influential. The AIDS crisis threatened to reverse this, but the courage and honesty of many AIDS victims won the admiration of the straight world.

Another single-issue movement was the Campaign for Nuclear Disarmament. This had been around since 1958, but the 1980s saw it rise in prominence, due to a sinister acceleration in the arms race. The Cold War had thawed during the early 1970s, but a new frostiness entered the international environment with the Soviet invasion of Afghanistan in 1979. Margaret Thatcher had already made her views on the Soviet Union clear – 'they are bent on world dominance'. In 1980, her ideological soulmate, Ronald Reagan, was elected US President. Their view was not without justification. In 1958 the Soviet Union had very few nuclear warheads, but by the 1980s they had more than America and were deploying ever more of them in Europe, on state-of-the-art mobile missile launchers.

The standard Western response to this was to deploy more, too: in July 1982 American Cruise missiles started arriving at Greenham Common airbase near Newbury. But was this really a rational response, given the mayhem these weapons could cause? Many people did not think so, and a peace camp was set up at the base. The camp was for women only, and a powerful expression of eighties radical feminism.

The missiles still came, and eventually the Russians began negotiating: their stockpile of warheads peaked in 1986 at

45,000, then began to decline as fast as it had grown. Out of altruism, or because their system was falling apart? Just as Lenin had beamed his ideas round the world from post-1917 Moscow, the message of the Thatcher revolution went global. Many other countries began privatization programmes. Even the People's Republic of China instituted free-market reforms, its leader Deng Xiaoping taking a new, pragmatic line from 1985 onwards (not that many people in the West took much notice: China was very poor and a long way away . . .). This global take-up is, perhaps, the ultimate tribute to this controversial politician.

The controversy continues to this day: Margaret Thatcher is a 'Marmite' figure, whom people either love or hate. Her critics say she created a culture of greed and selfishness. There's some truth in this – but it was not what she intended. These attitudes became most noticeable in the City, a place she never really liked. Her true heart lay with the hard-working small business person like her father, a successful grocer in Grantham. Alfred Roberts had been a patriotic and civic-minded man, who served as a JP and ran the local Workers' Educational Association (a traditional Liberal, he believed strongly in 'self-improvement'). His daughter always hoped that the 1980s' newly rich would react in similar ways, participating in their communities and giving generously to charity; in this, she was simply naïve.

She is also accused of failing to understand government and how it can create social value through institutions like Rowland Hill's Post Office or William Beveridge's National Health Service. Others say she split the country, not caring enough about the fate of the north: those values celebrated at Orgreave in 1935 and rediscovered at Jubilee street parties in 1977 imply duties for everyone – nationhood means sharing benefits and burdens – but instead, regional grants were cut at a time when unemployment was high (in the north it remained over 10% for the entire Thatcher era). Then, of course, there's the business of her personal tone. Once outvoted by 49 to 1 at a Commonwealth conference, she simply observed that she felt sorry for the other forty-nine. Her supporters say that the parlous state of the nation in the mid-seventies meant that this kind of bull-headedness was necessary. Others hear recordings of her voice and cringe.

These criticisms all stick. However, at the same time, Margaret Thatcher understood something that most politicians since the war seemed to have forgotten, that without sound currency and a vibrant entrepreneurial Wealth Machine there is little for the state to spend, even on the wisest projects. Victorian values? Possibly, but also ones that have become part of the modern political mindset.

CHAPTER TWENTY-SEVEN

DIVERSITY

YOUTH ORGANIZATIONS
COMMEMORATIVE, 26P, 1982

I N THE later years of the twentieth century, the number of stamps being issued increased markedly. Though this created great controversy in the philatelic world, the public seemed to like the new issues. Standards of design remained high. However, the kinds of story that stamps tell us changed as a result. They are not so much witnesses to eras as discussions about themes.

The 1982 26p, by Brian Sanders, celebrates the Cubs and the Scouts, as part of a series on Youth Organizations (other denominations featured the Boys' and Girls' Brigades and the Brownies and Girl Guides). The topic wasn't new – there had been a Scouting anniversary set in 1957. What was new about this issue was that the young Scout carrying the flag was the first non-white Briton to take centre stage on a British stamp.

Arguably, this is a rather late 'first', but stamps have always been a bit old-fashioned. In this century, more stamps have reflected Britain's diversity, a stylish 2006 issue, Sounds of Britain, being an excellent example.

As a trading nation with a relatively liberal political culture, Britain has always had an inflow of migrants. Back in 1330, Edward III shrewdly invited weavers from Flanders to come to Britain and add value to the wool being produced in East Anglia. In the late sixteenth century, many Huguenot Protestants fled France and, according to the memorial in the Huguenot cemetery in Wandsworth, 'found freedom to worship God after their own manner ... established important industries, and added to the credit and prosperity of their town of adoption'. Economic and religious freedom are two important strands of this story.

Did the Flemings and Huguenots encounter prejudice when they arrived? Sadly, the answer is yes. That's another strand. But they also encountered kindness, opportunity – and love: it is estimated that one in four Londoners has a Huguenot in their family tree.

The first wave of immigration in the era covered by this book was from Ireland. From 1830 onwards many came to assist in a task, the magnitude of which the nation had never known before: building the railways. A third of the 200,000 navvies were Irish. After 1846, a new flood of Irish emigrants fled the terrible famine: they were less fortunate than the navvies, finding little work (the great railway stock market crash happened around that time) and hostility from the locals. Like the famine, the situation was poorly handled: Liverpool was overwhelmed with starving Irish but received minimal assistance from central government. Typhoid fever broke out. In the end, some were forced to return to Ireland, while others took to the roads or found work. In the end, Liverpool adapted to the influx. Railway building resumed and rising trade meant work in the docks and warehouses. The Irish became part of that city's unique culture – the three front men of the Beatles all had Irish ancestors.

The next big influx came at the end of the century. After the assassination of Czar Alexander II in 1881, anti-Semitic riots spread across southern Russia. Millions of Jews fled, mostly to America but around 120,000 to the UK, many settling in London's East End, a traditional arrival point. They encountered a range of reactions, one of which was prejudice. The British Brothers League was set up calling for a ban on immigration. One of its founders, Conservative MP William Evans-Gordon, claimed that 'a storm is brewing which, if it is allowed to burst, will have deplorable results'. A young Liberal MP called Winston Churchill argued back, in favour of 'the old tolerant and generous practice of free entry and asylum'. As a compromise, the Aliens Act was passed in 1905, which did not, as the League had wanted, ban immigrants, but set some rules, including one that enshrined the principle of political asylum. Evans-Gordon's 'deplorable results' did not transpire. Instead, in the First World War over 40,000 Jews – an estimated 13% of the Jewish population (higher than the national average of 11%) – fought for Britain. Five of them won the Victoria Cross.

If there were deplorable results, they were brought about by the 1930s British Union of Fascists and their provocative marches into the East End. These met massive popular resistance: at the Battle of Cable Street in October 1936, an estimated 100,000 people turned out to stop a BUF march – many more than were members of the Union. Later, many Jewish families moved away from inner London by choice, as economic success enabled them to buy properties in the suburbs. The East End was ready for new incomers.

After the Second World War, many Poles who had escaped Hitler and come here to fight him settled down. Some German POWs decided to stick around, too. As the economy began to grow, another wave of immigrants crossed the Irish Sea – once again to help build Britain's infrastructure: the new towns,

the motorways. The booming brick industry employed many
Italians. The main source of post-war immigrants, however,
was the old Empire, now the Commonwealth. In 1948, the
MV *Empire Windrush* arrived at Tilbury with 492 Jamaicans
on board. Pictures of the disembarkation show smart, dignified,
cheerful people, clearly with high expectations of the mother
country. They soon found themselves trudging London streets
past endless boarding houses with signs in their windows
reading 'No coloureds'. Despite the turnout to defend Cable
Street, there was still a deep current of racial prejudice in
Britain. Nevertheless the new arrivals persevered, and communities from the various islands of the West Indies began to
form.

Levels of immigration rose throughout the 1950s and 1960s;
most immigrants now came from the Indian subcontinent,
though other parts of the Commonwealth, particularly Hong
Kong, also participated. Many moved into the East End, where
the story of the post-1881 Jews began to repeat itself: the mosque
on Brick Lane was formerly a synagogue (before that, it had
been a Huguenot chapel). The role of William Evans-Gordon
was taken by Enoch Powell, who made an inflammatory speech
in Birmingham in 1968, known as 'rivers of blood' (his actual
words were a prophecy from Virgil's *Aeneid*, of 'wars, terrible
wars, and the Tiber foaming with much blood'). The role of
the British Union of Fascists was taken by the National Front,
plus assorted gangs of thugs looking for someone different to
beat up.

As usual, liberal Britons fought back. A rather toothless
Race Relations Act was issued in 1965; a stronger one followed
in 1968, making it illegal to refuse housing or employment to
anyone on the grounds of ethnicity. Anti-racist parties formed
– including one of the more admirable spin-offs of punk, the
Rock against Racism gigs of the late 1970s. The rise of political correctness in the 1980s and 1990s is more controversial:
some people argue that it was a necessary part of exposing and

eradicating racism and other forms of prejudice; others say it was taken too far and did more harm than good to the cause of tolerance.

In this century, the most recent additions to the national mix have been from Eastern Europe, newly liberated from Communism and making use of the free movement of labour within the EU.

The 2001 census showed the result of these changes. The nation was 86% 'white British'. Another 6% were whites from other countries (about 1½% from the Republic of Ireland). Four per cent were from the Indian subcontinent, half of these Muslim. Two per cent were black, just over half Caribbean, just under half African. One per cent were mixed race: Britain has one of the fastest-growing mixed-race populations in the world. Half a per cent were Chinese and another half a per cent 'other'.

Many of the new Britons have a strong entrepreneurial streak, both commercial and social.

While I was writing this section, the sale of Euro Car Parts was announced. This business was started by Sukhpal Singh, a young Sikh refugee from Idi Amin's Uganda. In 1978, he borrowed £5,000 from his father to buy a bankrupt car parts shop in Willesden. It was not a business he understood well – apparently early customers usually knew more about car parts than he did – but he made his shop different by staying open into the evening six days a week, by promising to find any part for any car and by undercutting dealerships (in other words, by finding a smug oligopoly and taking it on: a classic entrepreneurial strategy). In 2011, the company – still a family business – had eighty-nine outlets across the UK, and an American buyer paid £225 million for it.

Kids Company, founded by Camila Batmanghelidjh, who came to the UK from Iran when she was eleven, is a remarkable charity that developed its own way of helping children who fall out of the education system. These youngsters have almost all been abandoned by parents who can't cope, and the organization provides a kind of substitute family for them, rather in the way Dickens and Angela Burdett-Coutts did at Urania Cottage. It has developed special educational techniques aimed at these children, for whom conventional classroom methods don't work: they are taught quick, practical mini-courses on topics like how to run your own home. The charity's Urban Academy has a 94% success rate of getting kids who were heading for crime, drugs or prostitution into job training or higher education.

Of course, not every immigrant to Britain has prospered. Riots broke out in several northern towns in 2001, with gangs of young Asian and white men fighting in the streets. The Mayor of Oldham, Riaz Ahmad, had his home petrol-bombed. A report on these events blamed the lack of interaction between communities, which it describes as living 'parallel lives'. Poor economic prospects – for everyone – did not help: these towns suffered in the 1980s and have yet to pick up. Riaz Ahmad is optimistic, but only in the long term, commenting at the time that it would take more than a decade for things to come good.

And then, of course, there's the spectre of terrorism. The appalling bombings on the London Tube on 7 July 2005 (and four attempted bombings two weeks later) were the work of young British Muslims who had been indoctrinated by terrorist websites and fanatical preachers. These preachers had been overwhelmingly rejected by UK Muslims, some of whom had actually alerted the security services to the threat they posed – sadly, the services did not act, possibly due to fears about political correctness. The preachers are no longer active but the websites remain: the danger has not gone away.

Despite this, the bombings do not represent the fissuring of British society, more the problems of a relatively small group of young individuals. The outcome was not a descent into communal violence, as William Evans-Gordon and Enoch Powell feared, but a coming together of all Britons in condemnation and sadness. Looking through the list of names of the victims, one is struck by its international nature: '7/7' was actually an attack on modern Britain's pluralism and diversity. As such, it failed.

And in the end, these problems are exceptions. The story of immigration to Britain is overall one of success. That success is often quiet: good neighbours, a successful local business, a happy mixed marriage, a young lad getting the honour of carrying the flag for his Scout troop. On the public level, immigration has added greatly to the nation's wealth – recent estimates show that the British South Asian business sector alone is responsible for 6% of GDP. It has made Britain fitter and more flexible for interacting with the modern, global world: one of the reasons why the UK won the 2012 Olympics was the bid's stress on the diversity of East London. It has added immeasurably to Britain's cultural and sporting prowess. It has, of course, meant changes for everyone – but cultures are always changing anyway: a black gospel choir, a Balti restaurant (a cuisine invented in Birmingham), a lion dance in Covent Garden are all parts of modern British life, which is brighter as a result.

It hasn't always been easy; it hasn't always been well handled; there are always going to be difficult cases at the margin about who is allowed in and who isn't – Britain is a small island and there have to be some rules about who comes to live here. But overall the country has done well following Churchill's advice and sticking, as close as is sensibly possible, with the old tolerant and generous practice of openness, of which this stamp is a quiet celebration.

CHAPTER TWENTY-EIGHT

LOOKING BOTH WAYS

SECOND EUROPEAN ELECTIONS COMMEMORATIVE, 16P, 1984

L OOKING THROUGH the catalogue of British stamps issued over the last fifty years, one sees that Europe features with great regularity. The first Europe-themed stamp came out in 1960. In 1967, stamps celebrated the short-lived European Free Trade Area. Stamps were issued in 1973 when Britain joined the European Community and in 1979 for the first direct elections to the European Assembly (no British election has ever featured on a stamp). In 1982, the Post Office began 'Europa' issues, an annual Europe-wide convention where each nation produces its own stamps, but on a shared theme, such as nature, bridges, invention or landscapes. This stamp, by Fritz Wegner, appeared in 1984, celebrating the second set of elections to the European Parliament.

From this, one might conclude that Britain is an eager participant in the European project. In reality, the relationship

between Britain and the European Union has been difficult
from the start, and shows little sign of improving.

After the Second World War, there was an intense feeling
of 'Never again!', especially in Germany and those countries
that had been occupied by the Nazis. Many people felt that
the very concept of the nation state was to blame; if Europe
was to avoid being consumed by another conflict, it would have
to transcend such thinking. Moves soon began to create
Europe-wide political / economic institutions. The first of these
was the European Coal and Steel Community (ECSC),
founded in 1951, essentially by France and Germany, but also
involving Italy, Belgium, Luxembourg and the Netherlands.
Under this, control of the named industries of member countries would be given to a central authority. If it wanted to close
a Belgian coalfield or Dutch steelworks, it could do so – the
governments of those countries would no doubt be consulted,
but in the end would be overruled.

This was unambiguously set up as a trial run for full-on
European government. Its first president, Jean Monnet, was
deeply committed to the European federal ideal. The first
bulletin published by the Community's delegation in America
was called *Towards a Federal Government of Europe*. (America
has always approved of European integration, which matters
much more to it than Britain's well-being, despite all the
rhetoric about the 'special relationship'. From the US point of
view, having been dragged into two European wars in the last
century, this makes total sense.)

Britain was asked to join the ECSC, but turned the offer
down. Subsequent historians have criticized this as blinkered.
But was it? Would UK voters have been happy if a British
coalfield had been shut by an authority based in France?

It's important to understand that Britain was not 'anti-
European' in some absolute sense. The country was already a
key part of a European entity: NATO. But Britain had its own
view of Europe as a group of nation states, co-operating in a

genuine and amicable manner where necessary, but otherwise letting each state get on with pursuing its own interests in its own way. This was based on a view that different cultures prefer different styles of government. Supporters of this view, such as Harold Macmillan, argued that many continental European nations liked a top-down system run by technocrats, while Britain preferred a more sceptical, democratic, 'let's try it and see' approach. Britain had political traditions developed over centuries, while many European states were less than 150 years old.

In this spirit, in 1960 Britain co-founded with Austria, Denmark, Norway, Portugal, Sweden and Switzerland a rival European political/economic entity, the European Free Trade Area (EFTA). EFTA clearly had disadvantages relative to the ECSC (which had by then been renamed the European Economic Community or EEC). For one thing it was a lot smaller, and for another the EEC was linked geographically while the countries of the EFTA were dotted around the place. But the EFTA countries shared ideals: free trade and national sovereignty.

The EEC, meanwhile, had been pursuing its clear federalist agenda. In the 1957 Treaty of Rome, it took its new name, set up a new European Parliamentary Assembly, which had few powers but was a trial run for an institution that would acquire many, and established the European Commission and European Court of Justice.

The problem for Britain was that this new entity started to do rather well. Britain found itself in the embarrassing position of doing more trade with the EEC than EFTA. The question arose: should the UK swallow both its pride and its vision of Europe, and join the EEC after all? Yes, it finally decided.

No, the EEC replied. France and Germany did not want British membership. From their point of view, it makes sense. Britain did not share their desire for closer political union.

They saw the British membership application as a simple piece of economic opportunism – which is exactly what it was.

For a while, Britain continued as a now rather unwilling member of EFTA. A pair of 1967 stamps, showing EFTA flags and a cargo ship and a BEA plane being loaded up with traded goods, tried to hide this unwillingness. The stamp issue, like the one for National Productivity Year, is notorious for the number of errors available to collectors: a Freudian slip, perhaps, because at the same time Britain was hammering on the EEC door.

In the end, the EEC relented. This is as much to do with personalities at the top as deep attitude changes: General de Gaulle, an arch-enemy of British membership, was gone, and in 1970, Ted Heath, the most Euro-friendly Prime Minister Britain ever had, came to power. Britain finally joined: cue a set of stamps depicting the EEC as a jigsaw into which an essential part was now, at last, being fitted. A referendum on British membership in 1975 was resoundingly won by Europhiles.

However, this positive mood did not last long. In the 1980s, the dislocation between Britain, whose view of Europe remained essentially economic, and idealistic federalists in the rest of Europe grew ever wider, reaching its maximum, perhaps, in the ill-concealed mutual loathing of Margaret Thatcher and 1985 EEC Commission President Jacques Delors. European negotiations became a battle between the two sides. The 1986 Single European Act benefited Britain with an expansion of free trade, while the European Parliament and European environmental agencies gained more powers in return. The decade also saw the Schengen Agreement (named after the town in Luxembourg where it was signed), which did away with passport controls between ten European nations. Britain was not one of them. And behind the scenes, work was going on developing a truly unifying project: a European single currency.

This currency was formally accepted as a goal on 7 February 1992, with the signing of the Maastricht treaty. Maastricht was another draw in the 'Britain v the rest' battle: many European countries wanted to further pool sovereignty on foreign policy, domestic social policy and law, but John Major largely prevented this. However, the currency became official policy, and Europe got another new name: the European Union. It wasn't just economic or just a community any longer.

Convergence criteria were set up, and governments sent away with the job of ensuring their economies met these. Inflation rates of participating currencies were all expected to move to within 1.5% of each other. Long-term interest rates shouldn't be more than 2% apart. No nation could join if its ratio of government debt to GDP exceeded 60%, or if its annual government deficit was more than 3% of GDP. All potential entrants would have to join an Exchange Rate Mechanism for two years, to make sure they not only fitted these criteria but adhered to them for that period (and were expected by financial markets to continue to do so). In this mechanism, all the participating currencies would be informally linked. If any one of them began drifting away from the others, its government would intervene to get it back in line, using a range of strategies which included interventions in foreign exchange markets.

Rather grudgingly, Britain joined this mechanism. However, the pound began to sink. John Major and his chancellor Norman Lamont pushed up interest rates to make UK bonds more attractive to overseas buyers and started to buy pounds on international markets. But to no avail: suddenly foreign exchange was pouring out of Britain and British interest rates were flying through the roof – on 16 September 1992, they were raised to 10%, then 15%. The game was clearly up: that evening, it was announced that Britain was leaving the Mechanism. The pound sank further, but ultimately found a new level. Figures show that 'Black Wednesday' cost the nation around £4 billion.

So no common currency for Britain. Making noises about

joining later, it sloped away, licking its wounds. Ironically, another UK stamp in celebration of Europe (this time, the single market) appeared less than a month after this fiasco.

In 1995, the new currency got a new name, the euro, and on 1 January 1999 it became a reality: the currencies of eleven countries were linked together at fixed rates; all government bonds in the eleven countries were now denominated in euros; the euro began trading on international markets. Three years later, the old notes and coins of the twelve nations (Greece leapt on board in 2001) ceased to be legal tender.

Britain continued its dalliance with new currency. Tony Blair, who had become PM in 1997, wanted to join, whereas Chancellor Gordon Brown was less keen. Brown set up five criteria for Britain to join which were never met. When he became Prime Minister, the euro disappeared off the agenda.

However, the new currency seemed to be succeeding. A bloc of over 300 million people was using it, and twenty-three other countries, with a combined population of 175 million, pegged their currencies to it. But underneath trouble was brewing. In 2002, the Maastricht rules were broken – not by Greece or Italy but by France and Germany. Nothing was done about this, and a tone of getting away with rule-breaking was set. Ten years later, this erupted into a full-blown crisis.

Britain can, up to a point, watch this crisis from the sidelines. But the long-term question of its relationship with Europe has not been settled. The early years of the euro were marked by a keenness by European central authorities not to interfere in the affairs of member states. This has now been replaced by an understanding that nations simply can't have a shared currency but totally different policies on taxation rates, tax collection, deficit levels or even the relative size of public and private sectors. Euro membership means greater political union.

Fritz Wegner's stamp makes a neat comment on the difficulty of Britain's situation in Europe: the bull is looking one way, the rider another. Despite all the Europe-themed stamps it has issued over the last fifty years, Britain clearly does not want to be part of political convergence – but unless the euro project is completely destroyed by the current crisis, which seems unlikely (though the zone may look a little different at the end of it), the euro nations will be forced to converge ever faster, driven by the realities of sharing a currency. Yet at the same time, Britain wants to be 'at the heart of Europe', its voice influential and its Continental trade flourishing. Quite how the nation will balance these two desires remains to be seen.

CHAPTER TWENTY-NINE

THE END OF HISTORY?

CHRISTMAS / 800TH
ANNIVERSARY OF
ELY CATHEDRAL, 1989

IVE DAYS before this stamp appeared, history came to an end.

Well, that's what Stanford academic and best-selling author Francis Fukuyama claimed. He didn't mean that nothing would ever happen again, but that the history of human social development was over. We had finally worked out the correct way to organize societies, liberal Capitalism, and subsequent events would simply be tidying up a bit at the edges. The event that precipitated this claim was the fall of the Berlin Wall.

Behind all its warheads, Communism had been quietly crumbling for decades. I visited Russia in the early eighties on a university trip, and found a nation ill at ease. The quiet people just wanted to get on with their lives; the wild ones wanted to hear all about Sid Vicious; nobody was interested in Marxist dialectic or the struggle of the proletariat. Everybody was narked at having to queue whenever they went shopping.

The young Russians I met were particularly embarrassed by their leadership: the Soviet Union had been led by a series of doddering old men since the late 1960s. Finally, in 1985, a more youthful leader took power: Mikhail Gorbachev. He was determined to fix things, and introduced new polices of *glasnost* (openness) and *perestroika* (economic restructuring). Meanwhile Russia's satellite states were pushing ever harder at the boundaries of central control – the most energetic being Poland. In September 1989, the Communist government in Warsaw was effectively voted out of office and replaced by a Solidarity one. What would happen to the rest of the Soviet Empire?

The answer is that it crumbled with astonishing speed – effectively between the date on which this Christmas stamp was issued, 14 November, and 25 December itself. On 27 November, a general strike in Czechoslovakia led to the government resigning. On 8 December Lithuania voted for a multi-party system. On the 11th Bulgaria announced 'free and democratic elections'. Most dramatic of all was the collapse of the Ceauşescu dictatorship in Romania. The world watched as Christmas approached and this old monster clung to power, massacring protestors in Timisoara. On 21 December he gave a speech in Republican Square in Bucharest. The crowd began chanting 'Timisoara!' Television footage shows a moment when Ceauşescu suddenly realizes what is going on, and a look of horror fills his eyes. On Christmas Day, he and his Lady Macbeth wife were executed. The Soviet Union lumbered on for a while, surviving an attempted coup by hardliners in 1991, but the truth is that by the time people sat down to Christmas lunch, 1989, the Cold War – the final legacy of Gavrilo Princip – was over.

Politicians, especially in America, started to talk about a New World Order. The idea was an intoxicating one: on 11 February 1990, Nelson Mandela walked free from Robben

Island. It really did seem that all round the world, the bad guys were simply giving up power, and that ordinary people everywhere would just be allowed to get on with living their lives in peace, in stable societies ruled by law and democratic principles. America would lead this process, but subtly, by example not by force.

In many places, that is what happened. But not everywhere. Even in Europe, the inhabitants of what had once been Yugoslavia fell on each other with shocking brutality. In the Middle East, Saddam Hussein invaded Kuwait. Both situations required interventions by force from America and her allies. Saddam was soon expelled from his new conquest – but at this point, the New World Order hit its limits. The Americans wanted to drive on to Baghdad and remove him. But diplomatically, they found this impossible. An uneasy compromise was reached, with Saddam still in power but prevented from bullying some of his people, such as the Marsh Arabs and the Kurds, yet free to bully others, such as the Shia. Confident talk of New World Orders ceased. American rhetoric became more about rediscovering its own values and fighting for them in a world that was still a bad place: the language of the neoconservative.

We had some new Conservatives in Britain, too. Despite the pleas of activists for 'ten more years', the country was beginning to tire of Margaret Thatcher. Around the time this stamp was issued, plans were being put in place to replace the old 'rates' with a poll tax that charged everybody, rich or poor, the same for council services. The aim was to show up spendthrift far-left councils, but few voters saw it that way: it just seemed bullying and unjust. The Conservative Party began to nosedive in the ratings.

In the end, what actually brought Mrs Thatcher's downfall was an issue that nobody on the street cared much about: the preparation of a timetable for formal entry into the planned European single currency. In November 1990 Sir Geoffrey

Howe, a senior minister, lashed out at her in a dramatic resignation speech in parliament; a leadership election was called, which she lost. Rather than go proudly, she went with tears and – worse for her successors – mutterings of treachery.

The new Prime Minister was John Major. The Conservatives could hardly have found a bigger contrast to Mrs Thatcher: a quiet man with a gentle sense of Britishness constructed around fair play and dignity, and with a strong will concealed beneath a rather comical exterior. He had the twangy voice of the London suburbs, where his father had run a garden ornaments business – but the voice was authentic; his predecessors, Thatcher and Heath, had clearly had elocution lessons.

At first he was an effective PM. He oversaw Britain's successful participation in the war against Saddam Hussein, negotiated forcefully at Maastricht and, in April 1992, won an election. The most memorable thing about the election campaign was Major's breaking away from a crowd of minders and standing on a soap box to address the crowd. In a world increasingly dominated by slick political marketing, this was a masterstroke, winning him more votes than any other leader of any other party in history. Oddly, this didn't give him a thumping majority, but it still overturned the predictions of the pollsters.

Or did he win? A more sinister explanation, which will come to echo louder and louder through the rest of Britain's story, was that the election was really won for him by the tabloid press. The press itself was in no doubt: 'It's The Sun wot won it!' proclaimed the nation's leading redtop when the result was announced. To anyone concerned with democracy this was a chilling claim. Not only had a commercial organization hijacked the democratic process, but it was so confident in its power that it would brazenly admit the fact. Underneath this claim lay a clear threat: take us on if you dare ... David Mellor, a junior minister in the Thatcher government, had tried to combat media influence, commenting at one point that the popular press were 'drinking in the last chance saloon'. Shortly after 'its' 1992 win, the *Sun* ran a story about an extra-marital affair of Mellor's, including the false accusation that he had worn a Chelsea FC replica shirt while making love and the possibly true one that his lover had sucked his toes. Mellor was the one who had to hastily finish his pint and shuffle out of the saloon. 'Toe Job to No Job' crowed the *Sun*.

Politicians started to court media barons: shortly after being elected leader of the opposition in 1994, Tony Blair went to address a News Corporation conference in Australia (News Corp owns the *Sun*). As any reader of Anthony Trollope knows, our leaders have always kept one eye on the national newspapers, but this was beginning to turn into an obsessive gaze.

However, our Ely Cathedral stamp speaks of higher things than redtops. As such, it was a good herald for the new decade. In their own way, the 1990s saw a move towards Christian values, though no longer expressed as such. As we have seen, formal organized Christianity was in decline. But informally, certain values began to reassert themselves, as a reaction no doubt to the 'devil take the hindmost' aspects of Thatcherism. The years became known as the 'caring nineties', reflecting what is surely a central message of the New Testament. The era saw a boom in therapy and counselling. The ideas of Carl Rogers came to the fore, where the therapist's job is to listen to the client and care about them – something for which you need to be an empathetic individual not a trained analyst.

The Green movement became more mainstream. The ideas were not new – Rachel Carson's *Silent Spring* had been on sale since 1962 – but the national mindset suddenly seemed ready for them. The 1986 Chernobyl nuclear accident, with radiation drifting across northern England, had frightened many Britons. In the euro elections of 1989, the Green Party won 15% of the vote. Organizations such as Greenpeace and Friends of the Earth grew in visibility – UK membership of the latter rose from 12,700 to 226,000 between 1984 and 1996. Global warming ceased to be the stuff of science fiction and became a truth accepted by most thoughtful people.

Government, of course, went on. The Major administration suffered a serious blow with 'Black Wednesday', and never really recovered its poise. A 1993 out-take in which Major described three of his cabinet as 'bastards' didn't exactly project the image of a confident, united party. Later, allegations of sleaze enveloped the administration: skulduggery about supplying arms to Saddam Hussein, MPs taking bribes to ask questions in the House, backhanders in Saudi Arabia, the latest episode of the Lord Archer saga . . . Behind this series of PR disasters, the government did a pretty good job: the economy grew, inflation remained low and (from 1994) unemployment fell steadily. But politics is as much about perception as facts. By 1997, an election was due – and Labour had a charismatic new leader with ideas more in tune with the age.

History didn't end in 1989. This stamp, celebrating a building that has watched over the Fens since a time before anyone ever talked about Communism or Capitalism or even Protestantism, is a clear reminder that history is bigger than any one era. But it's true that an era did end with the collapse of the Berlin Wall. After a brief dream of an informal Pax Americana, a multi-polar world began to develop, with countries like China and India quietly (and smokily) growing and growing. Would this multi-polarity later fissure into new, ideological blocs? Francis Fukuyama didn't think so – and a lot of people agreed with him. What was there to get divided about? Surely not the stuff of this first stamp of the new era, religion . . .

CHAPTER THIRTY

DEATH OF A
PEOPLE'S PRINCESS

DIANA COMMEMORATIVE, 26P, 1998

THIS PICTURE of Diana, Princess of Wales, was taken by photographer Tim Graham in 1995. She seems happy and confident in her new role as a kind of global ambassador for goodwill, despite the continuing after-shocks of her marriage break-up. The happiness, however, was something of an illusion.

The era of New Labour began on 5 May 1997. The claim to newness was genuine: this was a radical shift in government. The great themes of Britain's long revolution merged at this moment. Youth had been a catchcry since the rise of rock'n'roll. Now youth had finally earned its place at the top: at 42, Tony Blair was Britain's youngest Prime Minister since Lord Liverpool back in 1812 (and the youngest ever to be elected by a democratic mandate). There was a new social liberalism. New Labour genuinely wanted an inclusive society in a way that the

Conservatives still didn't (as their struggles to preserve a bizarre section in the Local Government Act that forbade authorities 'promoting homosexuality' showed). The percentage of women in parliament nearly doubled with the New Labour victory, from 9.2% to 18.2% (it has moved little higher since). The stiff upper lip was gone from politics: a level of self-knowledge and emotional intelligence was now expected in leaders.

Economically things had changed, too. While Labour were still in opposition, Blair had fought hard against Clause IV of the old party constitution, which committed it to 'common ownership of the means of production, distribution and exchange' – in other words state ownership of all enterprise. This had finally been dropped in 1995. New Labour had a healthy respect for entrepreneurship and for the Wealth Machine.

New Labour seemed to have taken the vigour and candour of the Beatles, the liberalism of Roy Jenkins and the economic realism of Margaret Thatcher, and blended them into a hugely impressive new political force.

The depth of its revolution was soon tested. In the early morning of Sunday 31 August 1997, Diana was killed in a car crash in the Place de l'Alma tunnel in Paris.

An extraordinary outpouring of grief swept the nation. Mourners from all over Britain brought flowers to Buckingham, St James's and Kensington Palaces, and to Harrods, owned by the father of Dodi Al Fayed, who had also died in the accident. Kensington Gardens and the Mall were soon awash with over a million bouquets. Many bore tributes from ordinary families: Diana, with her immense capacity for empathy with the suffering and disadvantaged, had genuinely touched hearts.

The new Prime Minister understood this. He probably didn't 'save' the monarchy by persuading the Queen to come down to London and to fly a flag at half-mast on Buckingham Palace – it's a more robust institution than that – but he certainly spared it an enormous amount of unpopularity. He also captured the mood of the nation in his famous speech on the morning of the death, written, it's said, on the back on an envelope and delivered on national TV from his constituency, Sedgefield in County Durham:

> *I feel like everyone else in this country today. I am utterly devastated. Our thoughts and prayers are with Princess Diana's family, particularly her two sons. Our heart goes out to them ...*
>
> *She touched the lives of so many others in Britain and throughout the world with joy and with comfort. How many times shall we remember her in how many different ways – with the sick, the dying, with children, with the needy? ...*
>
> *She was the People's Princess and that is how she will stay, how she will remain in our hearts and our memories for ever.*

His opposite number, William Hague, failed as thoroughly as Blair had succeeded. His initial reaction seemed to be annoyance that Blair was making 'political capital' out of the death. A gimmicky suggestion that Heathrow Airport be renamed in honour of the Princess did little to make up for that.

Diana's funeral, on 6 September, was a day of national mourning. An estimated three million people lined the route as her body was taken from Kensington Palace to Westminster Abbey. The service itself was remarkable for Elton John singing a specially rewritten version of 'Candle in the Wind', a song originally about Marilyn Monroe – how the old guard must have writhed – and a fiery eulogy from Diana's brother, who promised that her 'blood family' would protect her legacy. The body was then driven to Althorp, the Spencer family home, with well-wishers throwing flowers on the cortège as it passed along the M1.

Looking back on those days, some commentators regard

them as a national embarrassment, like a teenage diary suddenly found at the back of a drawer. But this totally misses the point: it may have been a bit over the top, but the tears were genuine; they were the tears of people who had spent their lives being told to bury their emotions and were now suddenly allowed to let them out. It was a substantial shift in the national sensibility.

Diana's story summed up the changes in British life since the early 1950s. In 1980, the royal family was still basically an early 1950s institution. Life was governed by rules, convention, appearance and hierarchy. Duty was the prime value; how people felt about carrying out that duty was not important. Ranged against this was the new, post-1960s world of personal authenticity, where to put on an act was to be shallow and false. Respect was something you earned by your actions, not something due to social position. Duty was negotiable: good people didn't dispense with the notion, but decided for themselves where it lay.

In essence, Charles belonged to the first world, Diana to the second. A match between them was always going to be an uphill struggle. Added to that difficulty, they brought baggage to the relationship. Both had had difficult upbringings, in that upper-class world where nannies did most of the parenting (Diana's mother had been thrown out of her life when she was six). Neither were particularly mature when they met: Charles, at 32, should have been but wasn't; Diana was 19. Neither received good advice: Charles, in particular, was surrounded by ageing, out-of-touch father figures, and put under intense pressure to marry a virgin bride. The media finally forced the issue with endless speculation about the couple and increasing intrusion into the life of both Diana and the royal family.

Their fairytale marriage on 29 July 1981 was never anything of the sort. Both parties had already experienced doubts: Charles had made his famous 'Whatever love means' comment, and Diana had confided in her sister about her worries, to be told it was too late, she was on the tea towel. Things went into a vicious downward spiral, with Diana finding Charles' old-school reticence (and Palace life in general) unbearable and reacting to this by suffering attacks of bulimia, and Charles unable to deal with this level of emotional intensity and going back to an old flame for support.

Many unhappy relationships enter similar spirals; what was remarkable about this one is that Diana found, alongside her personal unhappiness, a totally unexpected capacity within herself. Her detractors call it an instinct for manipulating the media; her admirers say it was a sincere capacity to reach out to the wretched of the earth and offer genuine compassion. Arguably, it was a bit of both.

Probably the most striking example of this occurred in April 1987, when she was opening the UK's first AIDS ward, at the Middlesex Hospital. Up to that point, most people were terrified of the disease, fearing it could be transmitted by simple physical contact. Diana shook hands with the twelve patients. Her later work on landmines showed a similar mix of compassion and courage. Conflict areas around the world were littered with mines, and politicians were flapping around doing nothing about it, partially out of fear of the arms lobby. Diana not only took up the cause of eradicating these vile weapons, but went to mined areas, embraced dying victims, and even walked across half-cleared minefields.

This capacity made her hugely popular all around the world. As her marriage deteriorated, this popularity emboldened her to take on the Palace. In June 1992, she went public in a confessional (and, it seems, embroidered) book. The couple separated, but carried on squabbling. A war mentality seemed to grip the media and the establishment; everyone taking sides. In 1993 illegally taped phone conversations were released by both sides, each making the other look foolish. The Palace removed Diana's formal title and started cutting her out of official engagements. In 1995, the year of Tim Graham's photograph, she gave her famous TV interview to Martin Bashir. In 1996, the couple divorced.

After that, Diana continued her double life of successfully building her global personal brand but failing to find happiness in personal relationships – except with her children: Prince Harry said of her that 'She never once allowed her unfaltering love for us to go unspoken or undemonstrated.' These words are a fine epitaph. Diana was a standard-bearer for change – in an institution, 'the Firm', clearly desperately in need of it. As such, she is a heroine in this story.

But it's too easy to tell the story as a simple one of brave, sensitive, modern People's Princess versus stuffy, conniving, heartless old order. Diana was not without weaknesses. She had a strong narcissistic streak: many of the friends who helped her out in bad times later found themselves frozen out of her company as she moved on to newer, glitzier environments. Everything that went wrong in her marriage was someone else's fault. She became adept at playing the role of victim – the Bashir interview is the classic example – then abruptly morphing into a 'passive-aggressive' persecutor.

Five stamps were issued in her memory. The Post Office donated all profits, estimated at around £6 million, from the issue to the Diana Princess of Wales fund. The stamps featured photographs from the last ten years of her life (thus obviating the need to refer to fairytale weddings). All the stamps were priced at 26p, the then first-class rate, unlike most issues that try and maximize revenue by including higher values: suitable, it was felt, for a People's Princess. The aim of the issue was to show the princess as 'glamorous and compassionate'. It succeeds – though the stamps also all show her alone.

The notion of 'celebrity' has been around for a long time – isn't the beautiful young queen on the Penny Black a bit of a celeb? Edward VIII certainly was. But modern media have sent the notion into overdrive. It is something British youth have learnt to crave: every *X Factor* contestant wants fame 'more than anything they have ever wanted in their life'. Yet in the end it is an empty promise, as Edward quickly found out. So did Diana, Princess of Wales. The paparazzi who hounded her to her death weren't unnecessary hangers-on but an essential part of the machinery of celebrity. If she was a martyr, she was one to a monster at least partially of her own creation.

The old Britain that was vanquished in 1997 looked down on emotion, glamour and drama from a patrician height. The new Britain embraced all of this, celebrating it as an expression of life. But the events in the Place de l'Alma tunnel on 31 August 1997 were not about life but its opposite. The new post-1997 nation would have a new set of difficulties to face.

CHAPTER THIRTY-ONE

THE MACHINE
(NEARLY) STOPS

LLOYDS OF LONDON 64P, 1999

T ONY BLAIR may or may not have rescued the royal family at the time of Diana's death; he certainly did his best to protect them at a time when many party traditionalists would have gleefully fed them to the media lions. New Labour also befriended another part of Old Labour's demonology, the City of London. It did this via a series of lunches with the big City players, in what became known as its prawn cocktail offensive.

The City had once been a secret, conservative world of middle-aged gentlemen with rolled umbrellas and bowler hats (or silk top hats, if they were partners in Mullens, the government broker). This was changing fast: the new City belonged to the yuppies. It was global, young, public and dynamic – symbolized by the Corporation of Lloyds HQ shown in Brendan Neiland's sharp, classy stamp. No stuffy old guard here, just healthy young moderns ... The trouble was that the new City was also rather scary: the old City had had a strict code of ethics; the new version seemed to have ditched this for a ruthless pursuit of money at all costs.

One thing the new City could not be was ignored. It was growing fast – by the end of the century, it would be producing around 10% of the entire nation's GDP. The markets in which it operated, and in which it claimed to have unrivalled expertise, were becoming ever more important. In 1983, François Mitterrand had tried to introduce a set of traditional socialist policies in france, and global currency markets had turned savagely on the franc, forcing him to change tack. Global financial markets were becoming all-powerful, and politicians ignored them at their peril.

Along with awareness of financial markets' power, a belief was arising that this power was just. The Chicago School of economists, then the dominant force in the discipline, argued that these markets were not only inherently stable but possessed inherently sound judgement. This was due to complex mathematics that seemed to 'prove' market efficiency, but also to the belief that financial markets reflected the pooled opinions of the most able people: a social Darwinian process weeded out the unwise through financial failure. To the historian, who revisits stories of bubbles and crashes from the Dutch Tulip Mania of 1637 onwards, these claims sound odd – but the belief in the efficiency and wisdom of financial markets was one that gained prominence as the old century ended and the new one began.

It's important to understand that the markets where the City operates are not the same as the markets Adam Smith talked about. Smith's markets are for real goods and services, markets where you and I (and businesses) shop around for things or services that we need. We use the things or the services, and soon assess whether they represent value. Providers of the shoddy or overpriced are usually spotted pretty quickly and punished. By contrast, City markets are virtual. A share certificate is a bit of paper; a commodity futures contract may even exist only on a computer. This means that the perception of value is less obvious. It also means that they can be speculated in with much more ease.

Speculation is a necessary part of City markets – it helps keep them liquid, ensuring there are always buyers and sellers. But these markets face a perpetual danger that speculation will overpower them and become their driving force. Against this pressure to over-speculate was the concept of Value Investing. Old-school stock market investors like Warren Buffett look for shares they consider to be underpriced and buy them in the hope that, over time, other people will come to recognize the stock's inherent value, too, and the price will go up. However, during the tech bubble of 1999–2000, a new investment approach became fashionable: the Greater Fool Theory. Traders bought dotcom shares purely in search of short-term gain. They suspected that the underlying companies were rubbish, but there was so much hype around that they calculated that however daft a purchase might have been on objective criteria of value, a week (or an hour) later an even greater fool would come along and pay even more for the stock. This worked for a while – until the greatest fool spent their last dollar.

Which brings us neatly to the financial meltdown (or near-meltdown, anyway) of 2008. Along with Greater Fool thinking, there were three factors at work behind this. One was the increasing deregulation of banks and of markets, the second was the development of ever more complex financial instruments. Behind these was a classic asset bubble whose effects were massively magnified by the first two factors.

Banks take our money and lend it out, many times over, to other people. They get away with this because we don't all turn up at the bank on the same day and ask for our cash. If this does happen, for example because a rumour goes round that the bank is in trouble, there is a bank run (a very good description of such an event is provided in *John Halifax, Gentleman*). This breaks the bank, and all the depositors lose all their money (or the government bails it out). Hence the need for banks to be strictly regulated.

The above is retail or 'high street' banking. Investment or 'merchant' banking is a much more complex activity which involves a great deal of speculation. Traditionally, the two types of banking were kept separate. In America, this separation was enshrined in law by the Glass–Steagall Act, brought in after the 1929 Crash, which made it illegal for financial institutions to participate in both. In Britain, these rules were more informal. These were relaxed somewhat in the City Big Bang of 1986. In 1999 America abolished the Glass–Steagall Act and did away with separation. Britain followed suit: it had little choice, as much of the City was by that time American-owned.

Further US deregulation followed in October 2004. Traditionally, all financial institutions had to adhere to rules about the amounts they could borrow to buy assets. This borrowing is called leverage. In boom times, it's a magic formula for making money. If you have enough capital to buy one x, you can only profit on the rise in value of that x. If you can borrow enough to buy ten xs, you can make ten times as much. Of course, if the market falls . . . But people didn't seem to think the market could fall. Hadn't the Chicago School proven it to be efficient? Old rules about how much leverage banks could use were binned.

The increasing complexity of the entities traded on global financial markets was another post-2000 trend. Ever more ingenious and abstract financial instruments were created. In theory, they were supposed to spread risk – and because of this, they were not controlled: the American authorities, now totally convinced that the market knew best, thought that regulating these instruments would simply lessen their risk-spreading effect. The new instruments were even trumpeted as bringing greater security to the world financial system.

In fact, they were financial time bombs. Collateralized Debt

Obligations (CDOs), were essentially bundles of debt, often mortgages. But nobody knew which actual mortgages were in any bundle. It was assumed that because there were lots of mortgages in any CDO, a few defaults here and there wouldn't matter: there was safety in numbers and thus no need to go through the bundle item by item. And, anyway, you could take out insurance against a CDO going wrong, via an instrument called a Credit Default Swap (CDS). Both instruments were tradable: financial institutions ended up with portfolios of these things with theoretical prices attached to them, but no under-standing of what they actually represented. This was Greater Fool investing, not a search for underlying value.

There had been concern about the US property markets long before the 2008 crash. Traditional standards for assessing mortgage risk had been abandoned. The initial result was that millions of poor people suddenly appeared able to buy really quite swish properties. This was trumpeted as a triumph for the American Dream. In fact it was the old American Nightmare: never give a sucker an even break. These 'sub-prime' mortgages offered terms that were easy to start with but soon became much tougher. People bought them on the old Mr Micawber principle that 'something would turn up'.

In Britain, mortgage lending rules relaxed, too. Traditional mortgage lenders, building societies, were allowed to morph into banks and to relax their once-tight rules. Most aggressive of the new lenders was Northern Rock, which began offering 125% mortgages – the value of the house and some extra money, too.

The assumption behind all this borrowing and lending – US and UK – was that house prices would keep rising. They didn't, of course. The US housing bubble burst in 2006. This should have alerted owners of CDOs, which were suddenly full of unsustainable mortgages on depreciating assets rather than glistening little chunks of the American Dream – but analysts who pointed this out were either ignored or sacked.

As 2007 unfolded, and providers of sub-prime mortgages

began to go bust, banks at last began to examine their CDOs – and realized the toxic rubbish that was inside them. In March 2008, the first big player went under: investment bank Bear Stearns. Bear had always been regarded as the flashiest of the 'big boys': the other large institutions assured the rest of the world that everything was under control. It wasn't. On 7 September, America's two biggest mortgage lenders, the oddly named Freddie Mac and Fannie Mae, had to be rescued by the government. On 15 September, the huge financial house of Lehman Brothers went bankrupt. Shortly afterwards, American insurance giant AIG collapsed under the weight of CDS liabilities and had to be nationalized.

Naturally, these events had repercussions all round the world – but especially in Britain, with its huge financial sector. The first major UK bank to suffer a share price collapse was Bank of Scotland. Its failure was not actually connected with CDOs or CDSs but with conventional bad banking practice – it had written too many sub-prime loans of its own. It was rescued by Lloyds Bank. But then this rescue began to hit problems: had Lloyds bitten off more than it could chew? Another bank looked to be in deep trouble, too: Royal Bank of Scotland, which had loaded itself up with CDOs and CDSs via a subsidiary, Greenwich Capital, then compounded this folly by buying a Dutch bank, ABN Amro, which had also been deeply involved in these instruments.

The stock market began to plummet and, worse, bank depositors to panic. By October 2008, Britain was threatened with a run on *all* its banks. On 10 October, plans were put in place to close every bank and prevent any transactions – even cash machines would have been turned off. The government would then have had to nationalize the entire financial system to prevent it from collapsing. Some commentators have said that at one point, the system was three hours away from this outcome.

Luckily, 10 October 2008 was a Friday. Over the weekend, Prime Minister Gordon Brown and his advisers worked out a rescue package, shoring up the weakest points. It pumped £20 billion into RBS (in return for a 58% stake in the company) and £15 billion into Lloyds. Money was also provided to boost interbank lending, an essential part of the financial system that had all but ground to a halt, as none of the banks trusted any of the others not to go bust.

The rescue worked. Depositors in all UK banks were sufficiently reassured, and decided to keep their money in them, and there was no giant bank run. However other, later interventions proved necessary: further props to RBS, quantitative easing (which sounds a lot like printing money), more funds to oil the interbank market. It is estimated that the British taxpayer has forked out £850 billion to save the financial system since the day the Machine nearly stopped.

These figures can become meaningless. A million pounds' worth of £20 notes makes a stack about as high as a London bus. A billion pounds stacks up to over 5½ kilometres – four times the height of Ben Nevis, the tallest mountain in the UK. The amount spent in saving Royal Bank of Scotland (which taxpayers may or may not get back, depending on how the bank performs in the future) would be a pile of over 110 km, which takes us beyond the Karman Line, the recognized boundary between the Earth's atmosphere and outer space. The rescue package for the entire financial system takes us to nearly 5,000 km – we're on our way to the Moon!

But at least we still have a banking system. What next? Many people would like to see the City taken down a peg or three; and the sight of banks continuing to pay out massive bonuses heightens this desire. Yet at the same time, the City is a necessary part of the Wealth Machine. With its virtual markets in shares, currency and commodities, it is not inherently bad; these are a part of a bigger whole, a part of a productive system that has been allowed to poach way, way more than its fair share of the wealth generated by that system. How can proportion be re-established?

A report in 2011 by former Chief Economist of the Bank of England, Sir John Vickers, came up with a set of proposals for re-regulating the UK banking sector. These include rules on leverage and splitting banking's investment and high-street aspects. However, Vickers does not insist that the investment–high street split be total; both can be carried on by entities owned by the same organization – a ruling that falls short of what Glass and Steagall made mandatory in America after 1929. Banks are also to be given some freedom as to which activities they place in which category. And, while Sir John recommends that banks be encouraged to implement changes as soon as possible, the date by which he says the changes should be in place is 2019. This is both to give the banks time and to fit in with new global banking rules, known as Basel III.

Many people fear that these recommendations do not go far enough (the banks, of course, think they are draconian). If our attitude to 10 October 2008 is really 'never again', then surely high-street and investment banking should be carried on by totally separate entities? The 2019 date gives the banks time to lobby ever harder, plead poverty and generally hope that by then people will have forgotten the meltdown.

Yet even if banks do ultimately comply with Vickers, this will only solve part of the problem. 'Virtual' City markets, which have turned out to be neither efficient nor wise but dangerously unstable, are in need of some kind of regulation. A tax has been suggested on trades in these markets, along lines originally suggested by Maynard Keynes and more recently by Nobel laureate James Tobin, which might dampen the excessive enthusiasm of speculators. However such reforms need to be carried out on the global level – which makes them impossible, some people argue. But without them, it will only be a matter of time before the Machine nearly stops again. Or will it be 'nearly' this time?

Prawn cocktail, anyone?

CHAPTER THIRTY-TWO

FIRE AND LIGHT

FIRE AND LIGHT
MILLENNIUM ISSUE, 26P, 2000

THE NEW millennium produced a flurry of philatelic activity. In the run-up to it, a series of forty-eight 'tale' stamps appeared, a tale a month, focusing on different aspects of British life – the Inventors' Tale, the Travellers' Tale and so on. After the big event (when 1999 became 2000), a Millennium Project series followed a similar format, with forty-eight more stamps on various themes, more poetic in nature – the example above comes from the second of this series, entitled Fire and Light. The Fire and Light quartet showed a millennium beacon, a bolt of lightning, city lights and this fire-driven steam engine from the Welsh Highland Railway by photographer George Kavanagh.

None of the ninety-six special stamps featured the Millennium Dome. The idea of a jolly to celebrate the millennium was originated by John Major's government; when he was replaced, the idea went into overdrive. The Dome was intended to become a symbol of New Labour's New Britain, 'a triumph of confidence over cynicism, boldness over blandness, excellence over mediocrity', to quote Tony Blair.

It didn't really work out like that. To be fair to the Dome, it was reasonably successful. Over six million people visited it and underwent its 'Millennium Experience', which is not exactly a failure. Most of these visitors were positive about the Experience – a set of themed (and corporate-sponsored) Zones, plus ambient entertainment – though the critics were uniformly negative. However, somehow the Dome didn't live up to the hype: we had been told 10 million people would visit and have their socks blown off by the show. And, of course, it ended up costing more than expected – the Lottery fund had to fork out £600 million rather than the £400 million it had originally been told to set aside. After December 2000, when the Dome closed, a decision had to be made as to what to do with it. For a while it sat there, costing £1 million a month and doing odd jobs – probably its best use was in winter 2004 as a shelter for homeless people. Finally, it found its niche as the O2 Arena, opening in 2007 as a venue for big rock and pop gigs plus a cinema and restaurants. The London Eye, another millennium attraction, was introduced with much less fanfare and quietly became hugely popular, remaining so to this day. Hype always runs the risk of disappointment. It's also rather un-British.

The story of the Dome captures what went wrong with New Labour: they just got too good at the talk. The new millennium became the era of spin. No policy was ever wrong, it was 'the message' that hadn't been 'communicated correctly'. This is the world as understood by postmodernist philosophers, where there is no reality, only constructs, and where politics (and everything else) is about who can create the best illusion, not actually do things better. Even the Post Office suffered at the hands of the spinners, undergoing a £2 million revamp of its image that lumbered it with a new and meaningless name,

Consignia, which people said reminded them of a deodorant or a walk-on part in an opera. Postal employees refused to use the name, and it was later quietly ditched.

Reality hit the new era with a sickening crunch on 11 September 2001. The attack on New York's World Trade Center was global: citizens of over ninety countries died, including sixty-seven Britons. It re-polarized the world, with a new set of bad guys, the terrorist organization al-Qaeda.

To fight this new menace, it was deemed necessary to invade Afghanistan, a country that had been harbouring the terrorists. As the Taliban government in Kabul had no intention of handing them over, this was probably inevitable: the West had to find out what other plans al-Qaeda had. But as with many invasions, there was no proper exit plan. Fighting terrorists is not like fighting a country: drive them out of one place and they will resurface somewhere else. The new millennium brought with it a new kind of war, which the West is still learning how to fight.

After Afghanistan, the next place to be invaded was Iraq. The campaign was controversial from the start. Iraq's dictator Saddam Hussein had no connection with terrorism: al-Qaeda leader Osama bin Laden despised him as a 'Scotch-drinking, woman-chasing apostate'. Yet President Bush had decided that Saddam must be destroyed as part of what he called his War on Terror. Tony Blair agreed. By 2002 it was clear that America and Britain were going, arm in arm, to war with Saddam. Bush and Blair launched a diplomatic offensive to get other countries on board, but it was not hugely successful – most countries coughed up a few hundred troops; many refused to participate.

On 15 February 2003, a million people marched through London to protest against the war – the largest demonstration in British history. Observers noted the wide cross-section of British society who attended. (Among the demonstrators was stamp designer David Gentleman, who had designed his own banner, featuring a bloodstain in the O of the simple slogan

'No!') However, the protest was ignored; Iraq was invaded on 20 March by 150,000 US and 46,000 British troops. The next biggest contingent was 3,600 South Koreans. The invasion was clinically effective; on 1 May President Bush announced 'Mission Accomplished'. Game over – by the old rules of war. In fact, the problems had only just begun.

Iraq collapsed into lawlessness. This was made much worse by the decision to disband the country's old army and police force. Attacks by suicide bombers became commonplace – on occupying forces and on other Iraqis: the destruction of the state had unleashed furious sectarian hatred. The attacks carried on for four years until, in 2007, a US troop surge – 20,000 extra soldiers – brought some order back to the streets, though it didn't prevent all the bombings, including a horrific attack on a minority Kurdish sect, the Yazidis, later that year, when nearly 800 people were killed.

The war probably did leave Iraq better off, though that is still debated – but for Blair it was a PR disaster. He was seen as having been a toady to Bush. The war was a powerful recruitment tool for al-Qaeda – the recruits later including the four young men who carried out the London Tube bombings. It did huge damage to Britain's reputation in the Arab world. Arguably worst of all, Blair was seen by many as having used deceit to convince the British public that the war was necessary.

The official reason for invading Iraq was that Saddam had broken his commitment not to make weapons of mass destruction (WMDs). However, the evidence for this was not strong. So, between 2 and 24 September 2002, what evidence there was got 'sexed up' by the New Labour spin machine, to create what later became known as the dodgy dossier. Part of this process involved highlighting a claim that the dictator could launch a chemical or biological attack on British troops in Cyprus within 45 minutes. This claim, which is believed to have originated with a Baghdad taxi driver, was later found to be false, and was quietly retracted in 2004. Once Iraq was invaded, no WMD were found.

Did Bush and Blair have any other justification for invasion? Iraq was a thorny problem. The US and the UK were applying sanctions to the country, which Saddam was ignoring, letting his own people suffer the consequences: estimates of what this implied vary, but 170,000 'excess deaths' as a result of malnutrition or polluted water is an accepted figure. So something different had to be tried. In addition, the concept of liberal intervention had been gaining ground through the late 1990s/ early 2000s. This had effectively worked in Kosovo (1999) and Sierra Leone (1999–2002). But the objectives had been simple: in Kosovo to liberate an oppressed ethnic group and in Sierra Leone to rescue a failing UN intervention in a country being torn apart by civil war. To march into a functioning sovereign state, depose its ruler and dismantle its apparatus of government were all steps beyond these.

The loss of faith in the new government caused by the Iraq war and the way it was spun was considerable. Defenders of the Blair government reply that it was not unique in its use of spin. Doesn't everybody do it? Arguably Winston Churchill's majestic speeches were spin. However, this administration did seem to take it to new levels. On the day of the World Trade Center atrocity, Jo Moore, a press officer at the Department of Transport and Local Government, circulated an email: 'It's now a very good day to get out anything we want to bury. Councillors' expenses?' Emails along similar lines were sent on the day that Princess Margaret died.

The death in July 2003 of David Kelly, a weapons expert who had questioned the dodgy dossier, added a new, sinister dimension to the debate. Did spinning include killing people who opposed the message? Answer, no: despite the usual conspiracy theories that spring up around events like this, it's clear that Kelly took his own life. But there's still a nasty suspicion that one of the factors in his suicide was the aggressive response of the spin machine to this gentle, conscientious professional.

Spin corroded public trust in politicians. This trust was in trouble already: since 1945, at elections had consistently been around 75%, but in the 2005 election it was 61%. In 2009, this trust received another body blow when details of MPs' expenses claims were published, in tabloid fashion, by the once-sedate *Daily Telegraph*. The paper milked this for weeks, coming up with ever more outrageous stories: the most infamous being the £2,000 duck island at the home of Tory MP Sir Peter Viggers. The new national mood was reflected by a notice seen in an Edinburgh shop: 'No more than two MPs allowed at a time'. Very funny – but dangerous, really. Democracy is still the best bulwark against leaders' creeping conviction of their total rightness. If democracy becomes a joke, then we are much less well protected.

The New Labour administration achieved a great deal. Best of all, perhaps, was peace in Northern Ireland – a huge topic that needs a chapter of its own. It also introduced a minimum wage, a civilized piece of legislation (wage levels are not the prime barrier to new employment; that is the bureaucracy attached to the process of employing people, something, sadly, the Blair government did little to improve). It doubled the number of women in parliament. It spent billions of pounds improving the stock of social housing. It worked to redress the north–south imbalance: Orgreave, for example, now boasts a Technology Park built by the Regional Development Agency in 2005. It provided nursery places for millions of preschool children. It doubled the international aid budget and badgered other rich countries into giving more to poorer ones. It spent money on the NHS and schools (whether all that money was wisely spent is another matter, but some of it certainly was). It presided over steady, non-inflationary growth, until an essentially global crisis knocked the world economy off its feet. It shunted mainstream political debate on social issues back to the centre: when Labour lost the general election in 2010, the new Conservative Prime Minister David Cameron took on many of its more liberal attitudes.

Sadly, New Labour also got so addicted to spinning that if you tell people the above, they simply shrug. It's politics. It's probably all made up ... Such is the tragedy of New Labour: the Fire and Light of Tony Blair's original and powerful vision dissolving into the Smoke and Mirrors of spin.

CHAPTER THIRTY-THREE

THANKSGIVING

CELEBRATING NORTHERN IRELAND, 78P

WE LEFT Ireland in 1850, hanging our heads in shame at the sufferings inflicted on the people of that island. This attractive stamp, based on an image by Belfast photographer Tony Pleavin, tells a different story. It shows a bridge, symbolic of dialogue between opposites, bright lights and a shining silver angel. What happened in between? The answer, sadly, is much stupidity, cruelty, bigotry and bloodshed. However, the story does appear to have a happy ending.

Even after the horrors of the famine, reform in Ireland was painfully slow. It wasn't till the 1870s that land ownership began to be prised away from the absentee landlords. Around that time, the movement for Irish independence (Home Rule) found its greatest champion, Charles Stewart Parnell – who might have enabled a peaceful transition to an Irish state, had he not been brought down by a scandal about his private life. Instead, the route to statehood became a violent one.

Maybe it always would have been violent. In six of the nine counties of the old kingdom of Ulster, a Protestant majority was vehemently opposed to Irish independence. When a Home Rule bill was passed in 1914, an armed insurrection looked likely to break out in the north; it was prevented by the outbreak of the First World War. Instead, the insurrection took place in the south, the 1916 Easter Rising. This was put down, but the message had got across. After the war, the only possible solution was brought about in 1921: a divided Ireland, with an independent Free State in the south, and the north opting to become part of the United Kingdom. It seemed, at the time, a logical solution, but there were still difficulties.

A third of the population of the new UK province of Northern Ireland was Catholic. But from very early on in the life of the province, electoral boundaries and the voting system itself were rigged to produce strong Protestant majorities on local councils and in Stormont, the legislative body. Protestants soon secured a stranglehold on the top positions in society. The civil service was largely Protestant – in 1943, Catholics held none of the top fifty-five jobs. The Royal Ulster Constabulary – an armed force unlike mainland bobbies – was 90% Protestant. A similar percentage was to be found in many of the province's big employers (at shipbuilders Harland and Wolff in 1971, the figure was 96%).

Behind this lay the power of the Orange Order, a Protestant organization to which you had to belong if you wanted to get ahead in Ulster life. This would have been bad enough had the Order operated quietly behind the scenes, but it flaunted its power in annual marches, often through Catholic areas. (Most towns in Northern Ireland were strictly segregated, with Catholics and Protestants living in different parts, attending different schools, getting different jobs and hardly ever socializing.)

The reaction of the Catholic minority was, for most of the time, to put up with the situation. There had always been the option for angry young men to join the IRA, but, apart from spikes of activity in the 1920s and 1950s, that organization had enjoyed little support before the Troubles began to turn really vicious.

What of the Protestants? Descendants of colonists who came over from Scotland in the seventeenth and eighteenth centuries, they had long been painfully aware of their minority status in the island of Ireland. They were also aware that the Britain that they so eagerly wanted to belong to – and for which many of them had fought and died in the First World War – seemed to want as little as possible to do with them. They were afraid of the power of the Catholic Church in the South: Orangemen saw themselves as the little guys fighting for freedom against an overweening medieval theocracy. This is the real irony of Northern Ireland: both sides see themselves as oppressed and threatened minorities.

As the 1960s came along, demands for change grew. The question was, as it had been in the days of Parnell, could this be achieved peacefully? A new Ulster Prime Minister, Terence O'Neill, tried to break down some of the barriers. This did not hugely impress the Catholics and split the Protestant community, with men like Ian Paisley denouncing such truckling to Popery. The Catholics, inspired by American Civil Rights activists, began to create political organizations such as the Northern Ireland Civil Rights Association (NICRA) which had, for the first time in Ulster Catholic political life, real energy.

The Protestants, suspicious that NICRA had links with the IRA, responded to this change with violence. The first sectarian murders were committed by members of the Ulster Volunteer Force in 1966. On 5 October 1968, a Civil Rights march in Derry (officially known as Londonderry, but Derry is the original name and is the one used by most of the city's inhabitants) turned into a fight between marchers and police. The marchers were unarmed; the police had batons and water cannon; seventy-seven marchers, and no police, ended up in hospital.

Violence escalated further in 1969. Tensions had been rising in Derry throughout the year: what set off the explosion was another march – a Protestant one, this time, by an Orange-style organization, the Apprentice Boys of Derry. Local Catholics gathered to protest; the protest was forcefully policed; a full-scale riot broke out, with some parts of the Bogside, a poor Catholic area, being barricaded and becoming a no-go area for police. The Northern Irish Prime Minister requested that London send troops to patrol the area instead. At first the Army was welcomed by the Catholics, who saw it as much more impartial than the RUC. But at the same time, rioting broke out in Belfast. Seven people died in these disturbances, five Catholic and two Protestant; 1,800 properties were damaged, most of them Catholic.

The IRA had been an insignificant player in the proceedings up to that point. In late '69, it split, with a new, more violent wing, the Provisionals, taking the initiative. In July 1970, the Army responded to this new threat by carrying out aggressive house-to-house searches on the Catholic Falls Road in Belfast. They found weapons (but few belonging to the Provisionals) and in the process did a lot of damage to properties. An attempt to place a curfew on the same area resulted in four deaths, none of individuals connected with terrorist organizations. These actions ended the honeymoon between the Catholic population and the Army.

In February 1971, the IRA ambushed and killed five techni-cians on their way to service a BBC transmitter, and murdered three off-duty soldiers. The new Northern Ireland Prime Minister, Brian Faulkner, responded with internment of known IRA members without trial – or tried to: the move was an operational failure (most IRA members got away) and a political disaster (thirty-five people died in violence in the three weeks after the policy was instigated). Throughout the year, killings increased – the IRA and the Army now being the warring sides, with the usual high level of innocent victims caught in the cross-fire. In December the UVF reappeared, blowing up a Catholic bar and killing fifteen people.

The year 1972 began with Bloody Sunday, where troops shot at unarmed marchers in Derry, killing thirteen. The IRA started using car bombs, a particularly sinister and cowardly weapon against innocent bystanders. The UVF preferred to pick off individuals it disliked. Nearly 500 people died in the violence that year.

Attempts at political reform did little to stop this downward spiral, which instead spread to the Irish Free State and the mainland of Britain: in 1974 the Dublin and Monaghan bombings of 17 May and the Birmingham pub bombings of 21 November between them killed over fifty people (as usual, individuals who had no connection to Ulster or its politics). Back in the province, murders continued, too: the shooting of three members of a popular group, the Miami Showband (recently commemorated on an Irish stamp) in early 1975 seemed especially pointless, as did the Kingsmills atrocity of January 1976, when an IRA unit stopped a rural bus, ordered everyone off and shot ten people. In Belfast itself, the ultimate depths were plumbed by a loyalist gang called the Shankill Butchers, who specialized in kidnapping Catholics at random, then killing them after subjecting them to torture.

The province seemed to be hurtling towards civil war, with its political leaders (and Britain's) incapable of providing a solution. Shamefully, its religious leaders also appeared incapable. On 10 August 1976, an IRA member was shot dead in a car chase. By then, this was not an uncommon event – but the car crashed into a family and killed three children. The mother, Anne Maguire, was so traumatized that the children's aunt, Mairead Corrigan, had to identify the bodies – after which she went straight to the studios of Ulster TV, asked to go on air and made a powerful appeal for the violence to end. Betty Williams, another local woman who had witnessed the tragedy, began petitioning door-to-door to stop the violence and soon had 6000 signatures. A rally was organized in Catholic Andersonstown, but people came from the Protestant Shankill to attend as well. The movement called the Peace People had started.

Its first manifesto ran:

We have a simple message to the world . . . We want to live and love and build a just and peaceful society. We want for our children, as we want for ourselves, our lives at home, at work, and at play to be lives of joy and Peace. We recognise that to build such a society demands dedication, hard work, and courage. We recognise that there are many problems in our society which are a source of conflict and violence. We recognise that every bullet fired and every exploding bomb make that work more difficult. We reject the use of the bomb and the bullet and all the techniques of violence. We dedicate ourselves to working with our neighbours, near and far, day in and day out, to build that peaceful society in which the tragedies we have known are a bad memory and a continuing warning.

Sadly, this message did not stop the killing. But it did introduce the voice of sanity and morality into the debate. Before these ordinary, working-class women spoke up, an average of 300 people a year were dying in the violence; after them, the level dropped and stayed around 125. Of course, other factors were involved in this fall in casualties: the end of internment, for example – a new policy was followed, of using the law to punish terrorists. A toughening up of anti-terrorist activity, involving the SAS, also helped. But these high-level policies would not have been nearly as effective without those voices from the street simply crying 'Enough!'

The new policy of using the law seemed right, but it back-fired. Interned paramilitary prisoners had been treated like prisoners of war; now they were treated like ordinary criminals. Protests against this change became ever more dramatic, culminating in a series of hunger strikes in 1981, in which ten men died. Throughout this horrific process, the new(ish) Thatcher government refused to budge an inch, a response that played into the hands of the IRA. By taking their claim of special political status to the ultimate end, the hunger strikers won their argument: ordinary crooks don't do this.

The immediate result of this propaganda victory was just more killings, some on the British mainland, some in the province. However, the leader of the hunger strikers, Bobby Sands, had been put up as a nationalist candidate at a by-election and had won. Until that point, the IRA had looked down on what it called 'electoralism', but it now realized quite how many people would vote for them: this was a new way of getting their voice heard. At the time, this was seen as a threat in London, but in the long term it helped bring about peace, the start of the process whereby militant nationalists progressed from simple terrorism through 'the Armalite and the ballot box', to finally putting down the Armalite.

The 1980s and much of the 1990s were a period of ten steps forward, nine steps back. An Anglo-Irish Agreement was signed in 1985, creating new structures for co-operation between London and Dublin, and overriding the traditional southern Irish insistence on a United Ireland. This infuriated Unionists, whose politicians went into sulk mode for years and whose terrorists upped their violence. In case anyone began to think the IRA, with its new political wing, had become a decent, humane organization, it developed a new technique: a Catholic man who worked in an army canteen was kidnapped, chained to a vehicle and made to drive it to an army checkpoint, where it blew him, and five soldiers, to bits.

High-level political changes came in 1990: John Major

replaced Margaret Thatcher in Downing Street and Mary Robinson was elected President of Ireland. Major took a more nuanced approach to Ireland than the Iron Lady. Robinson changed the image of the Irish Republic. She was married to a Protestant; she was a noted liberal with a genuine passion for human rights; she was also incredibly likeable, proving massively popular in her country. This remarkable lady and the support for her went a long way to dispelling the old Unionist perception of the South as a freedom-hating theocracy waiting to gobble up its northern neighbour.

But still the old ways reasserted themselves. In 1993, the IRA plunged the province back into the seventies mindset by setting off a bomb in the Shankill Road that killed ten people, including four women and two children. Reprisals followed. But, as in 1976, a groundswell of public revulsion at the violence prevented escalation into civil war. Meanwhile, John Major plugged away at the peace process, ably assisted by nationalist politician John Hume. In 1994 the Downing Street Declaration was made: nobody was entirely sure what it declared, but shortly afterwards, the IRA announced a ceasefire. Loyalist paramilitary groups followed suit, even issuing an apology for their actions. Ulster being Ulster, some people at both extremes distanced themselves from these moves, but the new tone had been set.

Of course, new arguments then began: how could one side be sure that the other had really abandoned their weapons? Despite the interest of US President Bill Clinton in the proceedings and the setting up of an independent panel on 'decommissioning' headed by a skilled American politician, George Mitchell, the peace process got bogged down in mistrust. It took a change of government in the UK to get it moving again: 1997, and the Blair revolution.

It wasn't Blair himself who made the big difference, but his Northern Ireland Secretary, Mo Mowlam. This remarkable woman insisted on talking with as many people as possible

– even visiting Maze prison where she sat and talked, one to one, with convicted loyalist murderers. On 10 April 1998, the Good Friday Agreement was signed. There are many strands to this: to simplify, it set up a new Northern Ireland legislative assembly, a power-sharing executive body, an independent review on policing, a human rights commission to tackle (amongst other things) prejudice in the workplace, and agreements on prisoner release and troop withdrawals. Referenda in the Republic and Northern Ireland endorsed this agreement heartily. Then in August of the same year, one of the worst atrocities of the Troubles was committed: the Omagh bombing, which killed twenty-nine shoppers, including four children and a pregnant woman, in a country town.

This bomb was placed by the Real IRA, a splinter group committed to carrying on violence. Such is the danger of Northern Ireland politics. The more the majority desire, work for and create peace, the more a tiny minority of fanatics try to rekindle the hatred of the mid-1970s. In the long run, the only remedy for this is to rise above the provocation. A shining and deeply moving example of such rising was provided by Gordon Wilson, whose daughter was killed by an IRA bomb in Enniskillen in 1987 and who soon after said: 'I bear no ill will. I bear no grudge ... I will pray for these men tonight and every night.'

In 2007 one-time Protestant hardliner Ian Paisley and former IRA man Martin McGuinness sat down together in the second Northern Ireland Assembly. The same year also saw the erection of the fine statue celebrated on this stamp, the Angel of Thanksgiving (also known as 'The Belle on the Ball' or 'Nuala with the Hula'). It is of a woman, standing on a globe, holding aloft a ring, symbol of unity and wholeness. Around it, the modern city of Belfast gets on with its busy life – hopefully, now, for good.

CHAPTER THIRTY-FOUR

CHIPS WITH EVERYTHING

WORLD OF INVENTION, 72P, 2007

ARGUABLY NOTHING has done more to change British life in the last fifty years than the rise of the computer. However, the world of stamps has been relatively silent about this revolution. A 1982 issue celebrated Information Technology (IT) Year with two elongated stamps featuring equipment that now looks as antique as a Chippendale chair. In 1991 the bicentenary of the birth of computer pioneer Charles Babbage was commemorated. Alan Turing has appeared twice, as part of the Inventors' Tale millennium issue and as one of ten Britons of Distinction in 2012. And there is the stamp above from 2007, a witty celebration of the World Wide Web by Peter Till.

The rise of the computer industry has created millions of jobs in Britain. Whole new professions have arisen: in programming, in software, in IT consultancy, in the manufacture and repair of computers and peripherals. This has created opportunities for bright young people from all backgrounds to sidestep old career ladders and find new paths to success. At the same time, robotics and automation have destroyed traditional manufacturing jobs. The overall effect has been to upskill the workforce but to make life tougher for the unskilled. The IT revolution is Joseph Schumpeter's creative destruction in full cry.

In private life, IT has radically affected the way everyone lives. Most of the products that we regard as essentially modern – DVD players, satnavs, mobile phones, iPods and iPads – rely on what are effectively tiny internal computers, often with more power than a 1960s mainframe. Traditional products have been revolutionized, too: cars and household appliances almost all feature chip-based control systems. This has made them much more reliable and responsive but at the cost of simplicity. Years ago, a competent enthusiast with a decent set of tools and a Haynes manual could fix their own car – easy! Now the gadgets that surround us are more wonderful but less approachable. We have traded a simple, homespun power for enhanced functionality, and a certain robustness has died in the process.

Arguably the first computer was Tommy Flowers' Colossus, built at the Post Office Research Station at Dollis Hill in 1943 – after which it was taken to Bletchley Park. This machine, which filled a room, used 1,500 valves, the best technology available at the time. By the early 1950s, the first commercial computers, built mainly in America, were using transistors, of the kind that teenagers had in their radios. The first chip – a tiny electronic circuit on a base of germanium (the base was soon replaced with silicon) – was made in America in 1959, by Jack Kilby, who later won the Nobel Prize for his creation.

Initial demand for the lighter but costlier computers that resulted from Kilby's breakthrough came from government: NASA needed onboard computers for the new Apollo spacecraft and the US Army needed guidance systems for its Minuteman missiles.

In 1965, Intel co-founder Gordon Moore predicted that the

power of chips – specifically the number of transistors that could affordably be fitted on to one – would double every two years. The prediction was more in the spirit of an intelligent guess than the announcement of a scientific rule, but since that date his words have turned out to be extraordinarily prescient, so that people now talk about Moore's Law.

As chips followed this 'law', a new and very different market appeared for them – personal computers. The first of these were developed not by government or big corporations but by hobbyists: in 1974, you could buy an Altair computer kit for $440 (an early purchaser was a young enthusiast called William Gates III).

Like many technology products, the new personal computers went through a cycle of public scepticism, interest (gosh, it does work after all!), hype, disappointment and finally equilibrium where workable, reliable products become available, with specific well-understood uses (for PCs, these were word processing, simple accounts and games). The end point of this cycle was reached in the early 1980s, with the arrival of the IBM PC and the Apple Mac, the latter with its user-friendly graphical interface (the old PCs used typed commands). In the UK, Amstrad introduced its word processor as well as a range of budget PCs. But these machines still sat in the corners of people's homes. It took another technological development to bring them to the central position they now hold: the Internet.

Computers were originally solitary beasts that didn't communicate with one another. In the late 1960s the American military changed this, linking its computing centres via a system called ARPANET. The first message sent across this network was the command 'Login' – or should have been: it got as far as L, O, then crashed. In the 1970s and 1980s civilian networks were set up, linking universities and other research organizations. (Note how these initiatives were, like Colossus and the first chips, government funded: the modern Internet is full of bloggers bemoaning the evils of the state, but these people are happily riding on an information highway originally provided by government.) In 1989, the basic principles of the modern World Wide Web were established by Tim Berners-Lee, a British scientist working at CERN.

The Internet went commercial in the mid-1990s, with the rise of big service providers. It was still pretty slow going, however: readers of a certain age will remember, probably with some amusement, that weird ululating as your modem tried to hook up with the system and the feeling of relief when something actually appeared on the screen. Once online, users could send emails, join online clubs, and chat with people round the world – often realizing after a while that a dull person in Lima or Medicine Hat was as dull as the local pub bore, but sometimes making real connections. There were a few pioneering online stores, where visitors could buy things as long as the site didn't freeze halfway through placing the order. There was a vaguely frontier feel about the whole experience. Despite the obvious clunkiness of much of the technology, a stock market bubble followed in 1999–2000, with worthless dotcom stocks changing hands for huge sums of money.

As the 2000s unfolded, broadband did away with the old, squeaking modems and crashing sites. Nevertheless, the net was still a place where you either exchanged one-to-one emails or looked at other people's sites: preparing your own site was costly and sites were hard to change once set up. This ended with the development of Web 2.0 technology: the rise of simple blogging software and social media sites like Twitter and Facebook meant that everyone could now have an online voice. The modern net is participatory, democratic – the conversation that its advocates had always said it would be.

It is also a gold mine. A 2010 report from Boston Consulting Group estimated the value of Britain's Internet sector at £100 billion – only a little less than the financial sector (and a lot more stable), and bigger than the transport or utility industries. Unlike the rest of the economy, it's scheduled to grow, too – the report estimates it may represent 10% of Britain's GDP by 2015. A chunk of this comes from export: British online business is imaginative and globally successful. It is also diverse: much of this money came from small e-commerce sites, which led the report's co-author Paul Zwillenberg to say that Britain has now become 'a nation of digital shopkeepers'.

The Net is not without its critics. Is it creating a nation of computer addicts, sitting alone at their terminals, apparently connected to the world but not really connected, in any deep sense, to anyone? Have twentieth-century critics like Martin Pawley who feared that technology was taking us into a totally 'Private Future' been justified?

Probably not. The World Wide Web has made Britons better connected, within the UK and globally. The rise of social media shows that, once technology makes it possible, what people want to do above all is to communicate with each other. The Net has allowed individuals with minority interests to link up and share mutual enthusiasms. It has enabled those with an entrepreneurial streak to set up small, low-cost businesses and find customers all round the world. It has enabled everyone to access more information and thus take more control over their lives: knowledge is power, and the knowledge is out there.

The obvious analogy is, of course, with Penny Post, a century and a half earlier. But the analogy raises the question: will the Internet kill the product of this earlier revolution? Growth in the Post Office's letter business had been almost constant since 1840, but since 2000 it has gone into a steep decline. Maybe it's not surprising that IT rarely features on stamps.

Philatelic optimists point out that the great era of letter writing was way back in the days of the Penny Lilac: the claim that email has killed the letter is excessive; the telephone was the real perpetrator of this crime. Much modern post consists of Christmas and birthday cards, which still need stamps. And the post remains busy: online shopping has actually given postmen more to deliver. Royal Mail is still delivering 59 million letters a day. Despite the rise of the World Wide Web celebrated so wittily in this stamp, stamp lovers need not despair.

CHAPTER THIRTY-FIVE

THE PRINCE AND THE MERITOCRAT

ROYAL WEDDING MINISHEET, 2011

A MONG THE range of souvenirs celebrating the marriage of Prince William and Catherine Middleton was a set of stamps. The set could only be bought as a 'mini-sheet', costing just over £3; people in search of more exclusive philatelic mementoes could buy the stamps in a range of formats, all the way up to a First Day Cover with a gold royal wedding coin in it, retailing at £1,750. They are attractive items: two photographs taken at St James's Palace by Mario Testino, one formal, the other more informal. But how many actually escaped the mini-sheet and were used to send something through the post? There is a strange, postmodern artificiality about this: stamps as keepsakes rather than actual things to put on envelopes and use.

The marriage itself seems to be based on more solid ground. William and Catherine met at St Andrews University in 2001, where they started going out. They broke up in 2007, but got back together again a few months later. This is a relationship that has had time to breathe and grow. The couple became engaged in 2010. Later, it was announced that the wedding would take place on 29 April 2011.

As usual, Britain surprised itself. A few weeks beforehand, polls showed a lack of interest in the event: only a third said they would watch the wedding on TV, with another third saying they weren't sure. There were grumbles about the cost, from the usually right-of-centre Taxpayers' Alliance and various anti-monarchist groups on the left. Employers' organizations whinged about there being a public holiday for the event. Then when it happened, Britain turned on its TVs and was blown away by the colour, the splendour and the sheer optimism of it all.

It was in many ways a deeply traditional occasion. The venue, Westminster Abbey, is reputed to have been founded in the seventh century, though the current version only goes back to Edward the Confessor, who began building it around 1040. Along with the uniform of an Irish Guards officer, the Prince wore the blue sash of a Knight of the Garter, an order founded by Edward III in 1348. The anthem that greeted the bride as she processed up the aisle was Parry's *I was Glad*, a relative newcomer, composed for the coronation of Edward VII in 1902 (along with *Land of Hope and Glory*). Many of the guests were ceremonial: world and Commonwealth leaders, members of the political and military establishment. Sean Brady, the Catholic Primate of All Ireland, was there, too; an attractively inclusive gesture towards a man who has done much to create dialogue in Ulster.

However, as William is not immediate heir to the throne, it was technically not a state occasion, so the couple could also create their own guest list. This included the owner of their favourite bar in Mustique, David and Victoria Beckham, Rowan Atkinson, Sir Elton John, Joss Stone and (from both sides) a smattering of exes. In its own way, the wedding marked breaks with tradition.

Nobody in direct line to the throne had ever officially married a 'commoner' before (in 1785, the future George IV and Maria Fitzherbert had had a secret, legally invalid ceremony). Diana, remember, was an aristocrat, Lady Diana in her own right (she once pointed out to the Windsors that her title was older than theirs). The Middletons are meritocrats. Catherine's great-grandmother worked in a shop and made clothes as a sideline. Her grandfather ran a haulage business. However the real family wealth comes from a business started by her mother, Carole. Party Pieces began as a mail-order company operating from a shed in the Middletons' back garden in 1978. Like many entrepreneurs, Carole was a frustrated consumer, in her case angry at the difficulty of getting decent trappings for children's parties, and reckoned she could do better herself. She was right: the business is now estimated to be worth millions of pounds.

The family is clearly one of strong women. As such, it dovetails with a key theme of the new century. In the 1980s women were moving into the workplace in ever increasing numbers. This trend has continued. A recent survey has shown that among new entrants to the workforce, young women now earn more than young men. This may mark the overturning of an age-old inequality: women are beginning to outperform men in the education stakes, and education is what the modern working world needs.

If the first child of the union celebrated on 29 April 2011 is a girl, she will be heir to the throne, a change long argued for and finally agreed at the recent Commonwealth conference. At the same conference, the Queen made a speech highlighting the role of women in the future:

> *The theme of this year is 'Women as Agents of Change'. It*
> *reminds us of the potential in our societies that is yet to be*
> *fully unlocked, and it encourages us to find ways to allow*

*girls and women to play their full part. We must continue
to strive in our own countries and across the Commonwealth
together to promote that theme in a lasting way beyond
this year.*

The women of Britain march on. Meanwhile, men have had
to find new roles and role models.

Back in the Victorian era, the ideal was clear: the gentleman.
Its hijacking by the public schools nearly destroyed it, but it
survived. Into the twenty-first century? In Victorian times, to
say a man was 'not a gentleman' was to seriously impugn their
character. Nowadays to be called one remains a compliment,
but it is essentially an optional extra.

A rival set of male role models came from the Angry
Young Men, for whom to be called a gentleman was an
insult: for them, the gent was the enemy, inauthentic and
rule-bound. But how viable was their energetic but self-
indulgent alternative?

A third male ideal, courtesy of the long revolution of 1956–97,
was the New Man, a well-meaning guy who shared the housework, changed nappies and took emotions seriously. John
Lennon, as ever ahead of his time, set the tone: the last years
of his life were spent as a house husband, looking after his
second son, Sean. However, surveys carried out since the heyday
of the New Man have not shown men doing much more
housework. This is at least partly due to economics: apart from
the newly employed, most men still earn more than their female
counterparts, so it is to the overall advantage of the family unit
that they stay later at the office or on the shopfloor (Lennon,
with a stream of royalties, didn't have to worry about this).

Commentators have started talking about a crisis of male
identity. This is perhaps to take things too far. The contesting
models still have power. Maybe the brightest young British
men should pick and mix, taking the reliability and politeness
of the gentleman, the Angry Young Man's determination to

live vitally, and the New Man's concern to own up to his emotions and to respect the emotions of others.

Another contemporary aspect of the royal wedding guest list was the presence on it of a deputy prime minister. This is a title never used before 1942 and only sporadically employed since. The need for it in 2011 came from the election of the previous year, which had not produced an outright winner. The result was a coalition, something the nation had not seen since the Second World War.

This was a radical change. The old party system had been adversarial. Policies were forged in the heat of debate: think Gladstone and Disraeli, thundering at each other across the floor of the House of Commons, which is designed like a chasm, with banks of seats rising on either side. Now two of the three main parties were having to work together, creating policy by negotiation. This is the way most parliaments in Europe have been for many years, but for Britain it is new.

Is it to be the future for British politics? Many people say, 'Yes, and a good thing too', citing the rather childish point-scoring that went on in the old-style House. But behind the point-scoring was a determination to keep the government of the day on its toes – which can disappear if there's too much palliness in the corridors of power. These corridors should, surely, be a little bit draughty.

The wedding service featured three hymns, all with stirring tunes, two of them Welsh, Cwm Rhondda and Blaenwern, plus another piece by Parry (*Jerusalem*, of course). A prayer written by the couple themselves was read out; it had a good-hearted simplicity to it, which was welcome amid all the magnificence. At the end of the ceremony, husband and wife processed out of the Abbey to William Walton's *Crown Imperial*, written for the coronation of George VI (the last Crown to be Imperial) and the pealing of the Abbey bells. Later in the day, they appeared on the balcony of Buckingham

Palace and gave the now mandatory kiss. The affection between them was clearly genuine.

Like all such events, the wedding was stunning PR for Britain. People who complain about the costs don't seem to understand this. It was viewed in 180 nations, on TV and over the Internet. (An estimate from the Culture Secretary of two billion viewers was probably excessive, but it was certainly watched – and enjoyed – by vast numbers.) The royal couple can now visit any of the 180 nations and be instantly compelling ambassadors for this country.

But underneath all the pomp and spectacle lay something deeper: love. It is a shame the royal wedding stamps were available only in 'ceremonial' mini-sheet form. They should have been sold for simple letter use, where the images of the couple could have celebrated this most important value as part of real, everyday life.

CHAPTER THIRTY-SIX

FIRST CLASS?

FIRST CLASS STAMP, 2012

THE 2011 royal wedding was not only a magnificent occasion in itself, but also a curtain-raiser for the year to follow. The stamp issues of 2012 brim with confidence.

But Jubilee Olympic Britain is in trouble. Personal, corporate and government borrowing are all at or near record levels, a combination never experienced before in the nation's history. The austerity measures that appear necessary to sort this problem out have slowed economic growth, and the slowdown has hit the young – Britain's future – with disproportionate ferocity. The measures have also forced cuts in the welfare system, reawakening the spectre of the 1930s divide between haves and have-nots. Outside its borders, Britain seems unsure of its role. It is uneasy in Europe. It is seen as having toadied to America over Iraq. And all the while, new nations are rising in productive and political power, threatening to surpass it . . . Are these little islands off the coast of Europe really still First Class?

A stamp collection may not look the most obvious place to find answers, but let's try.

Two Jubilee stamps tell of how Britain has been in economic messes before and survived them. Dick Guyatt's 1977 stamp shows how Britain can gain strength from re-considering its traditions and celebrating them. Barnett Freedman's, issued as the nation was climbing out of the mire of the Great Depression, recalls another aspect of Britain, its ability to both create and embrace change. H.L. Palmer's 1946 Victory stamp tells of ascent from even greater depths, of the work of reconstruction after the Second World War – which it managed, despite difficulties along the way. Britain's modern manufacturing sector may not be as mighty as those of Germany or China, but it is still world-class in many areas. The UK's GDP remains in the global 'Top Ten' and is not set to leave it.

Life is not just about GDP, of course. All the stamps in this book speak of a nation with artistic ability and sensibility. They cover an ever-widening range of topics, reflecting a busy, diverse people with enthusiasms in every possible area, proud of their past and richly capable of enjoying the present. More generally, stamps serve as a reminder that even in the grimmest times, what matter most are human feelings and relationships – now, of course, often transmitted and maintained by the new electronic media, but also still expressed in letters or cards (texts and emails are great, but you still can't beat a love letter).

What of Britain's future? A powerful message comes from the very first stamp in this collection, the Penny Black. Its story is one of enterprising creativity, of a problem understood and grasped, a solution imagined for that problem, and that solution then nurtured and built into an enduring social institution that provided benefit for millions. The future will no doubt throw up problems, but these can and will be met in this spirit. There are other Rowland Hills out there, entrepreneurs, leaders, artists, engineers, visionaries, waiting to make their mark. Such people have emerged in many of the stories told by these stamps: Isambard Kingdom Brunel, Dinah Craik, Charles Dickens, Joseph Bazalgette, Disraeli and Gladstone, Henry and Millicent Fawcett, James and Mabel Cantlie, Keir Hardie, John Maynard Keynes, Barnett Freedman, Stephen Tallents, Winston Churchill, Tommy Flowers, William Beveridge, Edmund Dulac, Roy Jenkins, John Lennon, Sukhpal Singh, Camila Batmanghelidjh, the Peace People, Tim Berners-Lee . . .

If this answer seems to put too much weight on individuals, it is because remarkable people like Rowland Hill are, I believe, what drive change. This is not to endorse yuppie, 'me first' individualism. Everyone on the above list has served a cause: the public good; art or science; (for the commercial entrepreneurs) the welfare of their customers. British stamps, with the monarch depicted on every one, serve as reminders of collective values without which the efforts of even the most able individuals flounder – as Charles Dickens understood.

One criticism that can be made of Britain as reflected in its stamps is that the topics chosen tend to be rather inward-looking while the future is, above all, global. I guess people don't want terrifying transnational issues staring at them from the envelopes on their breakfast tables – but in the coming century, the true test of a nation's worth will be in its ability to participate in the solution of global problems such as terrorism, poverty, the environment, the spread of nuclear weapons and uncontrolled financial speculation. Britain is a great trading power with worldwide links and an increasingly diverse home population. It has a proud record of achievement in science and technology. These place it well to play a hugely positive role in dealing with these mega-problems. A set of stamps showing British achievements in these areas would be welcome.

Finally, I can't help wondering how a set of modern stamps will appear in 2100, when they will be as ancient as my great-uncle's Edwardian collection is now. The above reservation about a tendency to insularity aside, they will, I feel, look good. The stories they tell are, by and large, of a nation facing difficulties but dealing with them: strong yet diverse, eager for brightness, tolerant, witty, enterprising and humane. First class? For sure.

TRYING TO cram the history of over 150 years into 75,000 words was always going to be a bit of a struggle. Some things are bound to get left out. I'd like to have said more about some of the great Victorian social reformers, like Elizabeth Fry and Lord Shaftesbury. I never found a way in for Charles Darwin's 'Origin of Species': stamps were issued in 1982 for the centenary of the great man's death, but I didn't want to leap backwards in time. The chapter on the 1980s should have mentioned Bob Geldof's remarkable Live Aid gig, a classic example of what one determined person can achieve, but it didn't fit into the narrative. And so on. History lovers tend to have favourite eras and favourite events, which they consider especially resonant: my apologies if I have left yours out. (Do email me and let me know what it is.)

My name is on the front cover of this book, but many people

have helped with it. My wife, Rayna, above all, who has read drafts and joined in many discussions on a huge range of topics. Andrew Thacker, David Frew, Graham Michelli and Gervas Huxley have also been great people to debate with. Then there's my agent, Diane Banks, and the team at Square Peg / Random House, especially Rowan Yapp and Caroline McArthur in editorial, Lily Richards who helped with permissions, Julia Connolly for the jacket design, Simon Rhodes for production, copy editor Beth Humphries and Kate Bland and Ruth Warburton in publicity. Thanks to all of you.

I owe a huge debt of gratitude to a number of stamp designers and photographers who have given permission for their work to be displayed in this book: David Gentleman, Brian Sanders, Brendan Neiland, Peter Till, George Kavanagh and Tony Pleavin. Dealing with such talented and generous-spirited people has been a huge pleasure. Thanks also to De La Rue for permission to use H.L. Palmer's stamp, to the executors of Richard Guyatt for permission to reproduce his Jubilee design and to both Clarence House and Art Partner for use of the Royal Wedding image.

The image of Diana, Princess of Wales, is by permission of Getty Images. The Olympic Rings symbol on the 1948 stamp is courtesy of the IOC. And, of course, all the stamps appear with the permission of Royal Mail. Particular thanks to Stewart Tyson.

Gregory Spencer, Alex Bramall, Nick Loughran, Arthur Gearing, Jocelyne Bernhard and Mark Paul have all helped me secure permissions – thanks to them, too.

I also need to thank certain people for permission to quote from written works: the Society of Authors for Alfred Noyes, Roland Asquith for Cynthia Asquith. Quotes from parliamentary proceedings come courtesy of the Open Parliament Licence, and from royals thanks to the Royal Archives (thanks to Graeme Paterson at National Archives for organizing these). Extract from *The Labour Case* by Roy

Jenkins is reprinted by permission of Peters, Fraser and Dunlop (www.petersfraserdunlop.com) on behalf of the estate of Roy Jenkins.

Rather than clog up the book with references, I have put the main ones on my website, www.chriswest.info. Do visit. I'd also be delighted to discuss the book – chris@ the above address will reach me.

Above all, thank you for reading this book. I hope it both informed and entertained.

APPENDIX

PHILATELIC INFORMATION

I N THIS SECTION, I shall go into more philatelic detail about the stamps: the designers, how many were printed and when, (for definitive stamps) what replaced them, and what they are worth. I'll give a few hints for anyone seeking to start a collection and comment on the varieties available.

Asking how much a stamp is worth is a bit like asking how long a piece of string is. Condition is paramount. The Victorian post office was obsessed with avoiding stamp reuse, and often tried to obliterate stamps with dense postmarks called 'spoons', which had all the subtlety of trampling on them with mud-caked boots. If the stamp escaped this fate, a collector could damage it by poor handling or by using sticky paper hinges to attach them to albums. Inexperienced collectors could also take perfectly good mint (unused) stamps, lick the backs and just stick them in (my great-uncle, God bless him, did this to a fine set of USA 1893 Columbus commemoratives as a boy).

'Centredness' is also important. Early stamp-printing was an inexact science, with some Victorian examples being wildly off-centre. And before Henry Archer invented the perforating machine – it was first used in 1854 – all stamps had to be hand-cut by postal clerks. A Penny Black with four neat white margins all round it is worth a lot more than one with only one margin and a corner snipped off by an overworked clerk faced with a queue of impatient customers.

Stamps in really poor condition are called 'space-fillers': they're just occupying the place in the collection till something better comes along.

In the other direction, there is enormous scope for a stamp's value rising above the usual due to unusual watermarks, printing errors or official overprints. Some examples below will show this.

Given the high value of some stamps, there is a perpetual problem with forgery. When buying expensive stamps, it is best to use well-established, reputable dealers – unless you really know your stuff and can spot forgeries. Stamps, once purchased, can be shown to 'expertizing' bodies, who will issue certificates of genuineness (for a fee, of course). For UK stamps, the leading body is the Royal Philatelic Society, of 41 Devonshire Place, London W1G 6JY, United Kingdom. For cheaper stamps, eBay is a great place to buy, though the old principle of *caveat emptor* applies. As a general rule, the more eBay stars the vendor has, the more reputable they are. But clever fakes can still escape their attention.

The values listed below are estimates. I take no legal or moral responsibility for them. Any serious buyer should do their own research. The Stanley Gibbons catalogue is the best place to start, though SG prices are on the high side. Other reputable dealers have comprehensive catalogues available online or by post.

In the material below, I talk of a definitive stamp's 'date of unique use'. This is the period during which the stamp was officially the one you brought at a post office. After the end date, a new stamp performed this role – but the old stamps could still be used, often for quite long periods: the embossed shilling, for example, was formally replaced in 1856 but remained valid for the rest of Queen Victoria's reign. And of course, the changeover was never instant; superseded stamps remained on sale at post offices until the supply was used up.

For commemorative stamps, I just cite date of issue.

Penny Black

DESIGNERS: William Wyon / Henry Corbould / Rowland Hill

ENGRAVERS: George Rushall, Charles and Frederick Heath

DATE OF UNIQUE USE: 6 May 1840 to 10 February 1841

REPLACED BY: Penny Red

NUMBER PRINTED: 68,158,080

Value

UNMOUNTED MINT IN OUTSTANDING CONDITION: $4,000

REASONABLY NICE USED STAMP: $200

'SPACE-FILLER': $60

FOR THE BEGINNER ... You can get space-fillers of this stamp, and I've seen some pretty terrible ones. But as this is such a special issue, why not push the boat out a bit? $200 should get you a nice specimen with four margins.

FOR THE EXPERT ... 11 different plates were used to print the Penny Black. Plate 11 is the most valuable: it came into use shortly before the decision to drop the Penny Black was made; its main use was to make Penny Reds. Only 168,000 of these stamps were printed. The next rarest is plate 10, with nearly 2 million. Penny Black plate identification is a subtle art – with   most Penny Reds, the plate number is given on the stamp, but this is not the case with its predecessor.

FOR THE PHILATELIST WHO THINKS THEY HAVE DIED AND GONE TO HEAVEN . . . The complete sheet of 240 unused Penny Blacks in the UK National Postal Museum. Gaze at this and imagine yourself at work in a Victorian post office, ready for the first customer of the day . . .

ONE SHILLING EMBOSSED

DESIGNER: Unknown (head by William Wyon – used on all Victoria's stamps)
DATE OF UNIQUE USE: 11 September 1847 to 1 November 1856
REPLACED BY: Shilling Green (surface printed)
NUMBER PRINTED: 5,655,420

VALUE
UNMOUNTED MINT IN OUTSTANDING CONDITION: $5,000
REASONABLY NICE USED STAMP: $400
'SPACE-FILLER': $30

FOR THE BEGINNER . . . You'll probably end up with a lozenge-shaped stamp that has been cut all round its edges. Examples where the stamp has been left in a square, as was intended, are much more expensive. In between are all sorts of strange shapes, some corners cut and others left squared . . . If you do get a 'cut-out', make sure you get a good deal on it: it really is worth a lot less than one in a square.

FOR THE EXPERT . . . There are no errors to boost the value of particular examples. Two different dies were used, but in roughly equal amounts, so there's no rarity here. Just go for quality – clean, bright, a nice square cut giving plenty of margin.

Penny Red

DESIGNERS AND ENGRAVERS: as Penny Black

DATE OF UNIQUE USE: 10 February 1841 to 23 February 1854 (imperforate); 24 February 1854 to 1 January 1880 (with perforations)

REPLACED BY: Penny Brown

NUMBER PRINTED

IMPERFORATE: 2,588,000,000

PERFORATE WITH LETTERS IN BOTTOM CORNERS ONLY (1854–1858): 5,116,000,000

PERFORATE WITH LETTERS IN ALL FOUR CORNERS (1858–1880): 13,464,000,000

ALL TOGETHER: 21,138,000,000

Value

UNMOUNTED MINT IN OUTSTANDING CONDITION: $60

REASONABLY NICE USED STAMP: $3

'SPACE-FILLER': No value

FOR THE BEGINNER ... Just to get the collection going, buy a job lot of Victorian stamps for around $20. There'll be Penny Reds in here. Collect one of each main type: imperforate, perforate with letters in bottom corner only, perforate with letters in all four corners.

FOR THE EXPERT ... Unsurprisingly, given the number of stamps issued and the length of time they were valid, there's a huge variety of watermarks, plate numbers and papers to interest the serious philatelist. Two common approaches are to collect examples from every issued plate number, or to assemble a complete sheet, using the 'check letters' in the stamp's corners. Others collect envelopes: for most of the life of the Penny Red, each post town had its own numbered mark.

FOR THE PHILATELIST WHO THINKS THEY HAVE DIED AND GONE TO HEAVEN ... Plate 77. A number of sheets from this plate were printed but were unsatisfactory; both they and the plate were destroyed. A few, however, slipped out into the real world. Experts disagree on exactly how many, but nine seems to be an agreed figure: four mint and five used. These stamps have had adventurous lives. The example with the check letters AC was stolen from a private collection in 1965 and has not been seen since. Another one found its way to America but was destroyed in the fire that followed the San Francisco earthquake of 1906. Some are still to be seen in the Royal Collection (brought, of course, by George V) and the British Museum. All have been through the hands of famous collectors.

Many a philatelist has had a moment of amazement – 'I've got a plate 77!!!' – only to discover on more careful inspection that they have plate 177 instead.

Five Shilling Red

Date of unique use: 1 July 1867 to 1 April 1884
Replaced by: Five Shilling Rose
Number printed: 6,018,000

Value

Unmounted mint in outstanding condition: $3,000
Reasonably nice used stamp: $200
'Space-filler': $25

For the beginner ... As decent examples are costly, you could always cheat and buy a deliberate forgery to fill the space. These cost a dollar or two, and look nice. Please don't pass it off as the real thing!

For the expert ... Most of these stamps were issued with a Maltese cross watermark. For the last two years of its existence, the stamp came with an anchor watermark: these are rarer (just over half a million were issued).

For the philatelist who thinks they have died and gone to heaven ... A complete set of perfect-condition unmounted mint early Victorian high values, from 5 shillings to £5, can be worth around $150,000.

Three Halfpence Red

Date of unique use: 1 October 1870 to 14 October 1880
Replaced by: Penny Halfpenny Venetian Red
Number printed: 42,638,160

Value
Unmounted mint in outstanding condition: $250
Reasonably nice used stamp: $25
'Space-filler': $1

For the beginner ... As with the Penny Red, a job lot of Victorian stamps should contain some of these.

For the expert ... Two plates were used, 1 and 3 (numbered on stamp).

For the philatelist who thinks they have died and gone to heaven ... The 1870 design actually dates back to 1860, when a change in postal rates was proposed. The three halfpence stamp was prepared – then the proposal was dropped. Most of the stamps were destroyed. 48,000 were sent out to postmasters overprinted with the word SPECIMEN. 9,000 others escaped into public use. The 1860 stamp can be recognized by its purpler shade of red and the blue paper on which it was printed.

Penny Lilac

DATE OF UNIQUE USE: 12 July 1881 to 1 January 1902
REPLACED BY: Edward VII Penny Scarlet
NUMBER PRINTED: 33,600,000,000 (!)

Value

UNMOUNTED MINT IN OUTSTANDING CONDITION: $2.50
REASONABLY NICE USED STAMP: 50 cents
'SPACE-FILLER': No value

FOR THE BEGINNER ... Another one from the job lot. If you feel more expansive, a block of four mint Penny Lilacs should cost $10 or less.

FOR THE EXPERT ... The earliest versions of this stamp have 14 dots in each corner and can change hands for $200 or more. After six months, a sixteen-dot version was introduced. Later, various errors occurred, including stamps printed without watermarks.

FOR THE PHILATELIST WHO THINKS THEY HAVE DIED AND GONE TO HEAVEN ... In 1889, the Post Office did a deal with Pears' Soap (famous for using J.E. Millais' painting *Bubbles* in its ads) whereby PEARS SOAP or USE PEARS SOAP would be printed on the back of the Penny Lilac. The idea proved difficult and was abandoned, but copies of the trial exist.

Jubilee 1½D

DATE OF UNIQUE USE: 1 January 1887 to 21 March 1902
REPLACED BY: Edward VII 1½d
NUMBER PRINTED: 492,960,000

Value

Unmounted mint in outstanding condition: $15
Reasonably nice used stamp: $1
'Space-filler': No value

For the beginner ... If, like me, you love this issue, treat yourself to a full set of all 14. You can get them (used, of course) for around $40 – buy a decent set rather than a load of space-fillers. Aim for ones postmarked with a 'CDS', a nice gentle circular date stamp rather than Size 10 boot obliterations.

For the expert ... The late Victorian (and early Edwardian) government service issued overprinted stamps. Common overprints for jubilees are Army Official, IR (Inland Revenue) Official, Gov't (Government) Parcels and O.W. (Office of Works) Official. Overprints are, of course, easy to forge: enthusiastic amateurs can get their hands burnt. For any expensive overprint, certification is recommended.

For the philatelist who thinks they have died and gone to heaven ... A number of the jubilee stamps exist without perforations: the ½d, the 2½d, the 3d, the 4d and the 10d.

This issue inspires huge loyalty. There is even a website dedicated to it, 1887jubileeissue.wordpress.com.

Hong Kong 5 cents

Date of unique use: December 1880 to August 1901
Replaced by: Edward VII 5 Cents Yellow
Number printed: Unknown

Value

Unmounted mint in outstanding condition: $50
Reasonably nice used stamp: $1
'Space-filler': No value

FOR THE BEGINNER ... Pure UK collectors could give this one a miss: I put it in my book because it told a story. Otherwise, plenty of cheap examples around.

FOR THE EXPERT ... Examples with inverted watermarks exist.

FOR THE PHILATELIST WHO THINKS THEY HAVE DIED AND GONE TO HEAVEN ... Probably the best Hong Kong set to collect is the one that came before this, which was issued in 1862. The stamps look very similar to this one, but have different values, from 2 to 96 cents. A complete set, mint, in excellent condition is worth about $15,000.

EDWARD VII 7D

DESIGNER: Emil Fuchs
DATE OF UNIQUE USE: 4 May 1910 to 1 August 1913
REPLACED BY: George V 7d Olive
NUMBER PRINTED: 5,963,000

VALUE

UNMOUNTED MINT IN OUTSTANDING CONDITION: $5
REASONABLY NICE USED STAMP: $5
'SPACE-FILLER': 50 cents

FOR THE BEGINNER ... As with the jubilees, the Edward VII stamps can be bought in a set. I think I paid £20 (around $32) for mine.

FOR THE EXPERT ... A 'deep grey-black' version is worth a lot more.

FOR THE PHILATELIST WHO THINKS THEY HAVE DIED AND GONE TO HEAVEN ... Forget the 7d, and imagine yourself the possessor of a Edward VII 2d Tyrian Plum. This attractive stamp was designed and printed, in great numbers, in 1910 – then the King died, and the stamps were never issued. They were almost all destroyed. Only one used example exists: it was sent to George V and it is now in the Royal Collection. In 2011 a mint example sold for $159,500.

GEORGE V 'SEA HORSE' 10 SHILLINGS

DESIGNERS: Bertram Mackennal / George Eve
DATE OF UNIQUE USE: 1 August 1913 to 30 October 1939
REPLACED BY: George VI 10 Shillings Dark Blue
NUMBER PRINTED: Unknown

VALUE

UNMOUNTED MINT IN OUTSTANDING CONDITION: $500
REASONABLY NICE USED STAMP: $40
'SPACE-FILLER': $7

FOR THE BEGINNER ... The entire 'Sea Horse' set (2s6d, 5s, 10s and £1) can be expensive, as the £1 is rare. Content yourself with the first three.

FOR THE EXPERT ... Various printers produced the Sea Horse over its working life. The first to do so were Waterlows. In 1915, the contract went to De La Rue, and in 1918 to Bradbury Wilkinson. It takes an expert to distinguish between the first two, and an accurate measurer to distinguish the last one (the picture is slightly bigger). In 1934, the three lower values were re-engraved and re-issued. These more recent issues, more common, are easy to spot: in the 1913–18 issues the king's head is surrounded by horizontal lines; in 1934 examples by dots.

FOR THE PHILATELIST WHO THINKS THEY HAVE DIED AND GONE TO HEAVEN ... The £1 value was only printed in 1913: any example will now be 100 years old. One of these, mint unmounted in excellent condition, can be worth $3,000.

George V Penny Red

DESIGNERS: Bertram Mackennal / George Eve
DATE OF UNIQUE USE: 8 October 1912 to 24 September 1934
REPLACED BY: Penny Red (SG 440), printed with new
photogravure method
NUMBER PRINTED: Unknown

VALUE

UNMOUNTED MINT IN OUTSTANDING CONDITION: $1
REASONABLY NICE USED STAMP: 25 cents
'SPACE-FILLER': No value

FOR THE BEGINNER ... As with all cheap definitives, buy a
job lot of 'KGV' stamps.

FOR THE EXPERT ... Various shades of the stamp are listed
in the catalogue. Different watermarks were also used over
the years. A classic error has some stamps with QNE PENNY
written on them.

FOR THE PHILATELIST WHO THINKS THEY HAVE DIED
AND GONE TO HEAVEN ... In a very rare error, this stamp was
issued in a *tête-bêche* pair: the two stamps are linked, but one
is the wrong way up.

German 200 Marks, overprinted 2 million

DATE OF UNIQUE USE: 10 October 1923 to 20 October 1923
REPLACED BY: 2 Million mark definitive
NUMBER PRINTED: Unknown

VALUE: Surprisingly little

FOR THE BEGINNER ... The low value of these stamps might

surprise collectors, as they were in issue for such a short time. However, many were hoarded: people realized they would be unusual. As a result, one can buy collections of these stamps cheaply. For a few dollars you can get a set which, while not complete,will tell the whole mad story, from a sensible 10 pfennig stamp dated 1921 right through to a 50 Milliard (50,000,000,000) mark blue.

FOR THE EXPERT ... A complete set of such stamps is not difficult to collect.

FOR THE PHILATELIST WHO THINKS THEY HAVE DIED AND GONE TO HEAVEN ... For some reason, a mint 500 mark green overprinted with '800 Tausend' is particularly valuable.

BRITISH EMPIRE EXHIBITION THREE HALFPENCE COMMEMORATIVE

DESIGNER: Harold Nelson

DATE OF ISSUE: 23 April 1924

NUMBER PRINTED: Approximately 17,000,000 BEE stamps were printed. I don't have a breakdown of how many of each type. The 1925 ones seem to be a little more valuable, so I assume slightly fewer were printed.

VALUE

UNMOUNTED MINT IN OUTSTANDING CONDITION: $10

REASONABLY NICE USED STAMP: $3

'SPACE-FILLER': Not a lot

FOR THE BEGINNER ... A wonderful piece of history at a very reasonable price. Buy the pair as a set (1d and 1½d).

FOR THE EXPERT ... This set was remarkably free from errors. I expanded my own set of BEE stamps with some cigarette cards and other memorabilia from the exhibition.

FOR THE PHILATELIST WHO THINKS THEY HAVE DIED

AND GONE TO HEAVEN ... A first-day cover from the 1925 reissue – the stamps appeared on the 9th of May – can be worth \$2,000.

SILVER JUBILEE 2½D COMMEMORATIVE

DESIGNER: Barnett Freedman
DATE OF ISSUE: 7 May 1935
NUMBER PRINTED: 14,200,000. This makes the 2½d considerably rarer than the other denominations in the set, which were issued in hundreds of millions.

VALUE
UNMOUNTED MINT IN OUTSTANDING CONDITION: \$5
REASONABLY NICE USED STAMP: \$1
'SPACE-FILLER': Not a lot

FOR THE BEGINNER ... As with the BEE commems, buy a set.

FOR THE EXPERT ... Hitler produced a propaganda version of the Silver Jubilee issue, with Stalin's head replacing the king's and the slogan 'This is a Jewish war' on it. By a bitter irony, these stamps were made by inmates of Sachsenhausen Concentration Camp (which shows what kind of war it really was).

FOR THE PHILATELIST WHO THINKS THEY HAVE DIED AND GONE TO HEAVEN ... A few sheets of this stamp were printed in a much darker, and in a way truer, blue, now known as 'Prussian blue'. They were all issued from a post office in Edmonton, north London. Many were bought by one individual, an eagle-eyed entrepreneur called A.J. Stavridi (who kept some, and mailed others to his friends for fun). It is estimated that there are now about 200 examples of this error in existence. In 2011, a block of four, certified as genuine, of course, sold for \$38,400.

EDWARD VIII HALFPENNY DEFINITIVE

DESIGNER: Hubert Green
DATE OF UNIQUE USE: 1 September 1936 to 10 May 1937
REPLACED BY: George VI Halfpenny Green
NUMBER PRINTED: 1,739,250,000

VALUE

The stamp is not valuable. None of the stamps from here
on are worth much as individual items, and I shall not
list values from now on.

FOR THE BEGINNER ... Only four denominations were issued
for the new king: this one plus a 1d, 1½d and 2½d. Buy the set,
or get a job lot of Edward VIII/George VI stamps. Trading up
a bit, I bought mint panes of four of each, which make a nice
page in an album.

FOR THE EXPERT ... 'Postage Due' labels were also issued with
Edward VIII watermarks. Blocks of these can be quite valuable.

FOR THE PHILATELIST WHO THINKS THEY HAVE DIED
AND GONE TO HEAVEN ... The British Postal Museum contains
early versions of a planned 1937 coronation issue. Low values
would show the King in the uniform of the three armed services,
and 2½d and 2s6d stamps would show royal castles. The coronation, of course, did not take place.

GEORGE VI 2½D DEFINITIVE

DESIGNERS: Edmund Dulac (king's head) and Eric Gill
     (surround)
DATE OF UNIQUE USE: 10 May 1937 to 21 July 1941
REPLACED BY: Lighter blue version (to save ink)
NUMBER PRINTED: Unknown

For the beginner ... Buy a job lot of George VI stamps.

For the expert ... Collecting wartime postmarks – from all round the world – can bring the historical context to the fore. Postmarks urged letter recipients to do things like 'Dig for Victory' or buy war bonds.

For the philatelist who thinks they have died and gone to heaven ... Like the George V Penny Red, this stamp also exists in a very rare *tête-bêche* printing error.

2½D Victory Commemorative

Designer: H.L. Palmer
Date of issue: 11 June 1946
Number printed: 307,832,000

For the beginner ... Complete sets of George VI commemoratives (minus the Royal Silver Wedding £1 of 1948) can be bought cheaply.

For the expert ... A first day cover of this issue in good condition can be worth $50.

For the philatelist who thinks they have died and gone to heaven ... Nothing special here. Just forget stamps for a moment and imagine what it was like on the day commemorated, when five and half years of total war finally ended ...

1 Shilling Olympic Games Commemorative

Designer: Edmund Dulac
Date of issue: 29 July 1948
Number printed: 32,187,000. The 3d and 6d in this set were printed in about the same numbers; considerably more of the 2½d.

FOR THE BEGINNER ... See above.

FOR THE EXPERT ... A good condition first day cover is of value – especially if posted from Wembley with a special Olympic postmark.

As we enter the reign of Queen Elizabeth, stamp issues become more frequent, and the results tend to have little monetary value – though, of course, they are still of interest to the historian and/or the lover of good design. With the exception of some early high-value definitives (datable by their watermarks), they have proven poor investments. The beginner can buy complete sets of an entire decade's commemoratives (or even all pre-decimal QEII commems) in mint form for very reasonable prices.

Note that some ordinary individual examples of QEII commems are on sale on eBay at inflated prices. Avoid!

For the more serious collector, there are still interesting errors and variations, especially with the introduction of multi-coloured stamps.

I shall cover the stamps of Elizabeth's reign in less detail than their predecessors.

CORONATION 1s3d

> DESIGNER: Edmund Dulac
> DATE OF ISSUE: 3 June 1953
> NUMBER PRINTED: 5,987,200

46TH PARLIAMENTARY CONFERENCE

> DESIGNERS: Frank Langfield, Michael Farrar-Bell
> DATE OF ISSUE: 12 Sept 1957
> NUMBER PRINTED: 10,472,160

National Productivity Year 3d

Designer: David Gentleman
Date of issue: 14 November 1962
Number printed: 182,580,000, plus 13,320,000 with
phosphor bands

As I said in the text, this stamp exists with a number of errors. Most of these don't seem to command a huge price – don't pay a lot just because there is an error in the stamp. One error that is expensive is one where the queen's head has been omitted.

Collectors might also buy versions of this set with phosphor bands on them – hold the stamp up to the light, almost flat, and you will notice alternating bands of matt and glossier surface. The purpose of the bands was to facilitate automatic letter sorting. The bands soon became standard and on later stamps phosphor does not command a premium, but on some early sixties issues it can make a great price difference. The NPY 3d is actually not worth any more with phosphor bands, but the 1s3d is.

British Landscapes 1s6d

Designer: Leonard Rosoman
Date of issue: 7 May 1966
Number printed: 5,462,640, plus 1,204,200 with phosphor bands

World Cup Winners 4d

Designer: David Gentleman
Date of issue: 18 August 1967
Number printed: 12,452,640

SILVER JUBILEE 8½P

DESIGNER: Richard Guyatt
DATE OF ISSUE: 11 May 1977
NUMBER PRINTED: 73,960,000

A 9p stamp replaced the 8½p in June, when postage rates went up.

LIVERPOOL AND MANCHESTER RAILWAY 12P

DESIGNER: David Gentleman
DATE OF ISSUE: 12 March 1980
NUMBER PRINTED: 23,425,600

An error exists with a strip of the five stamps in this set printed without one of the colours, lemon.

YOUTH ORGANIZATIONS 26P

DESIGNER: Brian Sanders
DATE OF ISSUE: 24 March 1982
NUMBER PRINTED: 8,669,000

EUROPEAN ELECTIONS 16P

DESIGNER: Fritz Wegner
DATE OF ISSUE: 15 May 1984
NUMBER PRINTED: 22,618,150

CHRISTMAS 1989 38P

DESIGNER: David Gentleman
DATE OF ISSUE: 14 November 1989
NUMBER PRINTED: 13,356,400

Note – over 200 million of the cheaper stamps in this set were printed.

DIANA 26P

Photograph by Tim Graham
DATE OF ISSUE: 3 February 1998
NUMBER PRINTED: 30,260,820

The presentation pack for this set issued in Welsh is a rare collectors' item.

LLOYDS OF LONDON 64P ('THE WORKER'S TALE')

DESIGNER: Brendan Neiland
DATE OF ISSUE: 4 May 1999
NUMBER PRINTED: 4,413,600

'FIRE AND LIGHT' MILLENNIUM ISSUE 26P

PHOTOGRAPH: George Kavanagh
DATE OF ISSUE: 1 February 2000
NUMBER PRINTED: 16,175,100

WORLD OF INVENTION 72P

DESIGNER: Peter Till
DATE OF ISSUE: 1 March 2007
NUMBER PRINTED: Unknown

ROYAL WEDDING MINISHEET

PHOTOGRAPHER: Mario Testino
DATE OF ISSUE: 21 April 2011
NUMBER PRINTED: Unknown

INDEX

ABOUT THE AUTHOR

CHRIS WEST has written widely in a variety of genres, but has never before been published in the United States. His titles include a bestselling business guide and a quartet of crime novels. He inherited a love of history from his father and an Edwardian "Lincoln" stamp album from his great-uncle as a child. His love for stamps was revived when he found that same dust-covered album in his attic as an adult. He lives in Cambridgeshire.